W9-ADX-980

Drawing on an ethnographic study of a remote farming community in the Auvergne, Dr Reed-Danahay challenges conventional views about the operation of the French school system. She demonstrates how parents and children subvert and resist the ideological messages of the teachers, and she describes the ways in which a sense of local difference is sustained and valued through a complex interplay of schooling and family life. This book explores the role played by history, identity, and power in local responses to a national institution. A significant contribution to the anthropology of education, it offers fresh insights into the ways in which French culture is transmitted to the coming generation. Dr Reed-Danahay also provides lucid and critical discussions of sociological theories on education, including those of Bourdieu.

Cambridge Studies in Social and Cultural Anthropology

98

EDUCATION AND IDENTITY IN RURAL FRANCE

Cambridge Studies in Social and Cultural Anthropology

The monograph series *Cambridge Studies in Social and Cultural Anthropology* publishes analytical ethnographies, comparative works and contributions to theory. All combine an expert and critical command of ethnography and a sophisticated engagement with current theoretical debates.

A list of books in this series will be found at the end of the volume

EDUCATION AND IDENTITY IN RURAL FRANCE

The Politics of Schooling

DEBORAH REED-DANAHAY
The University of Texas at Arlington

CAMBRIDGE
UNIVERSITY PRESS

PUBLISHED BY THE PRESS SYNDICATE OF THE UNIVERSITY OF CAMBRIDGE
The Pitt Building, Trumpington Street, Cambridge, United Kingdom

CAMBRIDGE UNIVERSITY PRESS
The Edinburgh Building, Cambridge CB2 2RU, UK
40 West 20th Street, New York NY 10011–4211, USA
477 Williamstown Road, Port Melbourne, VIC 3207, Australia
Ruiz de Alarcón 13, 28014 Madrid, Spain
Dock House, The Waterfront, Cape Town 8001, South Africa

http://www.cambridge.org

First published 1996
First paperback edition 2004

A catalogue record for this book is available from the British Library

ISBN 0 521 48312 3 hardback
ISBN 0 521 61617 4 paperback

Transferred to digital printing 2003

In memory of my parents

Contents

Illustrations

Tables

Acknowledgements

These comments must begin with the people of Lavialle, who allowed me to share and participate in their everyday lives. I have chosen to address only some of what I learned while living in Lavialle in this book, but I am as grateful to the Laviallois for their lessons to me about myself and about being an anthropologist as I am for the knowledge that I gained about them. Many people in Lavialle, in all stages of life, helped my research. I hope they understand that my hesitancy to cite individuals by name, and my use of pseudonyms in the text, are based upon a sincere concern to protect their privacy. I must also thank the teachers at Lavialle's school for their willingness to give me access to the school, and all those former teachers who shared their recollections and observations with me.

Others in France were also generous with advice and support for the fieldwork that I undertook in the early 1980s. I thank, in particular, Isac Chiva, Henri Mendras, Pierre Bourdieu, Jacques Maho, and André Fel for welcoming me to the world of French scholarship on rural France. Marc Prival, an ethnologist of the Auvergne, provided invaluable assistance in locating a fieldsite. When I would leave Lavialle to undertake archival and library research in Paris, Dominique Blaess helped in countless ways; and when I did the same in Clermont-Ferrand, Collette Valleix provided friendship and lots of good advice. Although I conducted my field research as a "lone" anthropologist, this wider support system connected me in important ways to various streams of French society and culture.

I am fortunate to have had many dedicated teachers and colleagues here in the United States. I would like to thank Norman B. Schwartz, Daniel Biebuyck, Juan Villamarin, and Ken Ackerman for first teaching me about anthropology. Later teachers who gave advice on this project in its early stages include David Kaplan, Marvin Davis, Pierre-Yves Jacopin, Helen

Codere, Roy C. Macrides, and George Ross. Several colleagues have read various portions and drafts of this book. I am particularly grateful for the detailed comments of Katie Anderson-Levitt and Susan Carol Rogers – both fellow anthropologists of France. Michael Herzfeld and Pam Quaggiotto read and helpfully commented on earlier versions of my introductory chapters. Two anonymous reviewers for Cambridge University Press provided important suggestions for revision. In preparing this manuscript for production, I have received much appreciated support from the University of Texas at Arlington. I would like to thank Dean Ben Agger for his help with funding for the preparation of photographic material, and the photography staff at the UTA media center for their expertise. Jill Brown, graphic artist in Atlanta, provided excellent skills in the preparation of maps and illustrations.

I received funding for this research from the National Science Foundation, the French Ministry of Culture – through a Bourse Chateaubriand, and from NIMH Post-Doctoral Training Fellowship #17058. Without this generous support, I could not have conducted fieldwork in Lavialle, and would not have written this book.

My family, and my many friends scattered up and down the East coast, have all encouraged me in important ways over the years. I would like them to know how thankful I am. My husband, Martin Danahay, despite his own academic projects, has often taken the time to read through portions of this book and has been a constant source of support. I much appreciate his having lived so graciously with this long undertaking of mine despite not having had the experience of living in Lavialle. My children, Emily and Ian, have provided many interruptions to the writing of this book, none of which I regret. Their contributions to my work and to my writing, while significant, are difficult to name.

1

Introduction: journey to Lavialle

Before moving to Lavialle,[1] the French farming community that would be my fieldwork site, I spent one month in an international student residence in Paris. Most of the graduate and post-doctoral students staying at the residence were from francophone Africa, and, like myself, had a grant from the French Ministry of Culture. My contacts with these students were rich and varied, as were their cultural backgrounds. One friend, with whom I developed the closest ties, was from Tanzania. She cooked native foods for me, introduced me to her uncle (a former ambassador), and took me to a wedding reception for some African student friends of hers, in which tribal dances and songs were self-consciously and politically per-formed as a way of asserting indigenous "culture." It was this young woman who drove with me to the train station when I left for fieldwork in rural Lavialle, six hours away.

In a departure from standard anthropological practice, in which peoples from non-Western countries become the subject of research, I was leaving what was to me a fairly "exotic" and "multi-cultural" atmosphere on the boulevard Montparnasse to live among inhabitants of "la France pro-fonde" – the very heart of French culture, and, in many ways, of Europe. Ironically, I found my relationships with the foreign students in Paris much less fraught with cultural misunderstandings than my initial contacts with the Auvergnats of Lavialle. I was aware that my African friend had lived a very different life from mine, especially when she told me stories of her experiences as a schoolgirl during her country's struggle for independence. We were, nevertheless, able to communicate in Paris on a similar footing. I shared some sort of urban, intellectual, cosmopolitan cultural idiom with her and other students from extremely different traditions that I did not

1

share with the people of Lavialle, on the surface much closer to my own Euro-American cultural heritage.[2]

My abrupt transition from an international student residence in Paris to an Auvergnat rural community – from educated middle- and upper-class African students to the farmers of Lavialle – brought into sharp focus the experiences of those who have, for whatever reason, rejected to some degree the claims of the school upon their children. The African students I met in Paris, who had succeeded in European-style educational systems back home, were much more committed to, and trusting of, schools and teachers than were the Laviallois. Families in Lavialle share neither the assumptions nor the cultural ease of the middle classes in France or post-colonial Africa concerning formal education.[3]

This book is about the educational strategies of rural French families living in a remote mountain region of the Auvergne, in the *commune* of Lavialle.[4] It is a study of families as much as it is a study of local schooling. Educational strategies are the ways in which families influence the effects and meaning of schooling for their children. They are part of wider economic and political strategies, but also operate within more particularistic meanings of childhood socialization at the local level. The educational strategies of families in Lavialle reflect "everyday forms" of resistance to French schooling, but also operate to encourage strong forms of local cultural identity among children. They do not, however, entail a complete rejection of education or of French national identity. Primary schooling in rural France is an important cultural site for the construction of both local and national identity, and for the negotiation of conflict between families and the state.

This study is somewhat different from most anthropological studies of education, because it is not exclusively a "school ethnography." I did more fieldwork outside of the school, learning about such things as social organization, kinship, politics, religion, and socialization, than I did within the two classrooms of Lavialle's primary school. This allowed me to understand better the ways in which Lavialle families actively shape the socialization experiences of their children. My approach to the study of schooling involves looking beyond the classroom, and, in some ways, "de-centering" the school. There are many strands in the story of family strategies for childhood socialization in Lavialle – which lead in and out of the classroom, in and out of the home, and in and out of the community.

The core of this study is based upon fieldwork conducted over a decade ago, during 1980 and 1981. Lavialle was at that time recovering from the dramatic post-war population losses that had touched all of rural France. There was a renewed optimism among younger families, and more young couples were choosing agriculture, rather than leaving for urban occupations. Population loss in Lavialle continues, but at a slower rate than occurred earlier in this century. Lavialle remains a resilient, productive agricultural community. This has not changed since I conducted the initial study, and helps to reinforce my thesis that Lavialle has remained vital in part due to the socialization strategies adopted by its families. In a changing economy, where many areas of central France have become depopulated and have ceased to rely on farming, Lavialle persists. It does so through a subtle mixture of resistance to and coexistence with dominant French culture.

Many of the grandparents of the children I knew in Lavialle, especially those from outlying hamlets, told me that they had arrived at school speaking not a word of French. They recalled the trauma with which they experienced teachers who refused to "understand" the local dialect (*patois*) – even though they were themselves of rural origin. Today, children are taught French at home in order to save them from a similar ordeal. The Auvergnat regional dialect has become part of an unofficial, local realm. It is now used by the Laviallois in order to exclude the teachers (middle-class suburbanites who only know French) from interfering in local affairs. Such uses of language are one way in which the Laviallois maintain a strong sense of local identity, and through which they undertake a complex manipulation of social identities in order to defend and assert local cultural meanings. *Maintaining identity thru language (reverse) exclusion!*

Schools are often said to play a central role in the construction of national identity in modern nation-states. Through their educational systems, European nations have created sites in most local communities for the spread of literacy skills and dominant languages, social stratification, and cultural homogenization. The French educational system is generally viewed as one of the most successful of these systems. It is well known for having extended its bureaucracy and influence not only throughout rural France, but into its colonies abroad. My argument in this book is that local schools, even in the centralized system of France, may work to reinforce local identity, as parents and children resist aspects of national culture and state power. → *Maintaing local identity*

The role of schooling in the formation of cultural identity has not yet received sufficient critical attention in France, largely because schools are assumed to transmit French national culture. Primary schools in French villages have long symbolized the presence of the "republic" and of state

Schools assumed to transmit nat'l culture

The pressures of the mil? of native dialect. exclusion + categorization = loss of

power. France has a reputation for running one of the most centralized and bureaucratic educational systems in the world. As a consequence, French schools are generally assumed to be part of a uniform system, with uniform effects. French education has been credited with the creation of a culturally homogenous nation out of a diverse peasantry (Weber 1976). At the same time, it has been criticized for the reproduction of a class-based system of social stratification (Bourdieu and Passeron 1990). Such claims about the role of schooling in French society must, however, be tempered by an understanding of the social and cultural context of education.

It can be argued that French schools were never intended as places to create a "unified" French culture, despite a rhetoric of national unity, but have always been class stratified (Green 1990). Moreover, the persistence of regional diversity, particularly in rural France, challenges any myth of cultural homogeneity. Social stratification is, itself, not a straightforward process. Local meanings are constructed in and around schooling which complicate and subvert the stratifying work of schools in crucial ways. Rural and working-class families challenge and resist the cultural hegemony of the middle class in French schools, so that the middle class must continually assert and protect its social position. Schools are sites of struggle, and of the contestation of meaning and identity. The case of France, which has always had a highly politicized educational system at the national level, is a fruitful one in which to examine, with an anthropological lens, those issues of power and identity that surround local schooling.

Introducing Lavialle

Lavialle is a French *commune* on the Massif Central, a high plateau in central France, and is nestled in a mountain valley. Most visitors to Lavialle reach it either by train or by highway, both of which wind up into the mountains of Auvergne from the lower-lying city of Clermont-Ferrand, about 45 km away. Two mountain chains border Lavialle, the Chaîne de Puys to the northeast and the Monts Dore to the southeast. The ancient volcano Puy-de-Dôme (1,465 m), of the former range, and the summit of Puy-de-Sancy (1,885 m), of the latter, are both conspicuous sights on Lavialle's horizon. There used to be a temple to Mercury on the top of the Puy-de-Dôme, and there is still something fascinating and grand about this oval-shaped silhouette that rises abruptly from the lower surrounding peaks and can be viewed from almost all points in Lavialle. When the Laviallois raised sheep, up until the 1950s, these were guarded by shepherds on the Puy-de-Sancy and other nearby mountains during the summer months. The remnants of many shepherd huts still stand as

A changing life, even in rural terms

reminders of the past. The surrounding mountains reinforce for the Laviallois those aspects of local identity based on notions of the hardship and remoteness associated with mountain life.[5]

The mountains also, however, point toward the future. The Puy-de-Dôme is now a popular summit for hang-gliding, and on warm days it is sprinkled with colorful gliders. The mountains to the south of Lavialle serve as spots for Sunday afternoon outings by local families. They also attract an increasing number of tourists to the Auvergne, especially those seeking the good cross-country skiing possibilities of its rounded peaks.

Lavialle's location between the Puy-de-Dôme and the Puy-de-Sancy serves as a useful metaphor for the ambivalence felt among the Laviallois concerning the historical roots of their Auvergnat peasant identity and their current position as farmers in an increasingly urban society. As one of their own responses, the children of Lavialle play a game on the school-yard. They roll old tires with a stick, pretending to be tourists, passing by on the national highway.

Despite its seeming marginality in French society, Lavialle is not a deserted village, and inspires neither nostalgia nor regret. Its inhabitants have found strength in their feelings of otherness *vis-à-vis* the urban bourgeoisie for quite some time, rather than crumbling under outside pressures to change in certain ways or disappear. During my fieldwork, Lavialle was actually experiencing a period of revitalization among younger families (native to Lavialle) committed to staying in the community.

As is the case throughout France, Lavialle's population continues to decline, but the rate of decline is much slower that it was in the immediate post-war period. A high unemployment rate in France, particularly among the young, provides little incentive to leave Lavialle for those with farming opportunities. The population of Lavialle had dropped from 454 in 1975 to 421 in 1982. By the 1990 census, it was down again, to 375. However, the population continues to have a growing proportion of 20–39 year olds – those most necessary to the continuation of farming and local social life. This age group constituted 22% of the population in 1975, but was 25% in 1982, and had risen to 26% by 1990. There is out-migration, but the birth rate continues to be strong. It rose from 7.8% during the period from 1975–82 to 9.4% from 1982–90. The birth rate in Lavialle is slightly higher than the average for *communes* of comparable size in the region.

Lavialle has 17 hamlets and a central village, also called Lavialle (Map 1). The *commune* has an elevation that ranges from 800 to over 1,000 meters, and is dispersed over an area of 3,619 hectares. Its shape is that of an elongated oval, with the village placed right in the center. Lavialle's

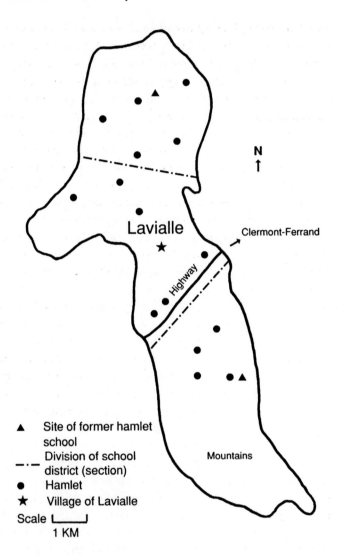

Map 1 *Commune* of Lavialle

primary school, as well as its Catholic church, are located in the village.

Lavialle's farmers live on small, family-owned and operated farms, which has been the norm for centuries. Beginning in the 1960s, Lavialle and its neighboring *communes* have increasingly concentrated on milk production to the exclusion of other economic activities that were important in the past – such as sheep and pig raising, cereal production, and cheese-making (LeBlanc 1975). Depopulation of the region since World War II has aided the development of milk production. Remaining farms have expanded at the expense of those farms that were unable to compete in the growing market economy. This has led to increased pressure on the land and competition among the remaining families for the acquisition of available land either through rent or purchase. The farms that operate in Lavialle today are all fairly strong, but this reflects a recent growth, following a period during the 1960s and 1970s of the dissolution of many smaller farms.

Lavialle's economy is based on farming and the few local services which support it, such as cafes, shops and artisanal trades. Eighty-five percent of Lavialle's adult population was employed in agriculture in 1979–80. There was no significant change in this during the rest of the 1980s. Although dairy farms predominate in the local economy, there are also farms that raise sheep, cattle, or veal. Most non-farmers work in artisanal occupations, such as house painting or plumbing. There are few employment opportunities outside of farming or artisanal work within the local area. During my fieldwork, several Laviallois were, however, employed outside of the *commune* – at small dairies, a chicken-processing plant, and a wood-cutting mill. Some residents of Lavialle, most of whom are non-natives, were employed in higher-status professions. These included non-Auvergnats: a forester who rented a house in the village, and a college professor and his family who lived in a former manor house near the village. A car salesman, who was originally from a farm family in a nearby *commune* and married to a woman from another region, lived with his family in the old rectory near the center of Lavialle. A native of Lavialle who lived in one of the southern hamlets was a Catholic schoolteacher who worked near Clermont-Ferrand. Her husband was from another region, and they had returned to Lavialle after living elsewhere for a few years, renovating an old barn from her family's property into a house.

Lavialle persists as a viable community largely because its families have reinforced ties to those who leave at the same time that they encourage many children to remain in agriculture. The extension of community life to family members who live and work elsewhere has occurred through the concept of *les nôtres* – a loosely defined kindred that reaches beyond the *commune*. Many of those who have left return for weekends and holidays, for weddings, funerals, and elections. They actively participate in family and community rituals, work, and decisions. It is mainly through the socialization strategies of Lavialle families that ties to kin are reinforced, and that local identity and meaning are renewed with each generation. Educational outcomes and processes are very much influenced by these overall strategies.

Beyond Lavialle

Lavialle, as a French *commune*, is part of a national government in which higher levels of authority are located at broader geographical units (as in the school system). Lavialle is in the district (*canton*) of Grosbourg, in the department of Puy-de-Dôme, in the administrative region of Auvergne (Map 2). With governmental decentralization, French regions have become increasingly important administrative units, fulfilling many functions that were previously carried out at the level of either the department or the nation. Rural depopulation has also led to the growing importance of the region, as social identity and social activity must increasingly be focused on a regional, rather than local, level (Reiter 1972; see also Rapp 1986).

The Laviallois go to the nearby town and district center of Grosbourg, located in the *commune* of Grosbourg, for goods and services not available in Lavialle. Located 6 km from the village of Lavialle, Grosbourg also has a state-run middle school attended by many Lavialle children. The population of the *commune* of Grosbourg was 985 in 1982 and 947 by 1990. Few of Grosbourg's inhabitants are now employed in farming, and most work in the service industries supported by the surrounding rural *communes*. Except for the busy summer months and its monthly outdoor market, Grosbourg looks from the outside like a sleepy provincial town, whose daily rhythms are punctuated mostly by the daily comings and goings of the bus to Clermont-Ferrand.

The *communes* of Grosbourg and Lavialle were almost equal in size in the early 19th century, but Lavialle now has less than one-half the population of Grosbourg. The population of Lavialle has dropped significantly from its levels in the eighteenth and nineteenth centuries, as illustrated in Table 1.

Because the town of Grosbourg has developed as a small-scale commercial center and attempted to attract tourists, its *commune* maintains a larger population. Lavialle, on the other hand, lost one-third of its population between 1800 and the start of World War I, and has lost another one-half since then. Some of this was due to a restructuring and annexation of

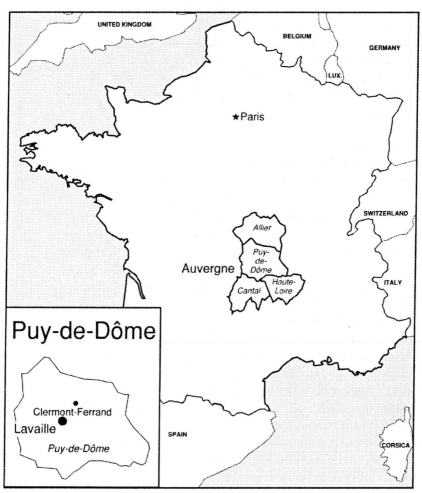

Map 2   France: region of Auvergne

Table 1. *Population of Lavialle and Grosbourg: 1806–1990* (Source: INSEE)

Year	Lavialle	Grosbourg
1806	1,287	1,306
1836	1,125	1,421
1856	1,166	1,551
1876	1,118	1,430
1891	1,100	1,448
1911	880*	1,361
1926	761	1,186
1936	784	1,230
1954	662	1,157
1968	519	1,077
1975	454	1,081
1982	421	985
1990	375	947

Note:
*Redistricting, whereby Lavialle lost some population to another *commune*, is partly responsible for the dramatic drop from the previous census.

some hamlets to other *communes*, explaining the sharp drop between 1891 and 1911. Most of this loss, however, was the result of rural exodus.

Like rural communities all over France, Lavialle has seen its regional context change from one in which most of the population lived in rural *communes*[6] to one in which urban life prevails. The urban and rural populations of the Puy-de-Dôme completely reversed their proportions during the past century. In 1872, 119,279 people lived in urban *communes* (population over 2,000) whereas 447,184 people lived in rural *communes*. The urban population exceeded the rural population in the Puy-de-Dôme for the first time in 1962, and by 1982 there were 396,238 people living in urban *communes* compared to only 197,967 people living in rural *communes* such as Lavialle. Despite its loss of rural population, however, the Puy-de-Dôme depends on farming more than most departments in France. It still had 12% of its population employed in agriculture in 1975, when the national average had dropped to 8%.

Clermont-Ferrand, with a population close to 140,000 in 1990, is Lavialle's closest major city. From Lavialle, the trip to Clermont-Ferrand takes about 45 minutes by car and even longer by bus along a two-lane national highway built in 1910. Daily buses along this curving, mountainous highway provide transportation for the older women and secondary schoolchildren who are their most frequent passengers. Teenagers from Lavialle who attend high school (*lycée*) must travel to Clermont-Ferrand, which has several public and Catholic high schools. Most of these students board in the city during the week and return home on the Friday afternoon bus each weekend.

Clermont-Ferrand is the major urban center of the entire region of Auvergne, and the capital of the Department of Puy-de-Dôme. It is also an historic religious center, having long been seat of the diocese of Clermont, and is dominated by an imposing cathedral. There is a major university, as well as a teacher training college (*Ecole normale*), in Clermont-Ferrand.

The post-war expansion of the Michelin rubber industry, which is based in Clermont-Ferrand, has been a crucial factor in the growth of the entire Auvergne region. The population of Clermont-Ferrand itself increased dramatically after World War II, in large part due to Michelin. This company dominates the local economy, and employed 30,000 workers in the late 1970s. Twenty-five percent of all workers in Clermont-Ferrand work for Michelin. The immediate post-war period represented the company's most intensive recruitment of workers from rural villages in the region, but employment at Michelin is still viewed in Lavialle as a major alternative to farming. During the economic recession of the late 1970s, which touched Michelin and other firms in the region, jobs were limited. The perception of few viable opportunities outside of farming helped bolster favorable attitudes to farming among younger Laviallois at the time of my fieldwork. Most Laviallois do not consider the factories of Michelin and other companies in and around Clermont-Ferrand to be within daily commuting distance. Therefore, those who seek industrial jobs leave the *commune*. This decrease in opportunities may be reflected in the slight population loss that the urban area of Clermont-Ferrand experienced during the 1980s.

A rural school

Lavialle's primary school has two classrooms and two teachers, and is the only school in the *commune*. It is technically both a nursery school and a primary school, and takes children aged 3 to 11. This school is a fairly typical school for rural France, and is not as unusual in France as one might expect, given its small size and rural location. One in four French primary schools was a rural, single-class school in the early 1980s (Lewis 1985:12; see also Fédération des Délégués . . . 1977). Over 30,000 rural *communes* (in which 16% of the total French population lives) had their own primary school in 1975–76, and almost one-third of all *communes*, like Lavialle, had populations of less than 500 and maintained primary schools.

The issue of whether or not to keep such small, one- or two-room schools open has been a topic of concern in recent years (see Belperron 1978; Cheverny 1981; Fédération des Délégués . . . 1977; La Blache 1990). A policy of closing or consolidating many schools has been actively pursued since the 1970s, and 10,000 schools were closed between 1963 and 1976 (Belperron 1978). Opposition to this trend among both teacher unions and parents led to the lowering of the number of students needed to keep a school open in 1976 and 1977. For two-room schools like the one in Lavialle, an enrollment of 23 students has been required since the early 1980s to keep both classes open (before 1976, the number was 26). To maintain sufficient enrollment levels and retain a two-room school in the *commune*, parents in Lavialle agreed to send three-year-old children to school in 1979 (the starting age had previously been four).

The Laviallois have generally supported the existence of the public school, both materially (through funds from the town council) and by sending their children to its classrooms. Families see many advantages to the basic education offered there to their children. They are, however, ambivalent about the ways in which Lavialle's school vividly represents the presence of the state in their daily lives.

The building which houses Lavialle's school is an important expression of the school's place in the community, and of its position at the intersection of the state, families, and local government. A two-story, box-like structure, the school (*l'école*) is of an imposing size, rivalled only by the Catholic church in stature. It is located in the village of Lavialle (Plate 1), on its own small lane, but in full view of the major road entering the center of the village. Ever since its construction in 1881, at the time of the Ferry Laws making French primary education free and mandatory, this structure has been a symbol of the presence of the state and its central role in socialization. Although there have been some internal renovations, the exterior of the school building has essentially the same appearance as it had when first built. Accentuating the alien nature of its statist architecture in the village context, the school looks almost as if it were set right down in the middle of a field: it is flanked by two dairy farms, one behind it and one on its right; to its front and left lie grazing fields.

Lavialle's school is the official secular building of the *commune*, in contrast to the official sacred building – the church. This was undoubtedly the intention of the architects of the Third Republic who designed schools. The early primary school teachers (*les instituteurs*) saw themselves as

Plate 1   *The village of Lavialle in winter.* This is a view looking toward the southwest. Visible are farms, the church (to the left), and the primary school (the large building with shutters toward the center of the photo). Winters in Lavialle can be quite severe, and this contributed to the region's physical and cultural isolation in the past.

secular missionaries, taking education out of the hands of the clergy, and spreading Republican values and French culture to unify the nation (Ozouf 1967, Villin and Lesage 1987). In Lavialle, however, both the school and the church symbolize the presence of large bureaucratic apparatuses of power lying outside of the community which exert influence at the local level. → Community supercedes school & church

   Although the school appears to be a daunting presence in Lavialle, it has important local meanings. Families have influenced teachers there for several generations, and fear of parental reprisals for various actions have constrained many a teacher in his or her behaviors. The school is a place where children learn to be both Laviallois and French, and is a vital part of the culture of childhood. Lavialle's school may very well be an "educational apparatus" of the state (Althusser 1971), but many social relationships that occur within and around it temper the effects and meanings of state power.

Fieldwork in Lavialle

Lavialle cultural meanings were vividly illustrated to me during an experience on my second day of fieldwork. I was invited to join a small party of Laviallois headed by car to a nearby town to place bets on a horse race and have a drink (*boire l'apéro*). This was at about 11:30 in the morning, and we were to return for lunch. I was feeling comfortable and at ease with my new neighbors, and glad to be included in this outing. It was a warm day, and I was quite thirsty. The waiter asked me first what I would like to drink, and I ordered a cold beer. A young male farmer in our group jokingly asked me if I really wanted to drink that. I thought he was just teasing me, since he had adopted this manner before, and I didn't change my order. When the waiter brought our drinks, the entire room became hushed, and most eyes were upon me. I immediately sensed that the beer was an inappropriate choice, and that I had somehow transgressed an important rule of drinking behavior.

In Paris, I had often shared a beer with friends. By the early 1980s, beer had become a common beverage, often replacing wine for lunch. When I tried to find out what I had done wrong at the cafe, I heard two versions of the rule not to drink beer in this situation. First, the female schoolteacher told me that women in Lavialle never drink beer, but only white wine and sweet liqueurs. Then, in a different conversation, a native Lavialle woman close to my age told me that people in France would never drink beer before a meal; it is not an appropriate aperitif.

The schoolteacher had appealed to a cultural model of the Laviallois as "backward," with strict gender roles, in explaining the beer episode (see Reed-Danahay and Anderson-Levitt 1991). Her explanation stressed the local situation, and its uniqueness. She was, thereby, culturally distancing herself from the women of Lavialle. The Lavialle farm woman, in contrast, had used a more general, "common-sense" explanation. To her, beer doesn't taste good before a meal, and, therefore, it is more appealing to drink a light liqueur at that time. She was using a national rhetoric, that distanced me as an American (with bad taste!). As I came to learn more about Lavialle drinking behavior, I found that both explanations were "true," but that the second seemed more valid than the first. On selective occasions, I observed Laviallois women drink both red wine and beer at home. More importantly, however, I rarely saw anyone drink beer in Lavialle, and never before a meal.

Most anthropologists have similar stories from the early days of fieldwork. My experience in the cafe, although I didn't realize it at the time, held great relevance for my understanding of relationships between families and schooling in Lavialle. It began my gradual realization that not only were many of my own cultural assumptions about such seemingly mundane issues as drink invalid in Lavialle, but that the Laviallois use shifting frames of social identity in everyday life. I learned that the teachers saw the families of Lavialle as different from themselves in important ways that colored their interactions within and outside of the classroom. I also learned that the Laviallois undertake a complex juggling of their identities as French, Auvergnat, Laviallois, and members of local families in their everyday lives. They were "French" to my "American," but Auvergnat to other French.

I arrived in Paris in September of 1980 knowing that I wanted to study rural education in the Massif Central, but with no clear possibility of locating a field site. Because one of my grants was from the French government, I received immediate access to the Parisian academic world of anthropology and rural ethnography. As I navigated through this culture, the most direct help in finding Lavialle came from Isac Chiva at the Collège de France. He introduced me to several French ethnographers in the provinces with contacts at schools. I chose Lavialle, after visiting several other sites, for two reasons. First, I was attracted to the seeming vitality of the school and its population, which differed from the situations in more deserted villages. Secondly, it fit my desire to find a marginal region in which I could investigate influences on schooling by families at some remove from dominant French culture. I was introduced to the teachers in Lavialle by a regional ethnographer and teacher – Marc Prival. They welcomed me and my research, and made arrangements for my stay in the *commune* and for my study of the school.

I lived in Lavialle from early November 1980 until late November 1981 – first in a room in the school building, and then in a small apartment in the village. I visited it again in the summer of 1984. When I arrived in Lavialle, during the month of November, I was struck early on by the naked volcanic peaks of the Puy-de-Dôme range, and the seemingly barren greyness of the terrain. When I had visited a few weeks earlier, investigating possible fieldwork sites, Lavialle had appeared picturesque and not unfriendly. Fall must have advanced considerably in the intervening time, however, because when I arrived to begin fieldwork, the landscape seemed very unwelcoming, as did the few Laviallois whom I met early on. I was not received with open arms by Lavialle families, and the posture of mistrust and wariness toward outsiders that I would later come to view as an integral part of Lavialle identity was unsettling when I was its object. I would

An 'outsider as any observer.

have been saved much distress if I had only known then that by springtime the entire region would be covered with green grass and spectacular wild-flowers, and that I would actually come to feel at ease among my neighbors and friends in Lavialle.

Morin nicely captures the importance of fieldwork "style" in his discussion of fieldwork in Brittany: "Adoption into the community involves adaption on the part of the visitor. He must be 'simple' and 'natural'" (1970:20). These were important values for the Laviallois, too, and I tried to adjust my behavior to this code. I also agree with Morin that "reserve and distrust are not the only obstacles to communication. Certain methods of inquiry may arouse resistance of another kind, which might be called the refusal to be categorized ethnographically" (1970:17). Although, as Morin suggests, this refusal is particularly pronounced among the French middle class, I sensed that intrusive research methods and interviewing techniques would not help me to gain the trust of the Laviallois. Most of my research was, therefore, conducted informally, with little or no note-taking in the presence of my informants. I am still convinced that, in a society in which literacy is such a culturally loaded phenomenon, my rapport with the rural Laviallois was enhanced by the predominance of oral, rather than written, inquiry.

Issues of power relationships between anthropologist and informants are always delicate, but especially so when the subject of study is education (since it is in this realm that most of the prestige of our discipline resides). As Bourdieu (1984) has so trenchantly shown, French society is very much stratified on the basis of educational attainment – through such markers as speech, dress, and lifestyle, as well as occupation and income. I was aware of my own status as student and of the possibility that I would be grouped with other professionals and outside agents in Lavialle. My foreign status, however, allowed me some freedom to avoid such easy markers. I was "other." My imperfect, if fluent French; my more casual American style of dress; and my attempts to accept and participate in the rural way of life, placed me in a more ambiguous role than that of French ethnographer.

My status as a single female in her mid-twenties permitted me easy access to the lives both of younger unmarried inhabitants and of people my own age who were married with young children. Although I did get to know many men, gender boundaries in Lavialle determined that I spend more time with women. The older women of Lavialle adopted a somewhat "protective" attitude toward me, and I was often invited to eat with neighbors and others, so that I would not be left alone. Although my being a young single woman living alone was a rarity in the *commune* itself, many families had unmarried daughters who lived alone and worked in the city. Lavialle families exhibit a flexibility, most likely connected to their continued strength, that allows unmarried daughters to leave and live on their own, yet keep in close contact with them. I was viewed by many older Laviallois as the daughter of a family in America who had just moved a little farther away than had their daughters, but who, like them, would return.

Because my study dealt with education, such a sensitive subject for farmers in France,[7] I attempted to keep myself distanced from the teachers and other "official" agents of government and religion. I hoped to gain the trust of the people of Lavialle in order to learn their own perspectives on schooling. At the same time, I wanted to observe the relationships between teachers and parents. Therefore, I always considered the teachers to be part of the study (as were the local families and children) not as privileged confidants. I also tried to avoid being seen as a teacher by the children, and did not take an authority role at school. I realize that in doing this I set up a sort of "othering" of the teachers, privileging the experience of the local families and my contact with them. This inversion was necessary, I believed at the time, in order to resist an identification with the teachers that would hinder both my ability to be accepted by local families and my ability to appreciate their version of the meaning and role of schooling. Since competing my fieldwork, I have become both a teacher and a parent, which causes me to view school-family relationships as much more complex than I had initially suspected. I am, however, still convinced that my approach was valid. I suspect that the identification with teachers that comes from the sort of study conducted by Wylie (1975), where the ethnographer takes on a role of teacher in a school, promotes another type of bias, in which school-family conflict is heavily colored by the perceptions of teachers.

Most of the children called me "Déborah" and used the familiar form of address with me (*tu*), as did teenagers and younger adults.[8] Older inhabitants of Lavialle called me "Mademoiselle Déborah," and used the *vous* form. The issue of form of address was negotiated soon after I arrived in Lavialle. This is a delicate business in France, and it often takes people in urban settings many months of acquaintance before the *tu* form will be used. There was a period early in my fieldwork when some younger adults used formal terms of address, but eventually all of my contemporaries used the *tu* form with me. I started early conversations with *vous*, wanting to be polite and being uncertain of the proper form of address; it was the

Laviallois who initiated more familiar speech patterns. (Chapter 8 takes up a discussion of parents' use of pronouns with teachers in Lavialle, and charts a shift from familiar to formal usage as conflict intensified.)

I spent the first four months of fieldwork carrying out intensive daily observations in the school, and then continued to visit the school about once a week when it was in session. In mid-March, I moved from my room in the school to an apartment in the center of the village, next to one of the cafes. My new lodgings permitted greater independence from the school and teachers, and was centrally located in Lavialle. My kitchen window opened onto the street, so that all passersby could see me if I was working at my table, and could stop and chat. The mailman (an important bearer of news) stopped every morning when he brought my mail, and I could see the bread delivery truck as it arrived in the village square. I was, most importantly, close to the local cafe. My landlady was the sister of the proprietor, and I became friendly with the family. This enabled me to enter the cafe freely for social visits with its owners, even though, as a woman, I would normally have been excluded such easy access to this male-centered domain.

It was mainly through the children and my contact with them at the school that I gradually gained entry to households. I spoke to the parents during a school meeting soon after my arrival in Lavialle, all of whom had already heard of me from their children. In my talk, I explained that I was a student interested in the life of children in a rural community. I began to get to know the Laviallois through visits to the households in the village where I lived. Later, in January, after I asked the children to write for me about the pig-slaughtering on their farms at that time of year, I was invited to attend several of these rituals, and thus began a deeper integration into family life.

Families were eager to let me see farm work at close hand, finding it easier to share this aspect of their lives with me than many others. When I visited farms, both men and women insisted that I accompany men to the barn at milking time to observe. Each time, the process and methods used were shown and explained. I was usually joined by the children during these visits, who would carefully tell me all the cows' names, little stories about them, and volunteer observations about which ones were pregnant. I also spent time alone with children at their homes, and followed them while they played.

Much of my fieldwork was spent with families, often helping in the fields or in the kitchen. I also participated in public activities and became an official member of the Youth Club and attended its meetings. As a

Youth Club member, I travelled with a group of Laviallois adults to a farming village in Normandy as part of an exchange program jointly organized with the school. I also accompanied the schoolchildren on their own trip to Normandy a few weeks later. I attended Mass most Sundays, was invited to holiday meals in Laviallois households, and participated in Tupperware and related types of parties in the *commune*.

In all of my dealings with the Laviallois, I attempted to demonstrate my willingness to participate in their lives – from helping with the haying, to feeding the animals and cooking, to slaughtering the pigs. They also knew that I spent a great deal of time reading and typing in my kitchen, which they gradually began to call my "work"; they saw my time spent with them in informal situations as a break from that "work." That my activities associated with literacy were seen as work by the Laviallois, while my labor on farms and fields was viewed as part of my leisure time, confirms the distance between us – despite my attempts to "fit in" – and underscores the role of education in social stratification.

"Work"

At the same time that I was doing participant-observation research in Lavialle, I carried out historical research on both schooling and regional socio-economic trends. I spent time in the communal archives and in regional archives in Clermont-Ferrand. I also interviewed former teachers of the school, and women who had worked there as cooks and aides. My interest in Lavialle's past was much more understandable to my informants than my interest in the present, and the work of folklorists was that to which I was most easily linked at first (apart from the usual suspicions that I was from the CIA). Early on during my fieldwork, I was often encouraged to visit elderly people who could tell me about how things "used to be." This was both a defensive move to distract me from current local affairs and a form of prideful self-presentation on the part of the Laviallois about their peasant past.

The Past

In addition to my research into the history of schooling, stretching my knowledge of Lavialle over time, I also went beyond the *commune* spatially, to visit other schools and families in the region. I spent time at both the public and Catholic middle schools attended by children from Lavialle, and observed a nursery school in Paris in order to gain some perspective on differences between center and periphery. In order to place Lavialle in its local regional context, I visited former Lavialle natives who had moved. I frequently visited a young woman from Lavialle who was a Catholic school teacher in Clermont-Ferrand, and a young family of Lavialle natives who had moved to another rural *commune* in the region. I lived for one week with a family in Grosbourg, and for two weeks with a farm

Other observations

family in a nearby *commune*. The wives in both of these families were Lavialle natives. My visits outside of Lavialle reinforced the message conveyed by the Laviallois to me that their community had retained its traditions more than had other *communes* in the local region. The strong network of Lavialle natives who had left, yet remained in close contact with their kin who remained, reinforced my view that this feature of social life was part of a desire to perpetuate a sense of belonging and of tradition, rather than a cultural lag.

On marginality

A flurry of rural ethnographies dominated the early years of Europeanist anthropology from the 1950s to the 1970s. There has since been much urging to address urban issues and global problems, such as those of immigrants, in European society. For some, the location of this study in a backwater region of central France may, at first glance, appear anachronistic (as well might Lavialle itself!). Many of the early community studies of Europe, and that of Laurence Wylie's *Village in the Vaucluse* (1975) comes immediately to mind in the context of France, relied upon romanticized and insular images of rural life. As a direct consequence of this, they often tended to ignore the wider socio-political context of those communities. Europeanist anthropologists have necessarily and quite rightly broadened their attention "beyond the community" (Boissevain 1975) since the 1970s.

There is a danger, however, in throwing the baby out with the bathwater in anthropological studies of Europe. The persistence of rural life, even as it changes, is vital to our understanding of global processes of power, resistance, and hegemony. This is not only of significance for European society. If our understandings of the influences of European hegemony on local communities in non-Western nations do not rely upon careful ethnographic study of Europe itself, then there is a strong risk of "occidentalizing" (Carrier 1992) – of reifying notions of European culture.[9] Recent studies of Europe "in the margins" help illuminate processes of change and persistence that have global significance (Herzfeld 1985 and 1987; McDonald 1989; Nadel-Klein 1991; Parman 1990; Rogers 1991; Wilson and Smith 1993).

In an age when popular images of contemporary urban life often depend upon either a nostalgia for the good old days in rural communities or a condemnation of the "ignorance" and "passivity" of country folk in former times, the study of schooling in Lavialle contributes to a more balanced view (see also Reed-Danahay and Anderson-Levitt 1991). This ethnographic journey questions prevalent assumptions about the French educational system and about relationships of resistance and power in European societies. The observation of national cultures from their own hinterlands is a vital enterprise, not to be forgotten by anthropologists, because it leads us to question the meaning of such dichotomies as traditional and modern, or margin and center.

2

Theoretical orientations: schooling, families, and power

This study combines the theoretical approaches of political anthropology with those of critical theory in education. I bring these perspectives to bear upon the understanding of family strategies for education and socialization – drawing from the work of social historians as well as from that of Pierre Bourdieu. In my attempts to understand schooling in Lavialle, I have been influenced by what Ortner (1984) has usefully labelled the "practice" approach in anthropology. I chose to study rural French education because this topic seemed well suited to the study of the interaction between social actors and social structure. Most policy in the French educational system originates in Paris at the National Ministry of Education. At every level, teachers are national employees, hired by regional educational authorities, who follow a national curriculum. Primary and nursery schools operate at the level of the *commune*, the smallest administrative unit in France. Thus, almost every French town and village has its own primary school for children up to the age of 11 or 12. Although the curriculum and the hiring of teachers are organized at the national level, the local government maintains the building and grounds of its school. This system has been in place for over a century, ever since the Ferry Laws of the 1880s making French primary education secular, mandatory, and free.

The centralized French system of primary education, superimposed upon diverse regional populations, provides an opportunity for the study of the manifestation (through social practices) in different local circumstances of a fairly uniform structure. I selected the remote mountain *commune* of Lavialle as a fieldsite precisely because it was far removed both spatially and culturally from the educational policy-makers in Clermont-Ferrand and Paris. In such a setting, I thought, the ways in

22

which local populations both shape and respond to national institutions would be more evident than in settings closer to centers of power.

I went to Lavialle to examine the ways in which the local population influenced schooling – in spite of the absence of formal mechanisms in the French educational system for parental or community input. I was looking for evidence of social agency within the structural constraints of French schooling, and my fieldwork in Lavialle confirmed my hunch that parents can informally influence schooling. More importantly, however, I learned that, in addition to strategies of influence over the school, families had adopted modes of defense against the intrusions of the state through education. Their power to influence the school was, thus, combined with forms of resistance to the power of the school. *Power of influence & resistance*

Despite the strong identification of French schools with the state, much of what occurred at Lavialle's school had to do with local matters. This was also a surprise to me, since I assumed that schooling would be dominated by state–local conflict. Parents used group parent–teacher meetings both to challenge and influence the teachers *and* to work out local political conflicts and rivalries. At school, children learned local cultural traditions of childhood at the same time that they learned French culture. An understanding of schooling in Lavialle entails a switch in emphasis from what schools do to what happens in and around schools. *Do vs. Surroundings*

This book lends an anthropological perspective to the pivotal meeting point of families and the state in France: a local primary school. Several excellent critiques of education have cogently alerted us to the aims of state control in education (Apple 1979; Bourdieu and Passeron 1990), and to the processes by which education was closely associated with the formation of modern nation-states (Anderson 1991; Boli *et al.* 1985; Cohen 1970; Green 1990). Western systems of education have promoted the state's goals of social stratification through elite and mass systems of training, and those of cultural homogenization and assimilation through dissemination of a common language and notions of citizenship. It is important, however, to distinguish between the overall intent of state educational systems and their incarnation in various local settings. The assumed monolithic nature of the French educational system is best viewed as part of an "officializing" (Bourdieu 1977b:40) discourse concerning the unity of France – rather than a *fait accompli*. A major aim of this study is to help dismantle the widespread assumption, held until quite recently in France, that, as Regine Sirota puts it, "the impact of a supercentralized educational system presupposes a great homogeneity in local situations" (1988:26; my translation).

Dismantle assumptions

Unity and diversity in France

The rural French primary school is a key symbol of the nation. A major concern in French rural historiography has been the role of village schools in the creation of a unified French nation, as teachers imposed a common language and culture which transcended regionalism (Grew and Harrigan 1991; Maynes 1985a; Thabault 1971; Weber 1976; Zeldin 1980). It is usually assumed that this process did occur, and that French peasants were, indeed, turned "into Frenchmen" (Weber 1976; see also Hobsbawm 1983) by the beginning of the twentieth century, or at least by its middle (Mendras and Cole 1991).

"The school," Eugen Weber writes, "notably the village school, compulsory and free, has been credited with the ultimate acculturation process that made the French people French – finally civilized them . . ." (1976:303). These comments by an eminent French historian are echoed in those made more recently by French rural sociologist Henri Mendras, who writes that "the spread of national education gradually broke down the old regional barriers, which had prevailed over much of France throughout the 19th century. It helped create a uniform, centralized nation, in which national identity overrode separate regional sentiment" (1991:91). The role of the Third Republic's rural schoolteachers, hailed as "secular missionaries," in this project of national unification is an important part of French cultural mythology (Ozouf 1967; Reboul-Scherrer 1989; Villin and Lesage 1987).

Primary schools in France have disseminated a common language and a common culture through a centralized bureaucracy, but these work to legitimize bourgeois culture, and have reinforced, rather than eliminated, regional and class-based boundaries. Andy Green, a comparative historian of education, has concluded that French schools worked to create difference among social classes through different types of training, rather than to promote a shared culture (1990:162). If the French did share some common culture, Green suggests, they were inserted into that culture in a variety of ways, depending upon their social class.

Despite centuries of effort to create a unified, homogeneous state, France is frequently characterized as a nation of deep cultural diversity and intense social stratification. Several ethnographic studies of rural France have stressed the continued development of regional attachments and local cultural forms (Reiter 1972; Rogers 1991; Rosenberg 1988). For the most part, these are interpreted not as traditional "hold-outs" from earlier times, but as ongoing responses to the universalizing tendencies of the nation. Susan Carol Rogers (1991) has recently argued that cultural diversity is not antithetical to modernization, and that regional variations persist during times of social change. She uses the resurgence of archaic living arrangements in a contemporary rural community to show that cultural forms do not necessarily disappear during processes of modernization, but follow different trajectories.

In an historical study of political economy in the Alps, Harriet Rosenberg (1988) stresses the active role of regional populations in the shaping of wider social processes. She emphasizes local attempts to resist the modernizing forces of capitalism and shows how tradition can be invented and reinvented during different economic periods. In contrast to stereotypes of French peasants as historically illiterate and apolitical, Rosenberg presents the case of a rural population in the "hinterlands" long interested in literacy and active in national politics.

The interest in cultural diversity in these rural ethnographies differs from the emphasis on more uniform processes in schools among ethnographers of French education. In her studies of urban and suburban French classrooms and teachers (1987 and 1989), and more recent comparisons with American cases (1994), Kathryn Anderson-Levitt stresses the shared basis of culture among French teachers. She has found striking similarities in the cultural assumptions and teaching practices of French teachers. When she and I compared criticisms of their pupils by teachers in Lavialle and in her own more urban setting, we found that quite similar cultural images of families and of rural and urban life informed all of the teachers' remarks (Reed-Danahay and Anderson-Levitt 1991). Our analysis of the ways in which teachers, often unwittingly, contribute to social stratification through criticisms of families sought to unpack French dominant ideology as used by primary school teachers. We suggested that, although this was not a coherent ideology, and was rife with contradictory images of the ideal family, it was used to justify the low status of contemporary working-class and farm families.

Although the two different views of France that one gets from rural ethnography and an urban study of French education seem to convey contradictory perspectives on French society, when combined, they complement each other in forming a more balanced view. France has certain institutions or structures in which all citizens participate and share to some degree. The social class divisions of French society appear to arise in the context of these overall structures, like education and industry – which explains the emphasis on social class among educational researchers. However, as ethnographic research among families and in communities shows, the people who participate in these more global institutions bring to them cultural backgrounds and social identities which differ. The important question to ask about French society (and perhaps any nation-state) is not, then, whether or not it is unified or diverse, but how it is that people learn to both participate in national structures *and* retain local and familial attachments. *Participate nationally, retain locality?*

Bourdieu, French education, and the peasantry

Many of the questions that provoked this study of schooling and power in rural France arose as responses to the work of Pierre Bourdieu. I will therefore turn to his theoretical and ethnographic contributions to the study of France at some length before returning to the case of Lavialle.

Bourdieu is most well known among anthropologists for his work among the Kabyle peoples of Algeria and more recent work on French class distinctions, language, and academic culture. Less known are his ethnographic writings on the Béarn region of rural France. All of Bourdieu's research and writings on France, whether focused on the peasantry or the middle classes, have dealt with the interplay between family-based systems of inculcation or socialization and formal educational systems in the construction of social-class differences. Unfortunately, however, Bourdieu has never combined these two foci within a single ethnographic study. Therefore, he writes either ethnographically of social practice in families or sociologically of social reproduction in schools. This has led him, I believe, despite his own protestations to the contrary (1990), to an overly deterministic view of the effects of dominant culture on the lives of rural French children.

Whether he is dealing with the marriage strategies of French farmers (1972), French students (1964), or the concept of "taste" in consumer culture (1984), Bourdieu relies upon a theory of "habitus" – a system of predispositions to action and belief acquired through what he calls "inculcation" in the family. External "conditions of existence" (which include class position), mediated by the family, determine the structures of the habitus "which in turn become the basis of perception and appreciation of all subsequent experience" (1977b:78). For Bourdieu, social systems and social actors are closely linked. He has recently written that ". . . the legitimatization of the social order . . . results from the fact that agents apply to the objective structures of the social world structures of perception and appreciation that have emerged from these objective structures and tend therefore to see the world as self-evident" (1990:135).

Family strategies, according to Bourdieu, are the product of habitus (1972:1124). Marriage strategies, like fertility strategies and educational strategies, are the means by which any group transmits to future generations "those powers and privileges that it has itself inherited" (1972:1125). Bourdieu shows, for instance, that farm families hope to make a "good match" (*beau mariage*) in the marriages of their children, in order to reproduce or augment the patrimony. Farm children, so the theory goes, are inculcated with just the right attitudes and tastes to choose a fitting spouse through what Bourdieu labels "la prime education" (which vaguely refers to all early childhood experiences). To paraphrase Bourdieu (1972), duty and sentiment are made inseparable, destiny given the appearance of free choice. Although Bourdieu acknowledges that there are sometimes breakdowns in this marriage system, he prefers to emphasize the high degree to which children do make the "right" marital choice.

Bourdieu has recently explained that his concept of strategy was developed in reaction to what he considers the over-reliance on a notion of obedience to rules among structuralists in their explanations of behavioral regularities (1990:65). It is also, however, meant to refute the concept of the calculating, rational individual assumed by theories of methodological individualism. For Bourdieu, the social actor is the "socialized agent" whose strategies are "more or less 'automatic'" and practical "and not the projects or calculations of any conscious mind" (1990:62). When he turns to the analysis of French education, Bourdieu argues that the educational strategies of families from different social strata, determined by their varying inculcated habitus, play a major role in educational outcomes. For Bourdieu, all strategies are primarily aimed at processes of social and cultural reproduction, rather than transformation. He writes that strategies are used by families "to produce and reproduce themselves, that is, to create and perpetuate their unit, and thus their existence as groups, which is almost always, and in all societies, the condition of the perpetuation of their position in the social space" (1990:74).

Statistical studies of education in France show that the children of small-scale farmers in France do not, by and large, advance beyond their parents' socio-economic status and tend to become either farmers themselves or low-skilled manual laborers (Daucé *et al.* 1972; Jegouzo and Brangeon 1976). As Bourdieu and others have suggested, the French school system plays a major role in this reproduction of the status quo (Baudelot and Establet 1971; Bourdieu *et al.* 1973; Bourdieu and Passeron 1990). Claude Grignon demonstrated the inequalities of the educational system in the 1970s through a study of social class differences in atten-

dance at various types of agricultural schools. The children of French
farmers who pursue agricultural careers usually attend rural vocational
schools (where they compose 83% of the pupils). In contrast, at agricultural high schools, only 53% of the students are the children of farmers,
and in the *grandes écoles* (elite institutions) of agronomy, only 23% of the
students are the children of farmers (Grignon 1975:78).

A pessimist when it comes to rural France, Bourdieu concludes that the
lower educational levels of farm children represent farmers' internaliza-
tions of a "practical acceptance" of their class position. As he so persua-
sively puts it: "Think for instance of the expression 'This is not for us' by
which the most deprived exclude themselves from possibilities from which
they would be excluded anyway" (1990:112). Bourdieu and his colleagues
portray those French farmers who encourage their children to leave
farming as unwitting accomplices of bourgeois hegemony: "One could not
suppress the peasantry without their own complicity. Emigration to the
city, the placing of children in institutions of higher education, and the
marrying of their daughters to urban men are the actions through which
peasants conspire against their own class future by becoming accomplices
to those who wish their extinction" (1973: 103, my translation). He pays
less attention to those who, like the Laviallois, resist such outcomes. For
Bourdieu, the strategies of rural French families ultimately reproduce the
class structure, and reflect an internalization of class position.

When he turns more specifically to the role of education in social reproduction, Bourdieu posits that the culture of the school most closely resembles the class culture (habitus) of the dominant classes in France, which, he
suggests, explains their school success. The school, he and his colleagues
have argued, has assumed part of the bourgeois family's role in cultural
and social transmission, and now serves to reproduce its class interests. It
is through the school that the symbolic (rather than purely material)
capital of the bourgeoisie is transmitted to future generations, assuring
their dominant position in society (1979). Bourdieu means by symbolic or
cultural capital those "cultural goods" (1990:30) which include linguistic
styles, values, interests, and tastes.

Members of the lower classes (such as small farmers) fail to succeed in
schooling, Bourdieu argues, because they lack the types of social knowledge and symbolic capital valued by the school system. They fail mainly
by opting out of the system, however, rather than being forced to leave.
Because of their "misrecognition" (Bourdieu's term) of the objective
structures of power and symbolic violence (operating through the
devaluation of their cultural capital and the legitimization of bourgeois

Making the only Choice they believe they have.

forms) which they encounter at school, the children of farmers internalize their failure and "choose" to enter farming and low-skilled careers – thereby contributing to social and cultural reproduction.[1]

Apart from Bourdieu's ethnographic observations in rural France, which led to his study of peasant marriage strategies, his writings on relationships between families, social class, and education are based upon statistical research. In most of his writings on education, Bourdieu focuses on the educational strategies of bourgeois families, rather than farmers or other lower classes, as they use schools to reproduce and assure their own dominant position.

Two recent qualitative studies influenced by Bourdieu's work use the concepts of class-based family strategies to explain differences in educational outcomes. One of these is Annette Lareau's (1989) study of parental involvement in two US elementary schools. The other is Regine Sirota's (1988) study of French classrooms, which infers family strategies from the classroom behaviors of children from different social classes in Parisian elementary schools. Both studies adopt Bourdieu's insight that families from dominant classes have more effective educational strategies because *Cultural Capital* their own cultural capital and class habitus are more closely in tune with that of the school than is the case among other families. This is also the underlying premise of Heath's (1983) study of families, language use, and education in the southern Appalachian region.

Family strategies
The strategies of rural and working-class families have received less focused attention than those of either the middle classes or the state. Studies of middle- and upper-class families show their active manipulation of education in order to achieve desired goals (Lareau 1989; Allatt 1993; LeWita 1988; Motley 1990). Bourdieu has examined French bourgeois strategies in much more depth than those of subordinate classes (1964; 1984) perhaps because, as he recently writes, he believes that other classes did not make much use of education until fairly recently (1990:44). *Formal Ed.*

The precise reasons why farm children enter farming and other rural careers, rather than middle-class professions, are complicated. In his study of northern Italian secondary education, Gambetta (1987) asks whether the structure "pushes" students to certain educational outcomes or whether the students choose to "jump." This metaphor is particularly suited to thinking about the education of minority groups, whose educational experiences often follow a downward turn. But are they moving off the educational bus, or over a cliff? Is the behavior of French farm children due to factors of elimination in the educational system that push children out of school early and into farm careers, or do they choose to leave for other reasons? Educational outcomes are, perhaps, best explained in terms of a dynamic negotiation between a structured system of inequality in the schools and the perceptions and strategies of families concerning the educational needs of their children.

What are usually termed the educational "failures" of children from rural and working-class families are most often assumed to result from a deficit in knowledge about the system, cultural capital, or language use – rather than from active strategies. Ogbu (1982) has usefully addressed this issue by clarifying the role of cultural discontinuities between home and school in school outcomes. In his work on racial minorities in the United States, Ogbu suggests that it is the type of cultural difference between families and schools, rather than difference *per se*, that determines educational outcomes. He argues that both immigrants coming in contact with schools of their host country and non-Western peoples attending Western-style schools experience different types of cultural discontinuity at school from those of native minority populations (or "castelike minorities") who are in situations of "stratified domination" (1982:298).

Although the Laviallois do not exhibit many characteristics of "castelike minorities," they are a regional minority population whose educational strategies are usefully viewed in terms of Ogbu's theory. The point most relevant to schooling in Lavialle made by Ogbu is that opposition to dominant culture is an important feature of such minority groups. He writes:

> subordinate group members . . . may . . . create certain cultural and linguistic features that differentiate them from their superiors in order to maintain their identity and sense of security or out of dislike for their superiors . . . they know a good deal about the culture of the dominant group but do not necessarily practice it, because their convention dictates that they should not act like members of the dominant group. *(300)*

Ogbu suggests that members of subordinate groups are "bicultural" because of their knowledge of dominant culture. Scott (1989) makes similar observations about the peasantry and other subordinate peoples. Families in Lavialle, for their part, accomplish what can be called cultural diglossia by selectively participating in national institutions and culture while at the same time actively reinforcing local identity and social life.

An understanding of the role of family strategies in schooling must take into account the relationship between culture and class. Although cultural discontinuities are frequently blamed for educational outcomes, an emphasis on culture alone fails to address the important class bases of

schooling processes. Similarly, an emphasis on social class and stratification in education can neglect the role of regional and class-based cultures
in responses to schools on the part of parents and students.

As Paul Willis has argued, low educational outcomes, such as those
among the adolescent males he studied in an English urban comprehensive school, can be explained on the basis of resistance to hegemony. In
this urban study, social class becomes the dominant explanatory mode.
The behaviors of the lads in rejecting school are explained as due to a particular cultural complex of gender and class attitudes among working-
class youth.

In contrast to urban-oriented research, much of the literature on class-
based resistance in rural settings places such resistance within the economic realm of the family economy, rather than emphasizing any link to
education or popular culture. James Scott, for example, links peasant
resistance to "the basic material survival needs of the peasant household"
(1985:295), and argues that it is the desire of the household to survive that
fuels both everyday resistance and outright rebellion to the claims of
employers, tax collectors, and landlords. In another analysis of peasant
resistance, Gavin Smith argues that "daily struggles" are closely connected
to "political struggles" (1989:17).

These perspectives link resistance to a notion of the "family economy"
and its role in family strategies. Louise Tilly and Joan Scott explain that
the family economy, which dominated rural life before industrialization,
was a system wherein "production and family life were inseparably intertwined. And the household was the center around which resources, labor,
and consumption were balanced" (1978:12). Mary Jo Maynes (1985b)
used the concept of family economy to understand the decisions about
their children's schooling made by rural families in nineteenth-century
France and Germany. She uses it to explain, for instance, that the family's
need for child labor and rural impoverishment often led to the attitude
that "children had more important things to do than to go to school"
(1985b:85).

Tilly (1980) identifies family strategies connected to the family wage
economy among the French proletariat in the nineteenth century in order
to provide a link between individual lives and collective behavior. Tilly
writes that family strategies were developed to deal with a variety of situations, such as schooling, labor, residence, and marriage (1980:203). She is
interested in the ways in which the family position of individuals, as well as
the overall social context of the family, influence the choices made and
strategies adopted by any particular family. Tilly was influenced in her use

of the concept of family strategies by Bourdieu's (1972) article on matri-
monial strategies among twentieth-century French farmers. She draws
upon Bourdieu's claim that in rural society "the household, not the individual or the society as a whole, acts as the unit of decision-making" (Tilly
1980:203).

The concept of family strategy is useful in understanding the educational behaviors of parents and children in Lavialle, where the household
remains the fundamental unit of identity and decision-making. For the
Laviallois, the educational strategies of families are predicated upon the
close identification of family and farm. As is the case for many rural
French families, decisions about how much and what type of education to
encourage in children are intrinsically tied to concerns about safeguarding
the family patrimony. As Henri Mendras writes:

> In the final analysis, the survival and continuity of the family depend on those of
> the farm, and vice versa. Thus, the father who knows that one of his children will
> take over the farm manages his enterprise differently than the one who has set up
> all his children in other occupations; and the father who wants to keep one son at
> home does his best to tempt him, when he comes of age, to remain and see that the
> "house" – the family and farm – survives.   *(1970:83)*

Family strategy is also a good place to identify female behaviors and relationships to power, particularly in terms of resistance. Most peasant
studies of resistance focus on male behaviors in public struggles over land
or politics (i.e., Scott 1985 and Smith 1989). Women's roles in power relations generally reside within the private realm of the family; therefore,
through the concept of family strategy, particularly related to children,
they become more visible in discussions of power.

Classroom strategies
Much of the literature on pupil resistance in education has centered on
overt challenges to authority among, primarily, working-class youth at the
secondary level (Foley 1990; McLaren 1985 and 1986; Willis 1981a). These
studies have usefully challenged views of students as passive victims of
hegemonic systems of oppression, and stress schools as sites of conflict
over, and the production of, cultural meanings. The schoolchildren of
Lavialle exhibit forms of passive, or "everyday" forms of resistance, and,
as such, their behaviors differ from the more self-conscious and overt resistance of adolescents.

It is useful, however, to consider this literature on adolescents here,
because of its strong theoretical attempts to link classroom behaviors to
wider social processes. One finds contrasting models of the meaning of

classroom resistance in William Schonfeld's (1971) analysis of authority relationships in French secondary schools, on the one hand, and more recent studies in Canada and England, respectively, by McLaren (1985 and 1986) and Willis (1977).

Schonfeld identified two poles in a complex of resistance and compliance in adolescent behaviors toward teachers. This complex varied from what he labeled the "authority-laden syndrome." where the teacher is a controlling authority figure and pupils are compliant, to the "chahut syndrome," where the teacher is not an effective authority figure and pupils adopt a stance of open opposition and noncompliance. Schonfeld, a political scientist, attributes the presence of these two opposed models to a preoccupation with "authority" in French national character. He claims that the chahut arises in part from the child's transition from the two "authority-laden" contexts of family and primary school, to a more diverse secondary-school experience. When children do not find a teacher to be sufficiently authoritative, he argues, they will develop overt means of opposition and "testing." Schonfeld defines the chahut as a situation in which "the teacher has lost basic control of the class" (27), and notes its pervasiveness throughout French secondary schools. He connects these alternating authority patterns in secondary schools to what some observers of France have identified as the profoundly contradictory nature of French culture: oscillating between anarchy and authoritarianism (1971:8). Contradictory French Culture?

This model from France differs from studies of resistance among working-class youth in other cultural contexts. Schonfeld's description of the chahut is reminiscent of the modes of resistance characterized by Willis for "the lads," working-class adolescents in a British high school (1977) or the "clowning" described by McLaren for working-class youth in a Canadian high school (1985 and 1986). McLaren, in direct contradiction to the explanation for oppositional behavior given by Schonfeld, however, writes that "breaching the rules is often a logical response to the oppressive conditions of the classroom and occurs most often when the naked authoritarianism of the teacher becomes too much to bear" (1985:87). For Schonfeld, French adolescents are noncompliant when they question the authority of the teacher, not when that authority is felt to be oppressive.

It may be that similar behaviors of resistance have different underlying causes, and that French and Anglo-Saxon youth have varying attitudes toward authority. This would certainly be an interesting comparative topic, but one which I cannot, unfortunately, address here. There are, however, other differences in the type of analysis of resistance offered by Willis and McLaren to that of Schonfeld. For Schonfeld, the school is a "mirror" of the wider French culture, and embodies contradictory attitudes toward authority, as does this wider culture. It is presented as a vehicle for the reproduction of these attitudes and behaviors, much as Althusser (1971) described both the school and the family as ideological state apparatuses working to reproduce class relations.

For Willis and McLaren, schools are sites of cultural production, as well as reproduction. As such, they produce contradictions and negotiations about control and authority, and are peopled by "social agents" who, as Willis writes "are not passive bearers of ideology, but active appropriators who reproduce existing structures only through struggle, contestation and a partial penetration of those structures" (1981a:175). These two perspectives place different emphases on social agency in their analyses of pupil resistance. For Schonfeld, French secondary pupils are behaving according to a code inscribed in ambivalent, but shared, attitudes toward authority in French culture. For Willis and McLaren, pupils are social actors whose behavior does not mirror, but, rather, creates cultural meaning.

Schonfeld's explanations, apart from their difference from those offered by Willis and McLaren, are less than satisfactory for the French context as well. In order to explain behaviors in secondary schools, he relied upon overgeneralized portraits of French home and school life at the primary level. Schonfeld bases much of his explanation on Wylie's monograph *Village in the Vaucluse*, from which he draws the conclusion that parents in France generally support teachers (1971:8). He claims that families and primary schools in France share similar patterns of authority, so that there is little discrepancy between home and school (1971:40).

Recent ethnographic work challenges this view of French schools. Anderson-Levitt has shown that, while, not surprisingly, urban working-class and immigrant families are labeled in their behaviors as deviant by French elementary teachers, upper-class families are also viewed as different from the preferred middle-class family model (Anderson-Levitt 1989; see also Reed-Danahay and Anderson-Levitt 1991 and Grillo 1985). The model of authority relations in French schools proposed by Schonfeld may reflect bourgeois contexts of family and home, but cannot be generalized to account for "the French" as a whole, and fails to incorporate social class differences into an understanding of family authority patterns. In order to understand the behaviors of children in Lavialle, comparative examples of classroom resistance in other cultures may be more useful than that of Schonfeld's for French adolescents.

Despite the observation that "norms of resistance are very common among schoolchildren" (D'Amato 1988:540), there are few studies of classroom resistance among elementary school children. The studies of D'Amato (1988) and Sieber (1979) suggest caution in forming generalizations about the role of classroom resistance in primary schools. D'Amato's study of Hawaiian schoolchildren describes a transformation in pupil behaviors toward teachers from resistance to compliance, despite general structural constraints on school achievement and social mobility. After an initial period of pupil resistance, he writes, "Hawaiian children and their teachers then grow very fond and protective of each other" (1988:540). This situation differs from that in Lavialle, where teachers and students rarely form close personal bonds.

In a study of elementary peer behavior in an urban setting in the US, Sieber (1979) argues against assumptions that peer groups necessarily subvert school aims. Peer activity in classrooms can, he suggests, be a form of "informal work organization" (1979:209), shaped by teachers, which corresponds to the needs of industrial work settings. The emphasis on peer groups as forming resistance to the school fails, Sieber argues, to take into account other meanings of such behavior. These studies suggest that the meaning of pupil resistance depends upon both the wider social context of the school and the specific organization of the classroom.

In Lavialle, families do not share a model of authority relations with the teachers, and have not done so in the past. Children in Lavialle are, indeed, conflicted as they face two hegemonic systems – that of their families and that of the school. These are not identical, as Schonfeld insists they are in French schools, but neither are they independent. They have, rather, developed through mutual influences. The children's resistance to teachers in school is informed by a long history of school-community relationships, whereby a "culture of childhood" at school and cultural models for dealing with school have been developed. Children have shaped resistance to teachers on the basis of stories they have heard from parents and grandparents about their own harsh experiences at school, and also from hearing their parents openly criticize their own teachers. They also learn about resistance from peers and model behaviors on older children, much like the "lads" described by Willis.

An important question to be raised about the resistance of children in school is that of the degree to which this is part of a common developmental process of child–adult relationships in Western society which involves the establishment of concepts of authority, and to what degree it relates to wider political processes and varies according to social position.

Put another way, how does what goes on in schools articulate with broader political processes, and how can this be conceptualized? An important place to start in answering this question, is to realize that schooling is informed by the strategies of families as well as by educational authorities. Wider conditions, events, and meanings influence schooling at both of these levels – through their effects on families and through their effects on educational policy.

The study of resistance

Schooling & Power

The analysis of schooling set forth in the remaining pages of this book concerns relationships between schooling and power – the power of the French state and its educational apparatus, and the power of Lavialle families to influence its effects upon their children. It seeks to reconcile the cultural and historical analyses of resistance to, or noncompliance with domination (Certeau 1988; Foster 1988; Martin 1987; Scott 1985 and 1990; Smith 1989) with the insightful perspectives of the sociology of education emphasizing the hegemonic nature of schools and their role in the reproduction of social stratification (Apple 1979; Bourdieu and Passeron 1990; Willis 1981a).[2] My approach shares with other recent anthropological studies a focus on social practice and cultural meaning in wider social, political, and historical perspectives (Behar 1986; Cohen 1987; Herzfeld 1985; Rogers 1991; Sider 1986).

A case-study challenging a theory?

Bourdieu's work on family strategies and on education as a vehicle for social stratification is crucial to an understanding of schooling in France and elsewhere. However, the case of Lavialle has prompted me to rethink some of his theoretical perspectives. Although I am much persuaded by Bourdieu's arguments about the workings of power in French society, I take issue with his seeming denial of resistance, which, as I see it, is the other side of the coin. Lavialle families skillfully employ modes of resistance as well as accommodation in their dealings with teachers and the school, and cannot be viewed simply as the unwitting accomplices of a powerful and hegemonic educational system. Research in education directed by a concern with social class tends to look for global processes associated with educational institutions, assumed to operate in fairly standard ways in various schools. This local study of schooling in Lavialle incorporates the more particularistic emphases of cultural anthropology, paying attention to both historical and local contexts. Like Heath (1983), I lend more weight to the values and attitudes of families, rather than interpreting them, as Bourdieu does, in terms of a misrecognition of power relations.

The Laviallois are not, I suggest here, playing out a cultural script determined by their position in the overall class structure, but are actively involved in the creation, production, and transformation of social life. *Active Agents* They have adapted to change and persisted because of their ability to manipulate and resist sources of power. For the Laviallois, social and cultural reproduction is not a straightforward matter to which all family strategies and educational experiences necessarily lead, but must be accomplished through struggle and negotiation. Bourdieu's analysis of education and social class in France is most usefully interpreted as an "ideal" model of an arrangement from which the dominant classes would most benefit, rather than a model of what actually occurs.

Except for Heath's detailed descriptions of children at home as well as at school, research on education and social class tends to focus mostly on schools. Family strategies are, consequently, viewed primarily in terms of parental behavior at schools. Although Lareau (1989) maintains that parental involvement must be viewed within a broader perspective, her *Shifts this / (2003)* observations were confined primarily to formal parent–teacher interaction. Bourdieu's theory of inculcation and family socialization, likewise, lacks ethnographic detail.

In this study of schooling and families in Lavialle, I incorporate an understanding of the wider context in which educational strategies are shaped by looking from the families to the school, rather than, as is often the case in school ethnography, working either exclusively within the *Families to the School* school or looking from the school outward (see Foley 1990). This allows for more emphasis on the meanings of schooling for people who attend educational institutions and send their children to them. Parents in Lavialle seek to influence the education of their children through whatever means available, and do so not only through their interactions with the school and teachers, but through the reinforcement of local identity outside of school.

I am especially persuaded by Foucault's argument, best expressed in his first volume on the *History of Sexuality* (1978), that power and resistance *Foucault* go hand in hand and are both "distributed in irregular fashion" (1978:96). Foucault articulates a view of resistance wherein it is intertwined with power, yet always offering a challenge to it. The role of small-scale forms of resistance ("a plurality of resistances" – [Foucault 1978:96]), which neither overturn the dominant social order nor simply acquiesce to its hegemony, has been of increasing importance in the literature on resistance. This has been illuminated by Scott – with the notion of "everyday resistance" (1985), and by Certeau – with the notion of "everyday practices" (1988). These are useful concepts in understanding the ways families in Lavialle approach the school. Their resistance does not entail a total, highly organized form of rebellion but, rather, "mobile and transitory points of resistance" (Foucault 1978:96).

Everyday resistance, as defined by Scott, constitutes unofficial (private) discourses and behaviors that subvert and undermine official (public) ideologies and actions. It is a form of political action among subordinate groups that is disguised, and characterized by "such acts as foot dragging, dissimulation, false compliance, feigned ignorance, desertion . . . sabotage . . ." (1989:5). Scott (1990) has more recently described these acts as "hidden" transcripts not readily apparent in the "official" transcripts and onstage behaviors controlled by elites. A similar concept is expressed by Certeau in what he calls "ways of operating," "everyday practices," or bricolage. Certeau defines these as "victories of the 'weak' over the 'strong' (whether that strength be that of powerful people or the violence of things or of an imposed order, etc.), clever tricks, knowing how to get away with things, 'hunter's cunning', maneuvers . . ." (1988:xix).

Concepts of resistance depend upon a notion of people as social actors. The degree to which social actors are truly aware of their objective circumstances is a subject of much debate in contemporary social theory. For Bourdieu (1977b), who advocates a theory of *méconnaissance* (or, misrecognition), social action, or "practice," does not occur with an awareness of objective social circumstances. It is a feature of modern society, according to Bourdieu, that the arbitrary nature of power relations is masked. Bourdieu argues that schools, therefore, are mistaken for "neutral" institutions, rather than symbolically violent and stratifying ones (Bourdieu and Passeron 1990). The necessity of misrecognition to the legitimacy of power relations at school, according to Bourdieu and Passeron, is such that: "Every power to exert symbolic violence, i.e. every power which manages to impose meanings and to impose them as legitimate by concealing the power relations which are the basis of its force, adds its own specifically symbolic force to those power relations" (1990:4). For resistance theorists, especially Scott (1985) and Willis (1981a), the ability to resist depends upon some ideological "penetration" of such masking, mystification, or, as it is most strongly phrased, "false consciousness." Social actors, according to this perspective, oppose and challenge the dominant ideology (Abercrombie *et al.* 1980) when they engage in behaviors of resistance. Their "misrecognition," to use Bourdieu's term, is not total.

A useful middle ground to this issue is suggested by Sider, who writes that "people act in terms of what they cannot understand, or understand in radically different ways, and in terms of relationships they cannot form, or sustain, or leave, as well as in terms of what 'works', what they think they clearly understand and probably do" (Sider 1986:10; quoted in Vincent 1990:405). Giddens says much the same thing when he writes that "all human beings are knowledgeable agents" (1984:281). He then goes on to address indirectly the issue of "misrecognition": "Since actors do what they do for reasons, they are naturally likely to be disconcerted if told by sociological observers that what they do derives from factors that somehow act externally to them. Lay objections to such 'findings' may thus have a very sound basis. Reification is by no means purely character-istic of lay thought" (1984:284). Herzfeld's concept of "social poetics" (1985) similarly values the integrity of the social and cultural meanings of informants and sees them as actively shaping and creating social realities.

The concept of "everyday resistance" is useful in understanding the educational strategies of the Laviallois. At the same time, a study of their behaviors helps clarify the relationship between compliance and resis-tance. Lavialle families have influenced the education of their children through "everyday" resistance, overt challenges to teachers, modes of accommodation, and active manipulation. I will argue in this book that the Laviallois resist state power, but do not do so in a calculated manner which is always based upon a clearly articulated understanding of pro-cesses of domination. Their resistance does not, moreover, reside in a sense of individual agency, but rather in the strength of extended family groups and local cultural identity. As Kondo has warned, it is important to guard against notions of the unified "self" who can "authentically resist power" (1990:224). Power and meaning are intertwined, she argues, drawing upon Foucault, so that it is important to look at the creation of and struggle over meanings in everyday contexts, rather than to focus exclusively upon resistance.[3]

The concept of resistance has become a kind of catch-all in social theory, as Abu-Lughod (1990), Giroux (1983), and King (1982) have reminded us. Ethnographers now have the task of sorting out more clearly the relationship between the public performance of either resistance or compliance and the cultural models informing these behaviors. This must be set within an overall framework of power – defined as the ability to influence behavior or thought.

A distinction between overt (explicit) forms of resistance and tacit (everyday or "hidden") forms of resistance is common in the literature (cf. Scott 1985 and 1990; McLaren 1985). I suggest that compliance can, simi-

Compliance

larly, be viewed as having both overt or tacit manifestations. A wide range of variation concerning behaviors of resistance and compliance has been described in ethnographic studies. Scott (1985 and 1990) describes every-day resistance as a form of overt compliance masking tacit resistance. In his model of the overt resistance of the lads, Willis (1981a) posits that this ultimately implies a tacit compliance with structures of domination, leading to social reproduction. Smith (1989) traces a situation in which overt compliance turns into overt resistance or rebellion among peasants.

In a slightly different approach, Sirota (1988:173) identifies "active conformism" among working-class pupils in French elementary schools who must work to conform to school rules, and "passive conformism" among the children of professionals, for whom it is easier to behave in a timid and respectful manner at school – since their own social class back-ground is closer to that promoted by the school. While both forms of behavior constitute overt and not hidden forms of conformity, they differ in the amount of effort needed to achieve them. This has interesting implications for the study of resistance and compliance.

Such studies suggest that resistance and accommodation have several components, and that they may operate along a continuum ranging from total compliance (tacit, overt, and passive), to total rebellion (tacit, overt, and active resistance). Resistance may be overt, tacit, and active or passive (depending upon the degree to which it must be achieved or comes more "naturally"). Compliance, similarly, may take tacit, overt, active or passive forms. An understanding of active and passive dimensions of resistance entails going beyond the view of everyday resistance as "hidden", espe-cially as articulated by Scott (1985). A consideration of the active or passive dimension of resistance does not depend upon the troublesome notion of intentionality, which Scott raises with regard to everyday resis-tance. For Scott, whether or not a behavior, like pilfering, was primarily intended to satisfy one's hunger or to resist domination does not under-mine its role in everyday resistance. In the same way, a behavior labelled as active is not necessarily more intentional, nor any more effective, than one labelled as passive. By characterizing tacit forms of resistance as either active or passive, these can be distinguished without regard to their inten-tionality.

The Laviallois, for the most part, express tacit, passive forms of resis-tance. Because their cultural identity has been formed in opposition to "outsiders" and the dominant culture, resistance for the Laviallois is a "natural" stance, and, therefore, in the sense in which I am using this term, "passive." How, and to what degree, have rural families in France been able to influence education and resist the hegemonic tendencies of the school? The families of Lavialle, located far off the beaten track from mainstream French culture, serve as my ethnographic example throughout the following chapters in order to address this question.

Main thesis/question!

3

Cultural identity and social practice

Geertz's famous dictum that "anthropologists don't study villages . . . they study *in* villages" (1973:22) usefully orients our attention to cultural processes rather than to the administrative or geographic unit which is the "locus of study." Places, like Lavialle, are not, however, irrelevant or redundant in social analysis. The important issue is to understand the ways in which villages (or towns or *communes*) are socially constructed, "imagined" (Anderson 1991),[1] and used by social actors.

Definitions of "community" are numerous (Bell and Newby 1974), and I do not wish to reject emphatically any claims to the use of this term for Lavialle. It is, however, necessary to move beyond the usual dichotomy between school and community in order to understand schooling in Lavialle. The *commune* of Lavialle is not self-contained, has many internal divisions based on kinship and hamlet residence, and provides only one among many social spheres from which individuals living there gain a sense of "belonging" (Cohen 1982). In Lavialle, as in many French rural communities, it is the household and kin group, rather than the *commune,* which is most fundamental to social identity (Mendras 1991; Rogers 1991). As the authors of a recent overview of French ethnography caution, "the *commune*, administrative unit, is not necessarily a 'community' . . . bearer of a sentiment of collective identity" (Cuisinier and Segalen 1986:83; my translation).[2]

Being French is at best a vague, general source of group identity for the people of Lavialle. They define their identity in terms of region in important ways. Kinship provides the most called upon source of social identity in everyday life. The concept of being Laviallois, including the rights and duties of participation in local social life, is linked primarily to membership in a family with land in Lavialle, rather than to simple residence

42

within its borders. Although a dominant core of people reside and work in the *commune*, one's affiliation in a kin group in Lavialle is the most important determinant of "insider" status. Social life is deeply marked by social division within the *commune* itself, but also by cultural distance between locals and outsiders.

Many of the conflicts surrounding schooling in Lavialle are shaped by contradictions between communal solidarity and fragmentation, mirroring broader tensions in French society between local and national identity. The Laviallois construct and negotiate layers of cultural identity through a shifting use of insider/outsider status. They also employ a concept of social manipulation, *se debrouiller*, that reinforces a fluid model of social relations and informs resistance to the school. Laviallois identity is based upon family, household, *commune*, region, and nation. These, in turn, overlap with age, gender, and occupation. In this chapter, I will focus on Auvergnat regional identity, the *commune*, and hamlet residence as sources for cultural identity among the Laviallois. I will also discuss the importance of insider/outsider identity and the concept of *se debrouiller* as these are used in Lavialle. In the next chapter, I will turn to families, households, and individuals.

Regional identity: Auvergne

There are many ways of defining and being Auvergnat, depending upon one's gender and social position. As Bourdieu (1977a) suggests for the identity of the French peasantry in general, regional identity is strongly informed by notions held by the dominant culture. It is, thus, mostly in response to French dominant culture that the Laviallois assert their Auvergnat identity. The dominant culture cannot be construed as a coherent system, however, and encompasses contradictory images of regional identity (see Mark 1987). Moreover, it does not dictate forms of expression to the Laviallois, who actively shape their responses to dominant cultural meanings.

There has been a recent renewal of interest in regionalism in Europe at the levels of both popular culture and scholarly research (Foster 1980; Esman 1977; Bertho 1980; McDonald 1989). France's strongest revival movements have been in the regions of Brittany, Corsica, and the Occitan. Because these often militant movements, which center on uses of language as a symbol of cultural identity, have received so much attention, the persistence of regional identity elsewhere in France is often overlooked. In the Auvergne, regional identity is not shaped as an outright rejection of French identity. One is Auvergnat precisely because one is French, and this identity asserts that there is the possibility of cultural diversity despite the homogenizing forces of the French state.

There are differences of opinion among scholars of French regional identity about the meaning of the strength and resurgence of regionalism in recent years. McDonald has viewed the tension between nationalism and regionalism in the highly politicized context of Brittany, concluding that "it is, in many ways, only through Brittany's incorporation into the wider French world that modern Breton identity came to be constructed, and it is only through the modern concern for the supposed 'loss' of this identity that there is any compulsion to seek, through history, the autonomy and independence lacking in the present" (1989:14). She has found that rural Bretons are less than enthusiastic about the symbols of modern "Breton" identity as articulated by more urban activists. In the Auvergne, where a strong regionalist movement has not developed, there is less of a sense of a "loss," and, consequently, a more mundane and locally based sentiment of regional identity. The notion of regional identity among the Laviallois is not shaped by activists, but constructed by rural peoples during their everyday lives within a national context of conflicting discourses.

As Vera Mark (1987) has argued, in the case of the southern French Occitan region, the notion of a deep opposition between region and nation has been perpetuated by scholars as well as by activists. She uses the example of Bourdieu's writings on rural Béarnaise culture, in which he emphasizes how the class-based nature of French society overrides that of region. Bourdieu sees recent uses of the Occitan language in official settings as a form of "folklorization," and a signal not of regional vitality, but as the death of marginal languages and culture. Mark proposes, in response, that the social meanings of regional culture are not unified, and that "folklorization may be a positive strategy of incorporation into the national domain, rather than a purely negative one of devaluation and self-distancing" (1987:68). In Lavialle, Auvergnat identity and language use have shifting meanings – sometimes opposing dominant French culture, sometimes serving as a variant of it.

The Auvergne names both one of the old provinces of France and one of twenty-two administrative regions created in 1972. The current official Auvergne region consists of the four departments of Puy-de-Dôme, Allier, Cantal and Haute-Loire. Broader historical definitions of the region sometimes also include the Aveyron, Corrèze, Lot, and Lozère. Lavialle's location near to Clermont-Ferrand, the ancient provincial center of Auvergne, places it in the very heart of the region – no matter how defined. The

Auvergne has historically been a marginal hinterland. It remained predominantly agricultural up until the mid-twentieth century, in large part because its remote, mountainous terrain was not attractive to industry until transportation and communications were improved (Fel 1962). Auvergnats from the higher mountains to the south of Lavialle engaged in migratory labor during the 18th and 19th centuries (as knife grinders, chimney sweeps, sawyers, etc.) because of the poverty of the region. It is doubtful, however, that many people from Lavialle participated in this trend (Fel 1977). Many Auvergnats migrated to Paris during the 20th century, but retain a strong regional consciousness. They support the largest regional newspaper, *l'Auvergnat de Paris*, and have an active social network.

Auvergnat regional identity is not a static concept, and its uses and meanings are culturally produced, reproduced, and changed in different social contexts (Reed-Danahay 1991). The Laviallois shape their regional identity in the context of two alternative images of the Auvergnat available in French popular culture: (1) the uncouth and wild Auvergnat, and (2) the sly, noble, cunning Auvergnat. In the popular imagination, the Auvergnat is most often portrayed as a male figure – in contrast, for example, to the prevalent image of the female Breton wearing the traditional lace coiffe (Bertho 1980).

The first image has both rural and urban versions. The dominant stereotype of the rural Auvergnat is one of an unpolished rustic, somewhat slow-witted – a sort of "country bumpkin." His urban counterpart is known as the *bougnat*. This is a slang term deriving from the charcoal seller, an occupation that many Auvergnats took up after migrating to Paris in the early twentieth century. Like the rural rustic, the urban Auvergnat is portrayed as rough and crude – the opposite of the stereotypical refined, cultured Parisian. In a second, more "noble" regional stereotype, the Auvergnat is known to be clannish, stubborn (*une tête*), hard-working, and tight with money. Many of these qualities are both feared and admired, and point to the clever, cunning nature of the Auvergnat. One Auvergnat popular author thus lists the Auvergnat's positive characteristics as including "a taste for profit . . . a certain cunning . . . a generosity, and a certain nobleness" (Pourrat 1976:45).

A Lavialle farmer once jokingly told me this maxim when describing the Auvergnat: "Un seul dieu tu adoras; les Auvergnats, tu te méfieras" (You will adore the one and only God; you will beware of Auvergnats). This quip is not without sexual innuendos, but is also a more general statement about the cunning nature of the Auvergnat. The Laviallois use positive stereotypes of the Auvergnat to justify local values of modesty, prudence,

and resourcefulness (or cunning). They are, however, less comfortable with
the more negative stereotype of the Auvergnat as a clownish, rustic,
buffoon-type character. Their ambivalence is expressed in a series of local
jokes about a humorous old Auvergnat who outsmarts the "modern" outsider (often a tourist). → Outwit the moderners.

Auvergnat identity is most relevant in relation to what is defined as not
Auvergnat. Someone is Auvergnat in opposition, therefore, to someone
who is, for example, a Breton or Provençal. There are intricate negotiations concerning who is or is not "truly" Auvergnat for the Laviallois. To
be Auvergnat in Lavialle means to belong to a loose category which
includes all of one's family and friends, and which distinguishes one from
the rest of the French. In Lavialle, to be Auvergnat is certainly, among
natives at least, to be "one of us."

Yet living in the Auvergne region does not automatically constitute a
basis for affinity. Insider/outsider status in Lavialle is a shifting category,
which depends upon the situation. At the local level, only rural inhabitants
of the Auvergne are considered to be true Auvergnats. The teachers in
Lavialle's primary school, born in the suburbs of Clermont-Ferrand, were
not wholly convincing to the Laviallois in their claims to a shared regional
identity. The teachers were identified as urban. They were, therefore,
viewed as outsiders, despite regional affiliation. Similarly, when politicians
from Auvergne attempt to appeal to people from Lavialle on the basis of
common regional identity, this does not alone provoke a strong sense of
loyalty. Thus, although Giscard d'Estaing was supported in Lavialle
during his presidency, the fact that he was from the Puy-de-Dôme, in the
Auvergne, had less of an appeal than the pragmatic issue that he would
probably be more likely to lend economic support to the region than
would politicians from other regions. As with the teachers, Giscard was
not considered to be an Auvergnat in the same sense in which the
Laviallois see themselves. Class issues complicate those of region in deci-
sive ways (see also McDonald 1989).

In the view from Lavialle, Auvergnat regional identity takes many
forms. It is employed by competing folklore groups (one left-wing and one
right-wing) who perform regional music and dance, mainly for tourists
and urbanites (Plate 2). Their colorful costumes, traditional instruments,
and their dance of *la bourrée*, capitalize upon a fixed image of the region
associated with the past and sought by visiting tourists. The brother of the
elderly mayor of Lavialle played accordion in one of these groups. Lavialle
parents proudly show their children these "traditions" when they are on
display, but do not seek out such entertainment.

Plate 2 *A Lavialle storyteller dressed in traditional Auvergnat attire.*This native of
Lavialle is telling a humorous story in patois before an audience from the local
region during a summer festival. A Lavialle dairy farmer holds the microphone
for him, and a local Auvergnat folk dance troupe stands at the back of the stage.

For the Laviallois, there are more private expressions and performances of regional identity, associated with a rural way of life. At dances in the community center, when accordion music is played, Lavialle men will, after a few drinks, interrupt the more modern couple-type dancing, and get up and dance the *bourrée*. The Laviallois claim that this dance is unique to their region. It is primarily a masculine dance in Lavialle, and for Lavialle men, dancing the *bourrée* is an important way of expressing Auvergnat masculinity.[3]

It is in the home that Lavialle children learn Auvergnat identity. An example of an explicit lesson in this identity occurred one afternoon during my fieldwork, when I was chatting with a four-year-old girl in her grandparents' kitchen. The girl suddenly turned to me and asked "Déborah, are you American or French?" She had obviously heard me referred to as "the American," yet was confused by my insertion into local life. She already knew that American and French were somehow opposed identities. I replied that I was an American who was learning about France, and then asked her "what about you, what are you?" Before she had a chance to answer, her grandfather, who was passing through the room, emphatically interjected: "Why you are an Auvergnat!"

There is not a lot of explicit talk of this sort about Auvergnat identity in Lavialle, mostly because it is taken for granted. Children are reminded of their local and regional identity each time they sit down to a meal. Women in Lavialle are quite conscious of the Auvergnat character of the foods they serve. These include Auvergnat sausage and cheeses, clafoutis – a sweet cake made with cherries or apples, pot-au-feu – considered a staple of the Auvergnat diet, and many other local foods. Gentian liqueur, also native to the Auvergne, is a popular aperitif among both men and women. Another cultural site of regionalism is the regional market system for produce and animals. When children accompany their families to such outdoor markets, they gain a sense of affinity with Auvergnats beyond Lavialle who eat, dress, and talk in similar ways.

The Auvergnat *patois*, a "langue d'oc," is still spoken at home by middle-aged and elderly members of Lavialle families. Many younger Laviallois can fluently understand, if not speak, this language. It is used by men in Lavialle during town council meetings, and by older women when they meet in the market. Words in *patois* pepper speech in French, and pronunciations of French words have a clear "Auvergnat" accent. The *patois* is a language for private business, family talk, and for joking. It remains a vital symbol of Auvergnat identity, but is also used to make distinctions between Auvergnats. Just as cheese-making is believed by the

Laviallois to have important variations from village to village, language use is seen as a particularizing action. I was told by several older Laviallois that they sometimes had trouble understanding the *patois* of neighboring *communes*.

In relationship to the nation or to those from other regions of France, the Laviallois are emphatically Auvergnat. This reliance upon regional identity became clear in conversations I had with Lavialle residents who tried to find out what my regional identity was in America. It was determined that because I lived near Boston at the time, I was from "Nouvelle Angleterre," and, although I was identified as American, my regional identity was important for my informants – much more important than it was for me. Not used to dealing with non-French persons on a daily basis, the Laviallois prefer to trade in regional identities rather than national ones.

In everyday life among neighbors, however, it is hamlet residence, *commune*, and kin affiliation, rather than Auvergnat identity, which are the most important sources of identity and bases for social action. I will now turn to the *commune*.

The *commune*

The village of Lavialle serves as the commercial and administrative center of the *commune*, although "center" implies a much grander scale than is found in Lavialle. Lavialle's only school, a public primary school, is located in the village, as are the Catholic church, mayor's office, cafes, and small grocery shops. The village also has five working farms located in it, as well as the homes of several farm retirees. It had 53 inhabitants in 1981. The other hamlets vary in size from 3 to 60 residents, and consist solely of clusters of houses and barns surrounded by fields.

Lavialle has three focal institutions that symbolize and express its identity as a social unit: local government, the Catholic Church, and the primary school. Voluntary associations are also based in the *commune*, but often have a more fluid membership that encompasses the local region.

Local government

Like all French *communes*, Lavialle has an elected town council (*le conseil municipal*) and a mayor chosen from the council's ranks. The ten council members in 1981 were all male farmers, and came from ten different hamlets within Lavialle. French *communes* are not autonomous units within the state bureaucracy, although their roles have expanded since the decentralization reforms of the 1980s. The major official function of a *commune* is to oversee public utilities such as electricity, water, and housing. The mayor and town council are also responsible for the material upkeep of the primary school. The French vote for all elections in their *communes*, and file most national documents at the mayor's office. In a small *commune*, such as Lavialle, the town council and mayor represent the major links to outside political power and influence. Lavialle has historically had a "federal" model (Mendras and Cole 1991:128) of government, with households and hamlets serving as the basic units represented on the town council.

Although strongly identified with residence in the *commune*, participation in local government in Lavialle extends informally beyond its borders. Many natives of Lavialle who have moved to Clermont-Ferrand and its suburbs return to Lavialle to vote, and contribute active voices in local politics. At the counting of votes for the Presidential election in 1981, for example, several "returnees" were present and took an important role in supervising the process. At the same time, non-natives who reside in Lavialle are excluded from political participation. One man who had purchased a vacation home in Lavialle had tried to gain a seat in the town council, but was repeatedly rebuffed by natives. It is primarily membership in a kindred that owns land in Lavialle that lends rights to political participation. Thus, those who have rights to family land in Lavialle, even if they do not reside in Lavialle, have stronger rights to a political voice than residents who are not members of Lavialle kindreds (see also Abélès 1991:11).

The Catholic Church

In addition to being a unit of the French government, Lavialle is a Catholic parish. Most *communes* in France were organized on the basis of earlier parish units. There is one church in Lavialle, served by a priest who lives in Grosbourg, a neighboring town, and divides his time between the two parishes. There was a resident priest in Lavialle until the early 1970s, but with his death, occurring at a time of severe priest shortages, Lavialle lost this post. Some Laviallois attend Saturday night Mass in Grosbourg, and there are occasional joint services between the two parishes. As with politics, many natives of Lavialle who live elsewhere return to the *commune/paroisse* for important church rituals, such as funerals, marriages, and All Saints' Day.

The Monts Dore region of the Massif Central, in which Lavialle is located, is a Catholic stronghold (Poitrineau 1979:265). Many of Lavialle's inhabitants attend church regularly and consider themselves practicing Catholics. Men, as well as women, regularly attend Mass in Lavialle, and this is indicative of a very religious population in rural France. However, men receive communion only on Easter, when it is said that one has "gagné son Pâques" (literally, earned or won his Easter). There are also many Laviallois who consider themselves non-practicing Catholics; that is, they attend funerals, marriages, etc. but not regular church services.

Anti-clericalism is prevalent among the Laviallois, even those who regularly attend church. This was mostly expressed through criticisms of the priest for what is perceived to be a lack of interest in the parish. Lavialle's priest in the early 1980s was very much of a "modern" priest. A naturalist who organized mountain hikes for tourists and parishioners (mostly from Grosbourg), he was also active in regional theater productions. This priest lived in Grosbourg, and came to Lavialle only to perform church services. Many women in Lavialle complained that he was more interested in these outside interests than in the parishioners of Lavialle. There was a perception that the Church had abandoned them, by removing a resident priest and then supplying them with one who showed little interest in their affairs. In my conversations with the priest, he seemed not so much disinterested in Lavialle as unsure of how to approach his parish. A progressive Catholic, he was uncomfortable in the traditional role of blessing barns and animals, and in holding archaic Church services that had been abandoned elsewhere in France. He wanted to help revitalize rural France, but found the Laviallois so resistant to his efforts, that he kept his distance from them.

Lavialle's church plays an important role in local social life and in the socialization of children, despite attitudes toward the clergy. Many life-cycle transitions are phrased in terms of religious rituals, as will be seen more fully in chapter 5. In addition, although several residents attend Mass on Saturday nights at Grosbourg, Sunday mornings are unique occasions for the assemblage of a large group of Laviallois. Men meet after Mass to exchange news at the cafe, while women do the same thing outside in the square while shopping at the butcher and baker's trucks from Grosbourg parked nearby. A sense of "community," at least among practicing Catholics, is created through this shared gossip and group social interaction beyond one's family or hamlet.

Although the Laviallois are Catholic and for the most part church-attending, they are, in general, much more anti-clerical than populations in other Catholic regions of France, such as Brittany, where the public vs. religious school question continues to be highly divisive (Hélias 1978;

McDonald 1989). The Laviallois do not, for example, overtly label themselves as *laïc* and *libre* or "red" and "white" (supporters of public or
private schools), in the same way that people have done in rural Brittany
(Badone 1989; McDonald 1989; Morin 1970). The division between public
and private school attendance does not occur until middle school for most
children in Lavialle, so that the village school is not directly involved in
these debates. ⟶ For the individual families?
                            — Is this not the village?

The primary school
The primary school is a third focal point for consciousness of Lavialle as a
social unit. Like the town council and Church, it is also associated with
bureaucratic sources of power that lie beyond the *commune*. Although
housed and financed by the *commune*, Lavialle's school is operated by the
state and under the jurisdiction of an administration located in Clermont-
Ferrand and Paris. The primary school is one of the few remaining institutions that is still located in the *commune* of Lavialle. There is no longer a
resident priest, a post office, or a bakery in Lavialle. These are all now
located in Grosbourg. Despite its association with a national, bureaucratic
system, it is this feature of the local primary school – that it has come to
symbolize Lavialle as a community, which complicates the role of the
school as a national institution. Much more will be said about this school
and its relationship to the *commune* in later chapters.

Voluntary associations
Lavialle's Youth Club (*l'Association des jeunes*) is a more recent arena for
the shaping of local identity, and plays an important role in the grooming
of political leadership in Lavialle. Although the Laviallois participate in
several voluntary associations, the Youth Club is the only group composed
exclusively of Lavialle natives and residents, since the others include
members from neighboring *communes* within the district. Lavialle's Youth
Club is composed of teenagers as well as young married and unmarried
people in their twenties and thirties, and was led by a core group of about
fifteen men and women in 1980–81. Its members are all native to Lavialle,
although they do not all live there. Many unmarried young adults who
work and live in Clermont-Ferrand, such as the group's treasurer, return
home to Lavialle on the weekends to participate in the Youth Club's leadership and activities. For the most part, the Club organizes social activities, such as community dances and trips.

Two post-war movements in Lavialle led to the formation of this club.
The JAC (*Jeunesse agricole chrétienne*), a national Catholic youth move-

ment, was active in Lavialle during the 1950s. Members of the JAC put on plays, learned about agricultural techniques and politics, and were involved in many other projects (see Moulin 1991: 165–67; Mendras 1991:63–4)). Following a decline in the JAC movement, a government-sponsored project of "social animation" came to Lavialle in the early 1970s, reflecting a national policy aimed at rejuvenating the population of this region after post-war rural decline. This project was led by a full-time salaried activities coordinator (*animateur*) who organized trips, plays, and educational projects for a group of 14 *communes* in the Puy-de-Dôme. Funding for this program was eventually eliminated, at which time the youth of Lavialle organized their own club in the spirit of the previous groups.

Lavialle was viewed as rare in the district for having such an active Youth Club, and few neighboring *communes* had any youth group at all. Members of Lavialle's club explained that it had been even more active in the 1970s, when trips to Italy and Spain were organized and plays were regularly performed each year. At the meetings which I attended, it was evident that only a small core of people kept the group going, but that its activities (such as an annual dance) were well attended.

The club is not a partisan group and its members are of mixed political views. It nevertheless provides opportunities for young men and, sometimes, women, to practice political skills and organize followings for future local elections. It was, for instance, widely speculated during my fieldwork that when the elderly mayor of Lavialle stepped down from his position during the upcoming elections of 1982, the Youth Club president would run for office. Rumor held that this young farmer (about 30 years old) was attempting to gain political support through his participation in the Youth Club. He did not launch a campaign during that election. However, the newly elected mayor in 1982 was a middle-aged farmer who had been active in JAC activities several years before and whose daughters were currently active in the Youth Club. In another case, the first woman elected to Lavialle's town council, also in that year, was herself an active member of the Youth Club. She was a Catholic schoolteacher who lived in Lavialle and was native to the *commune*. The links between age-related clubs and politics were made particularly explicit when the retiring mayor left office in 1982 to direct a new club for senior citizens in Lavialle.

Other voluntary associations in which the Laviallois participate include the Rugby Club, the social clubs of the hunting and fishing associations, and the War Veterans' Club. These are exclusively male organizations, with a few exceptions, and all draw from kinship networks that lead outside of

Lavialle. Women do not meet in groups for voluntary associations, but organize gatherings such as Tupperware parties in their homes. These take on the character of mutual aid groups, in that women help other women acquire domestic items by buying products from each other.

One other type of social group, in addition to that of the Youth Club, included both men and women and expressed Lavialle identity. Age grade associations, called "les classards," organized annual meals. These were most active among middle-aged Laviallois. Groups of people of the same age, symbolized by class in school, the associations were open to all eligible inhabitants of Lavialle. The annual meals resemble, on a smaller scale, the class reunions of small-town American high schools.

Hamlets: rural neighborhoods[4]

Lavialle as a *commune* has several mechanisms beyond its purely administrative function in the French government that reinforce its identity as a social unit. However, most Laviallois identify with the hamlet as a residence unit, rather than with the *commune.* Even beyond the boundaries of Lavialle, in the district of Grosbourg, people will identify someone primarily by hamlet (as well as family).

Most people in Lavialle live in a settlement (hamlet or village) containing several households, and these units, rather than the *commune,* constitute the setting of everyday work and family life. Those who live in isolated households are often affiliated with a nearby hamlet cluster. Many of Lavialle's 18 settlements have been in existence for quite some time. Six of these place names were mentioned as early as the thirteenth century, when they signified the dwellings of various notables (Tardieu 1877).

The Laviallois explain the clustering of farms into hamlets as due to factors which encouraged people to "stick together" in order to survive. They cite as examples of this the severe weather conditions of the region, as well as the large manors that had sovereignty in the area during feudal times. Historical geographer André Fel (personal communication) has a different interpretation, and suggests that the hamlets probably originated as isolated farm households (the ancient *mas*) which later expanded as families grew, adding new households. The present household composition of hamlets, Fel proposes, is the result of various marriage arrangements, and out-migration of some original families.

The Lavialle model of mutual aid for survival within hamlets reflects and reinforces an ideology of hamlet solidarity in local social life, which is likely to have originated in the historical kin-solidarity suggested by Fel.

The inhabitants of Lavialle view both the weather and an historically dominant group of feudal lords as threats originating from "outside" of Lavialle. These threats, the belief goes, promoted solidarity. This historical "myth" helps shape current attitudes toward tourists, politicians, and teachers – who also pose potential outside "threats."

Despite a general ideology of hamlet solidarity, however, daily interaction among hamlet neighbors is minimal for the most part – with some neighbors closer than others, usually due to kinship ties. The Laviallois do not congregate in public, even in summer, except for such ritual events as Sunday Mass, funerals, markets, and fairs. Almost all social activity occurs *inside* – either in the house, the barn, or, in some cases, the cafe (for men) or the grocery store (for women). There is little *voisinage* (social visiting) among women, and those who chat risk being considered nosey and lazy. There is always a lot of work to be done, people say, and it is a waste of time to stand around chatting. No woman wants to be labeled *curieuse* (nosey), and most conversation among women is considered to be gossip, a suspect activity. Men will meet each other in a cafe in the village of Lavialle, but they, too, are discouraged from spending a lot of time there. After a quick *canon* (glass of red wine), and a few pleasantries, men are expected to be on their way back to work – apart from some clearly defined social occasions, such as after Mass on Sunday.

Hamlet residence provides important social and economic rights and obligations. Despite little casual social visiting among hamlet neighbors, mutual aid among the households is a vital feature of hamlet life. In such cases as the difficult birth of a calf, for example, neighbors will be called to help at any time of day or night. In the past, all of the households in each hamlet shared a shepherd who guarded their separate flocks of sheep in the mountains. Hamlet ovens were also shared by neighboring households, who baked their own bread. Now bread is purchased in Grosbourg or from the baker's truck when it passes through the hamlets twice a week.

There is, however, a more explicit and enduring economic basis for hamlet solidarity. Surrounding forest land is owned jointly by all residents in a particular hamlet. The rule is that one share of the timber goes to each house from which there is smoke coming out of the chimney, so that profits from timber are divided evenly among households. Since most people in Lavialle use wood-burning stoves, inhabitants of hamlets rich in timber can heat their houses for free. This is an important benefit, as I learned myself, since I had to heat with coal and bear the costs of buying fuel.[5]

Some of the hamlets also have a representative to Lavialle's local town

Hamlet representation council. A council member is expected to represent the interests of his or her hamlet, and is called upon as a leader in times of problems. When there was a minor flood in the village of Lavialle, due to a back-up of the drainage system, it was the council member who called the fire department to pump out the water and who oversaw the entire clean-up and subsequent efforts to alleviate the problem.

Important social distinctions are drawn between hamlets in Lavialle, clusters of which served as separate educational districts in the past. There are three main sections: (1) those nearest to the village of Lavialle; (2) those in the northern section (*dans les bois*); and (3) those in the mountain valley, the southern portion of the *commune*.[6] The southern hamlets are cut off from the rest by the national highway that passes through Lavialle, dividing its area almost in half, and are the least populated. The northern hamlets are richest in timberland, and their residents have retained a more "traditional" character and way of life than have residents of other hamlet clusters. Kinship and other social networks in Lavialle sometimes exclude relationships with residents of different hamlets, so that there are people in the village of Lavialle, for example, who claim never to have set foot in some hamlets in the *commune*, and meet their inhabitants only in public gatherings, such as at Mass or at market. Each cluster of hamlets has important ties (especially through kinship) to *communes* that border their corner of Lavialle, and some hamlets are socially closer to hamlets in other *communes* than to hamlets within Lavialle's borders. Each hamlet section or cluster was, in addition, associated with a different primary school up until the 1960s, as will be discussed in chapter 7.

Insiders and outsiders

My apartment in the village of Lavialle was in a building called "the gentlemen's house" (*chez les m'ssieurs*). Another building in the village was known as "the secretary's house" (*chez le secrétaire*). Most dwellings in Lavialle had names such as these, which were associated with families or with the occupation of a former inhabitant. In general, these names had nothing to do with the present inhabitants; rather, they dated back to social life at the turn of the century. *Chez le secrétaire*, for instance, used to be the home of the mayor's secretary, an ancestor of the family living there now. My building, informants surmised (since no one could tell me for certain), used to house some important men in town – notaries, perhaps, or priests.

These colloquial names of buildings (expressed in French as well as in the local *patois*) were not revealed to me until the second half of my fieldwork. People first referred to buildings in my presence as the households of the current occupants (as in "Giraud's house"). When I later began to realize that other place names existed, mostly through conversations in *patois* that I overheard, and expressed interest, people would remark in surprise about how curious it was that so-and-so had referred to a building with such an odd, archaic name. For a long time, I remained baffled about this situation. Then, one afternoon when I was helping in the fields, a young farmer explained to me in a matter-of-fact tone that, yes, all buildings had these older names, although he was not always certain of their origins. Eventually, as my presence in Lavialle became more commonplace, speakers used colloquial names more often in conversations with me.

These house names reflect and reinforce important aspects of local identity in Lavialle. They arise from the European pattern of a close association between a family and its house (Mitterauer and Sieder 1982:7–10). House names connect the present inhabitants of Lavialle to historical uses and meanings of dwellings, and also fix the memory of former inhabitants by association with the buildings and spaces that outlasted them. These names lend a historical sense to Lavialle and its hamlets, a stability and continuity through time of place and social life, if not individuals. They are part of the *commune*'s mythic past, a time often spoken of by young and old alike as "dans le temps", when things were different; when the old traditions were upheld and life was tough (*dur*). The old house names also provide a vehicle for the shaping of local identity based upon notions of a common past which is distinguished from that of other French citizens.[7] That knowledge of these names belongs exclusively to the Laviallois, and is not readily shared with outsiders, reveals the defensive, "in-group" posture of the Laviallois *vis-à-vis* the exterior world.

Lavialle had many such local "secrets," often gleefully withheld from outsiders. Inquiring tourists are, for instance, never told where to find berries and wild mushrooms in the surrounding woods, even though the *commune* is profuse in both. The Laviallois always respond to a query about gathering wild fruits or vegetables in deadpan and with the remark that the kind visitor must go *là-bas* (elsewhere) to find such goodies. This is a great "in" joke, and the Laviallois laughed heartily at the expense of the tourists on such occasions. There was quite a shock, therefore, one morning when two couples spending a short vacation in Lavialle promenaded through the center of the village with some baskets filled with the choicest mushrooms that they had located themselves!

These examples of secrecy illustrate the posture of Lavialle's inhabitants towards what is considered the outside. Although Lavialle is in no sense insulated from the wider French state and society, there is an attempt to "hold out" and not to embrace the outside world with open arms. Certain things are local, and have to do with Lavialle, it is felt; such things are not to be shared with outsiders. One informant explained this "secrecy" as having to do with *pudeur*, a sense of modesty and pride. At the same time, however, there is also a desire to manipulate or resist the outside world, not just hide from it.

A notion of secrecy related to insider vs. outsider status also operates within Lavialle. Not unlike the ways in which the Laviallois conspire to keep secrets from tourists, local households defend their own privacy from neighbors. Among close family members, certain things are personal and *en famille*, and these things are not to be shared easily with others. Political beliefs are not openly expressed, for example, and information about family members is not freely divulged to others. I was once counseled by a young woman not to reveal my attitudes toward American politics, on which I was often queried early in my fieldwork, because, she told me, people will always try to use such information against one. When a little girl once started to explain to me that her aunt had left for a vacation (which I already knew and had learned from the aunt herself), her grandmother, also present, quieted her, asking how she was so sure, and speaking in vague terms about the aunt's whereabouts. There is, thus, an attempt to mystify what is most likely common knowledge among neighbors in order to maintain some sense of family privacy. Such attempts at privacy may be futile in a face-to-face community like Lavialle, but are connected to notions of insiders and outsiders at all levels.

When I visited a village in Normandy with other Laviallois as part of an exchange program, I was struck by the ease and willingness with which the Norman families gossiped about each other to us. In Lavialle, rarely was gossip about neighbors openly and willingly communicated to "outsiders," such as myself in the early period of my fieldwork. The value of "closing ranks" against outsiders is strong in Lavialle. There was a constant attempt to learn information about others in Lavialle, but this was not openly admitted and occurred through sly questioning. When visiting households in Lavialle, I learned early how to negotiate my answers to off-handed questions about neighbors or households I had visited, and to see that what seemed at first to be trivial matters could loom very large in the local gossip network.

The categories of "insider" vs. "outsider" in Lavialle are shifting, and the Laviallois draw from various frames of identity in order to define, in any given situation, who fits in which category. This is particularly evident in the opposition between *les nôtres* (our people, or "us'ns") and *les autres* (the others). In general, it is the household and kindred, rather than the *commune*, which provide the primary source of in-group identity for the Laviallois. Participation in the social life of the *commune* can, however, lend limited "insider" status in the absence of local kin ties. This involves a complex juggling of identities, such as the one which enabled me to be included after my first six months there in a certain type of "in-group" that was opposed to tourists and other more temporary French visitors. Such claims and acceptances of belonging by non-native residents of Lavialle only go so far, however, as I observed in a conversation between a college professor who had lived for over 20 years in Lavialle and some Lavialle natives. The professor, who was from another region of France but had become sentimentally attached to Lavialle, expressed his interest in being buried in the cemetery. The reaction of the Laviallois to this was quite striking. They quickly remarked that this would be *impossible* since Lavialle families had already spoken for all of the plots and that there would be no room for him. Burial in Lavialle is, perhaps, the major expression of local identity, and many elderly natives who move in with children outside of Lavialle in their later years, return to the *commune* to be buried. Membership in a Laviallois kindred is fundamental to claims of being truly Laviallois, not simply residence in the *commune*. This is as true for burial rights as it is for political participation.

Social relationships in Lavialle are defined and articulated through words acting as "group shifters." These constitute linguistic categories of "outsider" vs. "one of us," whose "exact meaning, as with all shifters, depends on who is speaking, to whom, about what, and in what context" (Herzfeld 1987:154). French uses of pronouns in this way have already been described in earlier ethnographies (Bernot and Blanchard 1953; Wylie 1975; see also Petonnet 1973 for urban working-class examples).

Bernot and Blanchard identified an opposition between the *ils* and the *nous* (them vs. us) in the northern French village that is the subject of their book *Nouville: un village français* (1953). These terms referred primarily to the opposition between villagers (*les nous*) and outsiders, especially agents of the state (*les ils*). Wylie further developed this theme in his study *Village in the Vaucluse* (1975), focusing mostly on the concept of *les ils* (them) in a southern French community. Wylie writes: "the ils within Peyrane are a nuisance, but since they are specific individuals whom one knows and sees everyday, one can guard against them. The ils outside Peyrane are danger-

ous because they are anonymous, intangible, and overpowering"
(1975:206). These outsiders were connected in the minds of the people of
Peyrane to the French government. Wylie writes that "Peyrane is one big
family, composed of individuals who disagree among themselves, but who
unite when faced by a common enemy threatening from outside"
(1975:210). The group shifters *nous* and *ils* help to define insider/outsider
status, but their use depends upon the context.

Like their counterparts in Nouville and Peyrane, the Laviallois use the
nous/ils opposition to describe shifting insider/outsider statuses. More
often, however, the phrase of *les autres* (the others) is used for *ils* in everyday contexts. *Les autres* can refer to members of another kindred, household, or *commune,* depending upon the situation. The term *ils* is mostly
used for outsiders from another social class or region – in particular,
politicians and bureaucrats. *Nous,* or *nous autres* (us) is sometimes used to
refer to a group with which the speaker wants to identify, particularly in a
regional context. For example, when an older woman in Lavialle was
trying to explain to me the difference between the *patois* used there and
that used in a neighboring district, she referred to the Laviallois as *nous
autres.*

For everyday occasions at the level of hamlet and village life in Lavialle,
the third person pronoun (*on*) is a commonly used group shifter to denote
insider status. This term is more vague than either I or we, and can refer to
both individuals and groups. Speakers in Lavialle rarely use the pronoun
"I" (*je*), preferring the more ambiguous *on*. A sense of ambiguity is lent to
the phrase "On est allée à la foire," for example, since it can mean, alterna-
tively, that I/we/my family went to the outdoor market, linking the individual to an inclusive social category. Another term, *les nôtres* is used for "us"
or "our people" in the most intimate groups – especially that of the
kindred (which can, itself, be a shifting category). I first heard the *les
nôtres/les autres* opposition when an old woman was describing the
process of barn-raising for her household. She said: "Les nôtres sont des
braves gens; ils viennent tous nous aider" ("Our kin are reliable; they help
out"). She then went on to speak of the problems *les autres* (other households and their kindred) had in gaining help.

The tension between local, regional, and national sources of identity
plays an important role in the ways in which families and children in
Lavialle shape education. Most Laviallois are either dairy farmers themselves or members of dairy farming families. They thereby have an important economic and cultural stake in rural life and in encouraging children
to take an active role in this. The teachers are perceived as outsiders, even

after over one hundred years of universal public primary schooling in Lavialle, who can both help and hinder the attraction of farming to children. Laviallois attitudes to teachers are not unlike their attitudes toward the priest. The school, like the Church, is an important institution in one's life, and has deep local meaning. However, like the priest, the teacher is not "one of us," and is to be approached with apprehension.

Debrouiller: social fluidity and resistance

An important feature of Lavialle world view that informs the manipulation of social life, including identity, is expressed with the notion of *debrouiller*: the art of "making do" and/or "making out" in social situations.[8] This concept was applied one day when I went to make a phone call in the public telephone booth in the center of the village of Lavialle. I noticed that the cash box had been removed, apparently by vandals, and went to tell a neighbor. I asked: Should we call the telephone agency (PTT)? And, did she know about this situation already? My neighbor laughed and replied that "il faut se debrouiller" in this type of situation. If a public phone is broken, she told me, then that is the telephone agency's problem. Anyway, she had herself already made several free calls to Paris on the phone. She suggested that I call my parents in the US, since the money just came back into the open box, making the calls free. I was a bit taken aback at the time, interpreting the broken box in terms of my own middle-class American view that this was a case of vandalism and should be reported to the authorities. Eventually, the phone was fixed. I never did make any long-distance calls for free on it, though, mostly out of concern that I might be criticized for having done so (especially since the phones are publicly run by a governmental agency). Later on in my fieldwork, I realized that I was probably criticized by my neighbors for *not* having done so, for not having taken advantage of this situation. *Local Context*

This incident represents one of the ways in which I learned about processes of resistance in Lavialle, and of attitudes toward the state and the outside. The Laviallois feel that one should protect and defend the interests of one's family and neighbors, but that one should exploit the outside world (and especially state institutions) as much as possible. To take advantage of a situation in which one can do this is highly valued in Lavialle, as the example of the broken phone booth illustrates.

Two words express this value: *degourdi* and *debrouiller*. It is good to be *degourdi*; that is, to be "with it," sharp, shrewd, and savvy. Lavialle parents often remark that their children are not sufficiently *degourdis*, especially in comparison with urban children. One young mother from Lavialle who

Debrouiller

had moved with her husband to another *commune* was concerned about its lack of a nursery school program (such as the one in Lavialle). She told me that children who attend nursery school are more *degourdis* when they reach primary school, and are thus better able to handle the teachers and schoolwork. She drove her daughter to a larger town so that she could attend nursery school there.

Debrouiller is a more commonly used term, connected to notions of shrewdness or cunning, and expresses the value of social fluidity. Many social analyses tend to focus on concepts that provide what are considered as a type of "social glue" to maintain the system. In Lavialle, social relationships depend most heavily on "social fluidity" – the ability [to] *se debrouiller*. This concept helps the Laviallois to manipulate the various and shifting outsider/insider identities in their lives. It is a means by which one expresses the defense of "us" and resistance to, or exploitation of, "them." In Lavialle, *se debrouiller* refers to the ability to make the best of, or take advantage of, a situation; and get out of, or manage to cope with, a difficult situation. It has to do with "making do" in the face of hardship, but also with trying to turn such circumstances to one's own advantage in order to "make out." To be able to exhibit this skill is highly valued for both men and women, and it is felt to be an important characteristic of the Auvergnat.

This term was used when farmers related stories of how they managed during difficult birthings among their cows, when they expressed understated pride in maintaining a viable farm ("on se debrouille," or we get by), or in describing what life was like during the last war. That contacts with "outsiders," especially those associated with the state (such as the PTT), should be described with the same terms as those used for hardship is revealing about the stance the Laviallois take regarding such outside agents.

Se debrouiller in difficult situations is, primarily, to be "cunning."[9] This recognizes a certain open-endedness in social relationships, within which one must maneuver carefully, particularly when dealing with "outsiders." Whereas it is positively valued to be *debrouillard* in Lavialle, however, behavior labelled *rusé* (*literally* translated in dictionaries as "cunning") is negatively valued and considered to be dishonest. For instance, a farmer who is rumored to have added water to the milk yielded by his cows in order to get a better price is called *rusé*, not *debrouillard*. Although he has "tricked" the dairy, this action works against the other farmers, who get less money for the same amount of milk (and work). There is no hard-and-fast rule for when a behavior will be labelled *rusé* or *debrouillard* – it depends upon whether or not the speaker admires or feels threatened by the action. In general, however, a person who applies "cunning intelligence" (Detienne and Vernant 1978) in dealings with outsiders is called *debrouillard*, whereas a person who applies it with neighbors is called *rusé*. Other terms for cunning behavior used frequently in Lavialle include *malin* (for a male) and *coquine* (for a female). That there are so many terms for the English word "cunning" in French is, in itself, suggestive.

Debrouiller literally means to disentangle oneself, and it is also related to notions of being clear about things. The French word *brouillard* means fog or mist, so that *debrouiller* is, metaphorically, to get out of the fog, or to see clearly. In this sense, *debrouiller* is strikingly similar to the concept of *de*mystification (Scott 1985) or ideological penetration (Willis 1981a) in revisionist Marxist theory. Demystification involves "seeing through" the ideological hegemony of the dominant classes, so that subordinate peoples become aware of aspects of their oppression. *Debrouiller* expresses, therefore, not simply being able to manipulate or outwit people, but also ideas (including dominant ideologies).

Debrouiller is part of wider, public French cultural meanings at the same time that its use in Lavialle expresses particular local meanings. *Le Système D* ("D" for *debrouiller*) is a common label for dealings with the French bureaucracy and, especially, ways to "get around" it. This concept has been widely described in the literature on France, and has vividly captured the imaginations of Anglo-American writers. Wylie states that it refers to "any devious and usually ill-defined means by which an individual can take initiative in spite of the restrictions imposed on him by society" (Wylie 1963:223). The use of the concept of *le Système D* by inhabitants of a rural Aveyronnais community has more recently been noted by Rogers, who writes that her informants "perceive such behavior as a response common to any reasonably alert and clever French person, as nationally uniform as the mandate inspiring it" (1991:195).

The Laviallois do not generally label their behavior as operating according to *le Système D* in everyday life. They are more apt to speak of cunning or resourceful behavior as *debrouillardise*. It is not so much that the more public concept is not part of their vocabulary or ways of operating, but, rather, that *le Système D* is associated with bureaucratic, urban behaviors. *Debrouiller* is a more inclusive term than *le Système D*, in that it relates to social manipulation of many types, but it is also, paradoxically, more specific, since it is connected to the identity of the Laviallois as rural Auvergnats. For the Laviallois, *debrouiller* relates to their strong sense of regional identity and self-view as resourceful, clever Auvergnat *paysans*, but also to their more general resistance to a state bureaucracy that presents not just red tape, but an attempt to undermine local cultural meanings and power. *Le Système D* is associated with "Frenchness," but *debrouiller* is associated with local and regional identity.[10]

Local identity

Although a recognized form of behavior in French society, *le Système D* is "officially" viewed with disdain. This was made clear in a school meeting for parents in Lavialle whose children attended the Catholic middle school located about an hour away. The religious Brothers who taught at this school handed out a sheet of paper to the parents which listed various behaviors, clearly labeled with the heading "le Système D." Most of the behaviors listed were associated with children, and included copying schoolwork, pilfering, lying, and stealing. The teachers also, however, indicted that parents were using this practice when they helped their children with homework; often, it was suggested, doing it themselves.

Most of the parents in attendance were mothers, and they kept silent during the remarks of the teachers. There was no outright challenge to this critique of their behavior, although the mothers with whom I was seated were visibly uncomfortable. The teachers were asserting a form of "everyday domination" (Reed-Danahay and Anderson-Levitt 1991) in their critical remarks and attempts to reform parental behavior. The parents resisted this, however, through *debrouillardise*. They knew that the best way to deal with such comments by teachers is to avoid open confrontation and simply to proceed as usual (including, in some cases, continuing to help with homework).

Silent Confrontation

The model for avoiding open confrontation in Lavialle is connected to the image of a respected person. In Lavialle, this is someone who is able to do well without revealing too much of him- or herself to others, either other Laviallois or "strangers." A man must conduct himself in a manner which is, for the most part, prudent (*serieux*) – without making waves. An admired woman is not prone to gossiping (*pas curieuse*) and is unpretentious (*simple*). Both males and females should be hardworking for the good of the family, and not ostentatious. There is sometimes a conflict between the value for getting the best out of a situation (as expressed through *se debrouiller*) and that of being modest and prudent. The aim is to strike a socially acceptable balance between the two. Those who are too resourceful threaten the others, because they can be seen as too innovative, and, therefore, disruptive to the status quo.

The value for resourcefulness (*debrouiller*) and the value for modesty (*être simple*) both reflect a defensive, "in-group" posture that is related to resistance.[11] In general, the value of being cunning or resourceful relates to the outside world (i.e., the state bureaucracy, strangers), or to hardships which are presented from exterior forces (i.e., the weather, God). It is mostly about being able to deal with, and, to some extent, fend off or resist, these influences. The other value, for being prudent and modest, is about maintaining good relations with kin and neighbors, primarily in order to keep conflicts from disrupting local life, but also to close ranks in order to minimize outside (especially urban) influences.

The implications of these values for education are immense. Children have learned from their parents and others in Lavialle that individuals are not supposed to promote themselves openly, but that they should band together when dealing with outsiders (including teachers). Being able to maintain an identity as both French and Laviallois involves a certain amount of *debrouillardise,* and the ways in which children express this at school will be taken up again in chapter 9. Behaviors toward schooling in Lavialle are shaped primarily in terms of this concept of *debrouiller,* which expresses elements of both resistance and accommodation as means of manipulating social situations.

4

Les nôtres: families and farms

Kinship plays an important role in social identity for the Laviallois. The main kinship unit is the household, but the wider kindred establishes "insider" status within Lavialle. I was first taken aback in early fieldwork by differing claims to kinship. One person would tell me that he or she was related to another person who, in turn, would deny such a link. This type of "flexibility" is discussed by Bourdieu, who also found it in his natal village in the region of Béarn (Bourdieu 1962; 1972). With the concept of *cousinage*, he points out that one picks and chooses among kin in French peasant villages, since there are so many "potential" relatives if the link is pursued far enough back in time. Two distant cousins may emphasize the kinship component of their friendship through *cousinage*, while some closer biological relatives may choose, for social or economic reasons, to downplay their link.

Bourdieu's observation is quite apt in Lavialle. It is a highly endogamous *commune*, especially if endogamy is viewed from the regional level. Over two-thirds of the 1980 population was native to Lavialle. Of those who were not, almost 90% were native to the department of Puy-de-Dôme; all were French. One-half of all adults in Lavialle who were not born there were born in the district of Grosbourg. These people are rarely seen as true "outsiders," and are part of local social networks that go beyond the *commune*. The families of these Grosbourg natives most often have had kin and other social links with families in Lavialle before the wedding. Through this local inter-marrying, family ties are spread throughout neighboring *communes* in the district. Eighty-five percent of all adults in Lavialle are native to either Lavialle or another *commune* in the district of Grosbourg. Lavialle was even more endogamous in the past, with only 18% of the population born outside of Lavialle in 1959, and only 2.3% non-native in 1876 (communal archives; census records). Since the present inhabitants of Lavialle are linked by generations of intermarriage, it is understandable that they appreciate *cousinage*, which enables them to manipulate claims to kinship.

The drop in Lavialle's population since World War II has led to a decline in marriages between Lavialle natives, and people say that finding partners among the limited choice now available is difficult. As recently as the early 1970s, however, there was considerable dating and marriage between farm teenagers from Lavialle. One man in his early thirties from another *commune* in the district, who was married to a woman from Lavialle, remarked to me that he had always found this practice of local marriages in Lavialle a bit odd. In his own *commune*, he told me, young people were encouraged to find marriage partners from outside. Many of the young couples establishing themselves on farms or in trades in Lavialle in the early 1980s were composed of both a husband and wife from different hamlets in Lavialle. Most of the parents of the children who attend Lavialle's primary school are, consequently, native to Lavialle; only one mother was not native to the local region. Those young people who leave Lavialle, however, tend to marry non-natives. Marriage within the *commune* of Lavialle or district of Grosbourg seems to go hand-in-hand with a commitment to remain in either Lavialle or a nearby *commune*.

Household and family size in Lavialle have both changed over the past century, but there were never large families in Lavialle.[1] Household size has, however, declined dramatically in recent years. The average number of persons per household was 4.89 in 1876, 3.77 in 1921, and 2.9 in 1982. In 1990, it was 2.5 – less than three persons. In 1982, out of a total of 148 households, 41 had 4 or more people living in them. By 1990, there were 134 households in Lavialle, but 41 still had 4 or more residents. Although it is difficult to define family size precisely on the basis of this census data (since it identifies only co-residents), it appears that family size could not have been great in the latter part of the 19th century. No households in the late 19th century contained more than five children, and about one-third of all households were childless.

Although the ideal may have been for a stem family in Lavialle in former times (as exists frequently today), it is likely that people simply did not live long enough to fulfill that model. As Wheaton (1975) points out, large households were usually wealthy ones in traditional French rural society. In earlier centuries, Lavialle was a community of small family farms in a poor region with a non-labor-intensive economy. Dairy farming, sheep raising, and cheese fabrication were the primary sources of income, neither of which required (or could support) large families (see also Rogers 1991 on household evolution in the Aveyron).

Most families in Lavialle with children under age 16 now have one or two children. No families have more than five children. Recent shifts in the proportion of children to adults in Lavialle, tied to the aging of the population, have important consequences for education and socialization. There are now more grandparents and great-grandparents than ever before participating in the socialization and care of young children, and with this has come increased continuity between generations in Lavialle. In addition, now that there are fewer children, they are more highly valued both for the family farm (as potential contributors to this economic and affective unit) and for wider social life (as perpetuators of a rural way of life).

The Laviallois use three major terms to describe families and households. *Les nôtres* defines the kin-group on a broad and loosely categorized level, mainly oriented towards those living locally, but not necessarily within the boundaries of the *commune*. *La maison*, the second term, more precisely defines the kin-related household and farm unit. It is similar to the concept of the *ostal* in the Aveyron (Rogers 1991: 75–78). This is most often the extended family co-resident unit. The local usage of this word in Lavialle can, however, also refer to a group of relatives who occupy adjacent buildings with separate kitchens on the same farm. The third term, *le ménage*, refers to the nuclear family (although it can also extend to those older relatives who are now dependent upon the head of household, such as a widowed mother). A more detailed description of each term follows.

Les nôtres

The kin group in Lavialle is loosely referred to as *les nôtres* ("us'ns" or "our people"). It is the "family" or kindred most widely defined, which cross-cuts communal boundaries. Martine Segalen defines the French kindred as "that flexible cluster of relatives with whom one can decide to have or not to have relationships, determines the networks that interlink the various related domestic groups and can be seen as the channels along which news, mutual help and goods and services travel" (1986: 69). *Les nôtres* is the most important social group outside of the household itself, and the one from which identity is most strongly derived. In Lavialle, those who mutually acknowledge close kinship relations are important to each other in matters of mutual aid, ritual functions, and economic concerns – such as land ownership and inheritance. *Les nôtres* signifies those with whom a household acknowledges kinship. They will be called upon to help raise a barn, will attend weddings, first communions, funerals, etc., and will aid in an emergency. *Les nôtres* is the bilateral kindred from the perspective of a household, rather than an individual. Furthermore, and of most relevance to this study, it constitutes the primary social and moral context for the socialization of young children. It is from this group that most godparents are drawn.

La maison

La maison (the household) is an economic as well as kinship-oriented group, and is linked to a particular farm. Since wage-earning farm laborers are rare in Lavialle, it is rare for unrelated persons to live with family work units. Most farms can only support two full-time male workers, and this is usually a father and his adult son or son-in-law. Ideally, *la maison* in Lavialle includes three or four generations: grandparents (usually retired), the head of household and his wife and dependent children, and the son or daughter of the head of household who will inherit (or has already inherited) the farm, along with his or her own spouse and young children.

Family size is not large in Lavialle, and, as was mentioned above, three or four children has been the norm for the past few generations. The trend has recently been towards a slight decrease in this number, to about two or three children. According to French law, inheritance is equally distributed among all children. In Lavialle, however, the practice is for one child actually to acquire the farm and then to "pay off " his or her siblings the shares owing to them, usually by taking out bank loans and then eliminating the debt little by little. Those siblings from more prosperous farms who move away and receive a cash share of the estate are often well set up with furniture in apartments in the city. Young unmarried daughters who move to the city, for instance, will often receive expensive bedroom suites and other furnishings when their brothers take over the family farm. In general, however, it is understood that the inheriting child on the farm receives the better deal in terms of real and emotional value in land.

The division of labor within the household provides a complementary work unit. Men carry out the all-day farm tasks of caring for and milking cows, tending to fields and machinery, and the selling of animals. Women care for calves, poultry, rabbits, and the family garden plot, and also carry out all domestic duties within the house itself. Grandmothers and older female children help with female tasks in the house, freeing the wife and daughter or daughter-in-law to attend to agricultural duties. Children do not help much with farm and household tasks, although teenage boys take on increasing responsibility with age. Teenage girls, tellingly, have the least to do with the farm of anyone. Mothers seem to grant a period of reprise to their daughters at this time, knowing that when they marry their lives will be greatly constricted.

Le ménage

All members of *la maison* do not necessarily occupy the same living quarters. More and more frequently, young farm couples, especially after the birth of their first child, will acquire a house (or apartment) of their own. This usually is adjoining or next to the parental house, and has a separate kitchen. Each group sharing a kitchen (formerly, a chimney) is known as a *ménage*, so that a *maison* can incorporate one or two *ménages*. This breaking off of the young nuclear family is attributed by the Laviallois to mother-in-law/daughter-in-law rivalry, and is permitted by changing values and economic circumstances (especially since there is more cash now for the construction of a new house). The setting up of this new, semi-autonomous unit is preferred by both parties, but especially by the young wives. The older women say that they, too, had difficulty adjusting to their mother-in-law's home, and feel that the younger women are lucky. The older women have much to lose in terms of social status and control over the new *ménage*, however, in this recent pattern.

The degree to which the new *ménages* are really autonomous is not clear-cut. Each continues to be seen as part of the *maison*, the basic residential, kin, and economic unit which situates each individual *vis-à-vis* her or his neighbors in other households. Recent laws in France have encouraged farmers to retire early and hand their farms over to their sons (or daughters), who become legally (if not yet socially) heads of household (Moulin 1991: 175). This has created some inter-generational problems in Lavialle. In one farm, in which the inheriting son and his wife occupied an apartment attached to the side of the parental home, a long dispute over uses of space developed between the mother and daughter-in-law when the inheritance of the farm was enacted as part of this early retirement policy. Although father and son continued to work together on the farm fairly peaceably as before, the daughter-in-law called upon her legal authority over her mother on several occasions, saying that it was *her* farm now. For instance, she constantly reprimanded her mother-in-law for allowing her chickens to roam on her side of the yard. Despite this bickering, however, doors between the two *ménages* were left open and the younger couple's toddler wandered freely between them. Reciprocity also continued to operate strongly, through the sharing of baked goods, of garden yields, and child care.

Family: conceptual issues

A word is necessary here about the English/American term "family" and its application in the context of Lavialle. In Lavialle, the family, in the sense of a broad kinship unit, corresponds to the *les nôtres* category of kin, since neither the household nor the nuclear family unit is considered to be a socially autonomous unit in Lavialle. However, whereas *les nôtres* is the recognized kin group in terms of self identity, *la maison* is the primary social and economic unit in Lavialle: it is "the farm." *Les nôtres*, as the kindred, is not a clearly defined unit, but one subject to manipulation and left vague – it is "our family" in a very loose sense. The importance of *la maison* is primarily economic, and its members share in certain rights and duties regarding land use and profit. *Le ménage* is a less inclusive term, and is usually used in Lavialle to refer to a couple and their children – the nuclear unit. A newly married couple will be called a *jeune ménage* (young family or household) whether or not they have a separate house. Both *ménage* and *maison* could be translated in English as the "household," but they emphasize different aspects of it.

The nuclear family is not a good model for the concept of "household" in Lavialle, if one hopes to define the unit in which children are raised and socialized. Although the nuclear family (*le ménage*) can exist as a separate residence unit (i.e., in a single-family home) it is *not* recognized as a meaningful *social* unit. The terms used to designate "family" of *les nôtres* and *la maison* more aptly represent the relevant units of child rearing. This is because in Lavialle a person is most strongly identified with the broader kin groups of the farm household and the kindred, rather than seen primarily as an individual or as a member of a nuclear family.

In Lavialle, it is one's broader kin group which gives one identity and which shapes one's understanding of and relationship to the world. This model differs from that of the educational system, which uses the model of the nuclear family as the relevant group to interact with the school. With changing laws and the recent trend towards neo-locality in Lavialle, as elsewhere in France (Segalen 1986), it is possible that the *ménage* will become more important in the future. In the 1980s, however, extended kin groups were vitally important to educational strategies in Lavialle.

The case of Lavialle has implications for the study of relationships between schooling and families in other cultural contexts. It is generally assumed that, in these relationships, family refers to a nuclear household of parents and children. However, this is a cultural model of the family that does not always reflect actual social arrangements. It is vital to determine the cultural meaning of "family" for all social actors, and to examine the lived experiences of children outside of school. The pioneering studies of Stack (1974) and Young and Wilmot (1962), while not focused on schooling, illuminate the importance of attention to kinship systems in Euro-American contexts.

Dairy farming and everyday life
It is difficult to understand fully the everyday lives of the Laviallois without taking into account the role and meaning of dairy farming (Plate 3). The educational strategies of families in Lavialle are deeply connected to the desire to maintain the family's "patrimony." This includes not only the farms and fields owned by families, but also the way of life associated with farming. Farming in Lavialle is a family activity, linking family and farm in a profound way. Since only four hired farm workers lived and worked in Lavialle in 1981, most farm labor came exclusively from family members.

There were 92 farms in Lavialle in 1980, and they were about average in size in comparison with others in its district, but slightly above national farm size averages. Most farms in Lavialle have about 20 milk cows, although some have as many as 60. During the 1970s, the number of farms in Lavialle decreased less than the overall population, and the number of cows increased. Whereas the population fell between 1968 and 1981 by almost 20%, the number of farms only decreased by 9% between 1970 and 1980.

Farm technology in Lavialle changed very slowly up until the 1970s. The first tractor was introduced in the early 1960s, but by 1980, there were 142 tractors. There is still a wide range of farming technology in Lavialle. Some families manually milk their herd of cows, while one large farm (still family-run, but with one farm laborer), had set up an automated milking system with a revolving platform. Most farms fall within a mid-range between these two extremes. Manual labor is still in demand on the farms of Lavialle, and during haying season (in which there are three cuts of hay), help is recruited from many family members throughout the region. The need for seasonal labor and my own willingness to help in the fields of Lavialle boosted my acceptance by farm families. It also taught me a great deal about the pleasures and pains of another kind of fieldwork.

Plate 3   *Cows returning for the evening milking in summer.* A common sight in Lavialle is that of herds of dairy cows being led from field to barn at milking time. This herd is being led through the center of the village of Lavialle. A garden plot belonging to a village farm family is in the forefront. The communal toilets and telephone booth are to the right. A "traditional" barn/house and a "modern" house can be seen in the background.

Lavialle's specialization in milk production has allowed its population to survive with a viable farm economy, especially since dairy farming has been fairly well subsidized by the French government. While this has led some farms to grow larger at the expense of others, there has been an overall process of economic homogenization among the remaining farms. The very small farms can no longer survive, so that huge disparities in farm size have been almost eliminated. Competition among the remaining farms, for the land of the smaller farms which is being rented or sold, has been intensified by this trend. For the most part, however, this is a conflict among more or less "equals."

By far the most important daily activity in dairy farming is the milking of the cows (*la traite*). The milking in Lavialle organizes family life, influences values and ideals of farming and farmers, sets the farmer off from the non-farmer, and structures the pace of all local social activities. Vital to the farmers, milking also punctuates the day for everyone else.

At about seven o'clock in the evening, those of us in our homes would hear the familiar sound of the cows being led through the village or hamlet from pasture to the barn. There would be the calls of "allez" and the alternating spurring on and restraining sounds of the farmers' voices as they led their herds down the narrow roads and paths, the clanking of the cows' hooves, their mooing, and their smell. Then, when all the herds were safely delivered to the barns, there was a period of intense calm, and only the low humming of the milking machines and, in the summer, a light evening breeze. In the winter months, the villages would be pitch-dark except for the barn lights. The sequence was reversed in the morning: first the milking, then the trip to pasture.

Since most people in Lavialle are members of dairy farming families, activities in Lavialle are planned so as never to conflict with milking times. As the local farmers say: "the cows can't wait." For about two hours every morning and every evening, at least one member of the family (usually male and head of the household) must go to the barn to milk his cows. When going to the barn at milking time, a male farmer usually announces: "Je vais tirer mes vaches" (literally, I am going to "pull on" my cows).

Except for a handful of farms in which there are a great many cows and the need for women to help with the milking itself, *la traite* is a male activity in Lavialle. For the most part, a man and his adult son will be responsible for actually milking the cows. Viewed more generally, however, milking involves several activities in which women take part. When a woman goes to the barn, she will say: "Je vais soigner mes bêtes" (I am going to care for my animals). Women help lead the herds from pasture to the barn (grandmothers are often recruited for this task), and feed young animals during the morning milking. They mix powdered milk to administer to baby calves, and care for their chickens and rabbits. Women also do most of the clean-up after the milking, and take care of the milk tank. This type of job usually goes to the young daughter-in-law, while the wife of the head of the household stays in the kitchen minding young children and preparing a meal.

The Laviallois combine ambivalence about farming with poetic descriptions of the tasks of farm work and a sense of pride about the work. The milking is linked to anxiety about getting the cows led into the barn and then about how much milk will be produced, but it also includes moments of quiet satisfaction and relaxation. One young farmer, in a philosophical mode, revealed to me his awe that the cows are able to produce this milk from the green grass and hay they eat. Many farmers spoke of the peaceful atmosphere in which they moved among their cows, gently coaxing them and gathering their yield of milk. Children learn early that there must not be any loud noise or commotion during the milking; the cows need to be at ease.

The same farmers who waxed eloquent about their farms at some moments, would, however, at other times describe the milking as an extreme burden and constraint on time. Now that vacations were becoming more fashionable, farmers resented the ease with which artisans, factory workers, and (especially) teachers could take time off for travel. Getting away for even a day is difficult for farm families, since someone always has to be back for the evening milking. The special time requirements associated with the milking set up a conflict between farmers and the artisans and shopkeepers of Lavialle. Although the farmers have sizable holdings and increasing cash flows resulting from their milk production, they do not have the same amount of free time as do non-farmers, and they resent it.

Adding to conflict between farmers and non-farmers are the differing gender relationships in the two types of family. There is a much closer cooperation in work and daily living between husbands and wives in the farm households, and fathers are often present throughout the day for their children. In artisanal households, husbands leave for work during the day and return at night, although some do come home for lunch. These wives are left at home alone with their children and domestic chores. Norms of social life in Lavialle do not encourage much social visiting among women. This produces a feeling of isolation, especially for elderly and non-farm women, who are alone much of the day. For younger farm women, this is less of a problem, since they are often in the company of their husbands, children, and parents. These differences set up feelings of resentment on the part of non-farm women, and deepen the chasm between farmers and non-farmers.

Even though Laviallois farmers will readily admit that it is *dur* (hard, difficult), farm life is positively valued most of the time. In contrast, I never heard any such "fond" accounts of schooling among the Laviallois, and memories or descriptions of schooling, as evident in their stories, were always phrased in terms of harsh experiences and discomfort. With few exceptions, stories about schooling involved mean schoolmasters and traumatic punishments. This relative valuing of farm life and devaluing of schooling experiences is at the crux of an understanding of the socialization strategies of the Laviallois.

Plate 4   *A farm family from a northern hamlet.* This shows a multi-generational family (*la maison*). The father and mother stand at the left. Seated are three of their four children – two sons and a daughter. Also pictured are the eldest son's wife and young son. The family dog sleeps in the background. This photo was taken after a leisurely Sunday dinner.

Lavialle families: a series of vignettes

The farm families in Lavialle who had children in school all expressed the desire that one child would remain and take over the farm. Plate 4 shows a farm family from a northern hamlet, and Plate 5 a family from a southern hamlet. When mothers and fathers talk about encouraging a child to stay in farming, they recognize that, as they say, "c'est pas evident" – it is not obvious that one will stay. This requires some strategizing and flexibility on the part of the family. One can no longer assume or desire that the eldest son will take over the farm, which has historically been the ideal model for the stem families of Lavialle. There is an expression in France, "faire l'aîné" (literally, to make the eldest), which captures both the idea that the eldest is the proper heir and the practical realization of parents that the first-born will not necessarily take over the farm. Thus, it is necessary to mold other children with the desire to do so (see Bourdieu 1972:1112). This is well illustrated by the following case of the Rochette family, in which a daughter may become heir.

Plate 5 *Members of a farm family in a southern hamlet.* The wife of the head of a Lavialle farm household stands in the center, with her sister and mother-in-law to her left. Her youngest daughter and her nephew are at her right. Her grandson (the child of another daughter), who was visiting, as well as the family dog, are in the front. Visits from extended kin, even those who do not live in Lavialle, are common, especially during the summer.

This Rochette family lives in a nuclear household (two parents and three children) in a northern hamlet in Lavialle. Mme. Rochette's unmarried sister and father live nearby in her natal household. M. Rochette is also from Lavialle, and native to a farm household in another hamlet in this northern section. Their farm is of moderate size in Lavialle, and considered strong. The eldest son, Pierre, was in his early teens in 1981. He was enrolled in a technical training school for aircraft repair in another department, and only came home during vacations. His two younger siblings, Nathalie and Henri, both attended Lavialle's primary school. Henri did better at school than his sister, even though he was the youngest. Mme. Rochette told me that she expected that one of these two would remain on the farm, but that she just had to see which one was better suited to farming. She suspected that it would be Nathalie, but hesitated to rule out her younger son at that time. She was proud of Pierre and his acquisition of a trade, and recognized that the farm would only support one of her children in the future. Because Mme. Rochette and her sister had stayed on her own family's farm, it seemed natural to her that her own daughter would want to remain.

A similar attitude was voiced by the parents of a boy and a girl who also lived in a northern hamlet, but their preference for their daughter to take over the farm was even greater. The Villars farm was in the hands of females. Mme. Villars and her mother had both brought husbands into their family's farm. It was a large, wealthy farm, with the only automated milking platform in the *commune*. During my several visits with this family, it was obvious that the Villars' daughter, Jeannette, was being groomed for life as a farmer. She was encouraged to help with farm work, and although she attended the middle school in Grosbourg, she did not board there as many children did. Rather, she was picked up each afternoon by a family member and participated in daily farm activities. In contrast to other families in Lavialle, the grandparents, parents, and children in this household shared the same roof and kitchen. Both Jeannette and her brother, Claude, were treated with a great deal of indulgence and affection by both the father and mother. M. Villars often kissed and hugged his ten-year-old son, which was an uncommon display of affection in Lavialle. The children accompanied their parents on trips to inspect other properties and land that they owned, and were made to feel very much a part of the operation of the farm. Even though it was strongly hoped that Jeannette would remain to take over the farm, affective ties to Claude were strengthened so that he would remain close to the family and kindred.

At the Martin farm, located in a hamlet near to the village of Lavialle, the case was somewhat different. Like the Rochette family, the Martins had a first-born daughter and a younger son. Mimi Martin was enrolled in middle school at the Catholic school, where she boarded during the week. Jean, her brother, who was in the upper primary grades in Lavialle's school, was the obvious choice for heir. This was a farm controlled by two brothers – Luc Martin, the father of Mimi and Jean, and his bachelor brother, Marcel. Marcel tended sheep, while his married brother carried out the dairy farming business. Their widowed mother lived with Marcel in a separate house from the married couple, who had a more modern residence. Talk about the future of their farm always assumed that Jean would stay and continue in his father's footsteps. Mimi was much less involved in farming. When it was the time for the pig-slaughtering, she hid upstairs in her room to avoid the squeals of the pig, while her mother, Lucy, drained blood from its neck and her father and brother helped hold it. Lucy Martin was not native to Lavialle, but came from a neighboring *commune* which had supplied many wives to Lavialle farm heirs. For the Martin family, it seemed more "natural" that the son would inherit the farm.

There were other cases in which grandparents, who continued to farm without their own children having stayed, hoped that a grandchild would take to farming. The Batisse family, located in a southern hamlet, had three daughters, none of whom has remained on the farm. This is a small farm that cannot really support two adult families at the same time. The eldest daughter married a prosperous farmer in another *commune*. The youngest lived and worked in Clermont-Ferrand. The middle daughter lived in a hamlet in the northern section of Lavialle. She was married to an artisan (painter/plasterer) and had four young children – three boys and a girl. During the summer months, the boys were rotated to live for several weeks with their grandparents, and the two households were in daily contact. The children and their mother often helped with farm tasks, and it was hoped that one of the boys might wish to enter a farming career and take over the farm.

In another case, nine-year-old Etienne Charel, the only child in his family, was quite adamant that he wanted to be a farmer when he grew up. His father worked in the sawmill, but he and his parents lived near his grandparents, who farmed alone. Despite the father's having left farming, the two households were closely connected, and the boy spent a great deal of time with his paternal grandparents on their farm. They encouraged him in this. Several existing farms in Lavialle already follow this model of a grandchild taking over the farm of grandparents who had no farm heirs. It was indicative of a renewed optimism concerning the future of farming in Lavialle that younger families were entertaining this option for their children.

These family stories are fairly representative in Lavialle. Even those children whose parents are not farmers, or who will not enter farming careers themselves, are encouraged to have positive attitudes toward farming and to recognize their rights and obligations within the kindred. The multi-generational Lafont family illustrates the continued pull of farming in many families, and leads to a consideration of the renewed interest in farming and rural life for Lavialle's youth.

The Lafont family ran a farm in a northern hamlet of Lavialle. M. and Mme. Lafont had four children – two boys and two girls. The two male children both lived on the farm in the early 1980s. Their youngest child, André, lived with them in the main part of a large farmhouse. Their eldest child and farm heir, Roger, lived with his wife and small son in an apartment that took up a portion of the house structure. The Lafont dairy farm is moderate in size and affords the family a comfortable income. By 1981, M. Lafont had already handed the farm over legally to Roger, who was then about thirty, but they continued to farm together. Roger's wife, Marie, was from a farm household in another hamlet of Lavialle. As is increasingly common among French farmers, Roger supplemented their income – by driving a milk truck for a dairy cooperative a few days a week.

All of the children, except for Roger, the farm heir, had received some post-secondary education. The girls, now adults, had left Lavialle. The eldest daughter, Irène, lived and worked in Clermont-Ferrand, but regularly visited Lavialle and was active in the Youth Club. Her younger sister, Thérèse, had trained in agricultural school and farmed with her husband in another *commune*. André was currently enrolled in agricultural school during my fieldwork, and was involved in a farm apprenticeship at another farm. He hoped to become a farmer, but knew that he could not permanently settle on his parents' farm.

When I returned to Lavialle in 1984, André was living and working on the farm with Roger – not yet having found another "situation." Roger and Marie by then had two children, a boy and a girl, and had built a separate, more modern house behind that of M. and Mme Lafont. They were confidently hoping that one of their children would remain in farming. Marie Lafont told me that she knew that women in previous years had not wanted to be farm wives, but she felt that life was easier now. She pointed to the modern appliances in her new home, like the blender and washing machine, and said that life was not so bad now on the farm.

This general optimism in Lavialle was evident in other stories from Lavialle when I returned in 1984. Bernard, the school van driver, a thirty-year-old bachelor at the time of my fieldwork, had recently married and had a newborn baby. His wife, Odile, was the granddaughter of the old village baker. Odile's father, the baker's son, was a house painter who had left Lavialle for Clermont-Ferrand as a young man, and she had returned often to visit remaining relatives in Lavialle. Bernard and Odile were living with his parents, and planned to take over the farm. Bernard's parents had moved to Lavialle years ago from a neighboring *commune* to assume this farm, which had belonged to the grandparents of Bernard's mother. One of two children, Bernard had an elder sister, married to a farmer in another hamlet in Lavialle, who was raising two small children. Odile and

Bernard are representative of the new vitality of Lavialle's population, and of a renewed commitment to farm life, as well as the importance of the kindred in retaining social ties among those who leave – like Odile and her father. In an inversion of a widespread trend in France during the 1950s when farm daughters left to marry urban husbands, resulting in a high number of rural bachelors (Bourdieu 1962), Odile was a city girl who came to the village to marry a farmer!

Lucette, the school aide, a young unmarried girl of twenty during my fieldwork, was also newly married with a newborn in 1984. Her husband, Jean, was from a neighboring *commune*. He and Lucette had been part of the same group of youths who attended Saturday night dances as teenagers. Although he was the son of farmers, Jean worked as an artisan. Lucette and Jean had settled in Lavialle, renting the old presbytery, and hoped to remain in the area. Like Bernard, Lucette was from a farm family in the village of Lavialle. Her elder brother was heir to her family's farm, and lived there in a separate *ménage* with his wife and school-age daughter. Her elder sister had married a farmer in another *commune* in the region. A younger brother, still in school, hoped to become a farmer himself.

There are countless other family stories in Lavialle of farm families managing to keep the farm and keep children interested in staying close to the family – even if they will not, themselves, become farmers. This was not always the case in previous generations, however. An elderly widow in Lavialle, Mme Jussat, had been left alone with three small children and a small farm when her husband died. She explained to me that it would not have been possible for her children to become farmers, given the small size of the farm. This had been recognized by the teachers, who encouraged her children in school and helped them to continue their studies. Her son, who remains fluent in *patois* and deeply attached to regional culture, has a bureaucratic job in Clermont-Ferrand. One daughter also lives in the region and works as a teacher. The youngest daughter lives and works in Paris. Mme Jussat's children continue to hold an economic interest in the remaining family land, which is rented to other working farms in Lavialle. Her husband had been a town council member, and her son continues to be active in local politics, even though he does not reside and work in Lavialle.

The renewed interest in farming among the youth of Lavialle, evident in the increasing number of young families staying in farming, is not typical of all of rural France or even of the region of Auvergne. There is a great deal of poignancy in the story of a young farmer who stayed for a few

weeks on a Lavialle farm as part of his training at the agricultural high
school. Pascal was from the plains of the Limagne, north of Clermont-
Ferrand. His elder brother had done well in school and entered a professional job, and his parents, therefore, looked toward him, the only other
child, to take over the farm. Pascal felt enormous ambivalence about his
situation and the pressure on him to become a farmer. An active puppeteer
in his spare time, he was very familiar with life in Clermont-Ferrand and
surrounding towns. Pascal desired a more urban lifestyle, less tied down to
the land, he told me. His parents were cereal farmers, with a fairly large
operation in comparison to the smaller dairy farms in Lavialle. I visited
them for a few days, and was keenly aware of the tension in that household
over the perpetuation of the farm.

Perhaps, to return to Bourdieu's observations about the French peasantry (1973) cited in chapter 2, Pascal's family had participated in their
own destruction by encouraging him and his brother to cooperate with
schools and teachers, become educated, and yearn for alternate ways of
life. Their community's close proximity to Clermont-Ferrand and their
fairly high standard of living marked their strong connection to urban life.
The family's social status, as cereal farmers on the plain, was much higher
than that of the mountain-dwelling Laviallois. The educational strategies
of Pascal's family were different from those of families in Lavialle. They
operated in a much different social context involving proximity to alternative occupational choices and the greater availability of cultural models
encouraging farm-leaving. Although Pascal's parents, like those in
Lavialle, desired their child to become a farmer, their strategies had not
been effective in this context.

I heard of no story in Lavialle of a young person struggling over the
dilemma of not wanting to take over the family farm. On very small farms,
parents rarely urged children to stay. On most farms, it was expected that
one child would stay, and for the most part, retention of an heir was
accomplished. In Lavialle, it was often the case that a younger son or
daughter who had no hope of becoming a farmer would be distraught
about leaving farm life. In several Lavialle families, these younger siblings
continue to train in agriculture, like André Lafont, hoping eventually to
find a situation (through marriage or the purchase of another farm).
Although all children will not enter farming, and many have always left,
there is no scarcity of heirs in contemporary Lavialle. This has a lot to do
with family strategies which encourage positive attachments to the kindred
and to farming among children, and is dependent upon a continued strong
regional consciousness. As other recent studies of rural France confirm

(Clout 1989; Moulin 1991; Rogers 1991), the family farm is still a vital part of French agriculture.

In the next chapter, I will turn more specifically to those socialization strategies and rituals of Lavialle families which encourage attachment to family, farm, *commune*, and region.

5

From child to adult

Childhood in Lavialle is a time to learn one's place in society, and one's relationship both to the kindred and to wider social spheres such as *commune*, region, and nation. Learning to be Laviallois is, in many ways, learning how to juggle these sometimes conflicting loyalties and identities. Children learn about this both at home and in school.

Family-based socialization[1] of childhood in Lavialle stresses attachment to family, farm, and region. Schooling in Lavialle is immersed within the overall context of the meaning of childhood for local families, and the behaviors and attitudes of parents and children toward the school are caught up in this wider web of meaning. The socialization experiences that children in Lavialle have in the context of home and hamlet life are aimed primarily at producing responsible family members, who will defend and protect the interests of their families and those of the local collectivity. These aims have developed in the context of, and in response to, the influences of schooling. Family-based socialization in Lavialle is part of an overall family strategy aimed at influencing the effects of schooling on children. It encourages them to foreground their identities as members of local families (*les nôtres*) and as Auvergnats.

There are four major stages in the phrasing of childhood and adolescence for families in Lavialle that will form the basis for this chapter: early childhood, middle childhood, late childhood, and early adulthood.[2] These are marked by three key rituals which express important religious and family values, and define the stages and their transitions: baptism, first communion, and the communal festival. These childhood rituals do not specifically relate to schooling experiences; rather, they are tied to the concerns of families regarding the perpetuation of cultural meanings and

84

attachment to local region. The dominant emphasis in family-based socialization is on the rights and duties that children will assume as future *adult* members of Lavialle kindreds. These three rituals in the phrasing of childhood play an important role in providing "counter-narratives" for children to those of the formal socialization practices they encounter in school. They transmit and reinforce a sense of local identity, and of being a member of a Laviallois kindred.[3]

There are also less formal modes of socialization at home, which transmit these values in everyday life. Important settings for socialization at home include activities associated with farm work, family meals, and play. As I now turn to the stages of childhood in Lavialle, I will discuss and analyze each of these childhood rituals and family-based modes of socialization in turn.

[handwritten: KG: Farm, meals, play!]

Early childhood: *les petits*

Birth and baptism take place within the context of only the closest of kin in Lavialle. Later events in a child's life will occur in broader social surroundings. Most children are now born in Clermont-Ferrand, so that the first days of their lives are in the setting of the rituals of modern medicine. Upon return from the hospital, babies are cared for by their own mothers, who breastfeed them for a period varying from about two to six months. One mother told me that she nursed her son until he was "growing well," at age two months. *[handwritten: Kindred thru baptism & not birth?]*

It is through baptism, which occurs early in the first year of life, that a child is incorporated into the kindred. All children are baptized in the Catholic Church, whether or not their parents regularly attend Mass. Godparents, one of each sex, are chosen from among the *les nôtres* category of kin – usually a grandparent, aunt, or uncle. Non-relatives are rarely chosen as godparents, especially for the first-born. Godmother and godfather develop a special relationship with the child and play the role of indulgent adult throughout his or her childhood. A child will refer to a relative who is also a godparent as *la marraine* (godmother) or *le parrain* (godfather), instead of another kin term. For example, a grandmother who is godmother to one child in a household will be called *marraine*, and not *mémé* (the common term for granny), by the godchild as well as all of his or her siblings.

Baptisms usually occur on Sundays, in the early afternoon. The baptism party, with the child under the care of the godparents, usually stops for a drink at the nearby cafe before entering the church and meeting with the priest. *Boire l'apéro* (to have a drink) is an important marker of social

[handwritten: Drinks]

occasions and festivities in Lavialle. After the baptismal ceremony, the family returns to the child's home for a meal.

Although it is an important and obligatory religious event, which also recognizes a new child in the family, baptism does not play a very significant social role in the wider community. It involves only the household, godparents, and the child. By appearing with the newborn in the public ritual space of the church and the secular place of the cafe, families are announcing the arrival of a new member. However, the absence of a wider network of family and friends, and of elaborate ceremony, signals the gradual nature of the child's incorporation into the social group, and the primacy of the family over the community.[4]

The child becomes a "social self" later, at around age two. A professional photograph of the child is taken at this time, which is then distributed among relatives and shown to friends. For little boys, this photo also marks the date when their infant curls are cut, and their sexual identity as males is established. Several young mothers expressed their regret to me that their son's locks were sheared, remarking on how "pretty" the boys had been and how much they resembled little girls before their photos. They also said that it had been their husbands who had insisted on the haircuts. One mother, at least, was successful in staving off the barber until after her two-year-old son's photo had been taken, and proudly displayed the picture of the little boy and his long golden curls.

Young children in Lavialle are indulged and spoiled by all. Since births are spread out, with at least three years in between, children rarely have siblings close enough in age to compete for attention during this period. There is little harsh discipline, and a child of this age is believed to be *sauvage* (a little wild and uncivilized). Toddlers are neither expected nor encouraged to display the same type of self-discipline and manners as are older family members. At mealtime they may freely leave their place at the table, eating as they come and go from their seats and from those of others. Toilet training is a gradual process, in which children are first encouraged to defecate or urinate outside in the garden. In the summer, they run naked.

There is little constraining of the movements of toddlers. They run freely in and out of the house, or next door to Grandma's, at whim. Although mothers complain about having to keep track of their little rascals (*vilains*), few means are used to restrict their movements. While visiting one young mother and her son (aged about 18 months), I observed the little boy run outside to his toy tractor and ride it almost into the road about five times, and five times watched the mother go fetch him and bring him inside, scolding him for his dangerous behavior. It was only after the fifth episode that she finally moved the tractor out of his reach. Most of this chasing after toddlers is taken with the same good humor as that used when chasing after stray calves or cows: it is an expected feature of life.

Women coax and cajole young children into good behavior through the use of treats, especially candy. This ranges from the doling out of sugar cubes from the sugar jar to keep a child pacified during a social visit, to a threat to withhold a certain treat (for example, a trip to the upcoming fair) if good behavior is not exhibited. A good child is told that he or she is *sage,* or is acting like *un grand* (a big kid).

I observed this type of gentle coaxing of children in a farm kitchen one afternoon. Present were mother, grandmother, great-grandmother, myself, and a four-year-old girl. She had a flu and her grandmother was preparing a mixture of aspirin, sugar, and water for her. She didn't want any. Her mother took the role of observer during this whole process, letting her mother-in-law and grandmother-in-law handle it. The child's grandmother administered a couple of spoonfuls to her by gently encouraging her to take it, despite the child's continued protestations. Finally, when the child would not take the last spoonfuls, her great-grandmother said that she would give her a piece of candy if she took it. The child still refused. Then the grandmother suggested that maybe the child would take the spoonful for Déborah (myself). I offered a spoonful to her, which she took. She received no candy after this, and went off to play with her young uncle. This episode was marked by sympathy for the poor sick child, combined with a great deal of patience. It seemed expected that she refuse, almost ritualistically, and she expected to be coaxed.

Whenever a guest comes to a home in which a young child lives, she is obligated to bring a small gift (usually candy or cookies) for the child. This obligation is unspoken, but I never observed a social situation of this kind in which a gift was not brought for the child. Apart from this initial "fussing" over the child, however, children do not receive much focused attention in social situations. Children are simply there. Young children are neither segregated from adult life nor ignored, but they are expected either to amuse themselves quietly or just to sit with the adult group.

No institution of "babysitting" exists in Lavialle, and children are always present in social contexts with adults. Since most get-togethers, usually centered around an evening meal, must occur after the milking of the cows, they begin late and end at midnight or later. When families or friends visit, they bring their children along, and the children participate.

As the evening wears on, very small children might be put into a bed in the house; but children aged three and over most often just fall asleep in their mothers' arms, or slumped in a chair. It is not that the parents do not care about the children, or ignore them; rather, children are considered to be an integral part of their lives. When there are community dances, children are always there. Only one activity, which is considered masculine (although some women do join in) was considered inappropriate for children – that of card game tournaments. The schoolmistress was fiercely criticized in private, especially among mothers, for having attended one of these games while pregnant, since the smoke-filled room was thought to be bad for the fetus.

Although formal schooling in Lavialle begins at age three, early childhood extends beyond this point. School entrance is actually a gradual process, since many children attend nursery school irregularly during the first year, and some for only half a day. Mothers expressed their reluctance to have their children spend an entire day at school at so young an age. Even though the parents agreed in 1979, at the urging of the teachers, to lower the school entrance age to three in order to ensure that the school stay open (by having a higher enrollment), they were not all convinced that this was best for their children. Parents seemed torn between what they were told by educational authorities – that children who enter school earlier are at an educational advantage (*plus degourdis*), and their own emotional reticence to see their young "babies" go off to what was, in their own experience, an often harsh ordeal.

Early childhood modes of family-based socialization continue for these children at home despite their introduction to the more strict ways of schooling. Parents only gradually come to expect different behaviors, more controlled and well-behaved, up until about age five or six. They seem reluctant to deliver up their children totally to the control of the school.

For the next couple of years, children go through various stages of being either "little kids" (*les petits*) or "big kids" (*les grands*) in relation to older or younger peers. In general, they are promoted from the nursery/kindergarten class to the primary school proper at age seven. By this time, the attitudes toward their behavior by both parents and teachers are more closely in tune, although discipline continues to be more lax at home.

The ranking into "big kid" or "small kid" categories is an important social status marker for children. Age ranking is important in the community, and children learn early to locate themselves on the scale. The emphasis on whether one is big or little is used among peers at home and at school. Five year olds will refer to three year olds as "little" in relation to themselves, while five year olds are considered "little" by older children. This recognition of one's place on the age scale helps to solidify the age grades which continue to be strong bases for friendship and mutual aide in later life. As mentioned in chapter 3, adults of the same age in Lavialle are called *classards*, and organize annual banquets. Age ranking is also used as a disciplinary tool by parents, and sometimes by teachers, in order to reward or punish behavior: a good child is "big"; a bad child is "little."

Family life: meals and social learning

Mealtimes are important arenas for socialization in gender roles, family identity, and regional identity. Occasions for social eating in Lavialle families are not a strictly circumscribed area of everyday life, but must be seen as part of a wider stream of activity. Much of life within the household takes place in the "hearth" area, in the kitchen. Everyone enters the house through the kitchen, and it is here that social visits, and family gatherings take place. Even though newer houses, built within the past twenty years, may have added a dining room or formal sitting room, these rooms are rarely used. As with the shower stalls also built in these newer houses, they often become places for storage.

Because so much social life occurs in and around the kitchen table, food and drink are served numerous times throughout the day. When a neighbor or kinsman stops by, or an animal trader pays a call, some libation is always offered. A woman will make coffee and offer sweet cake, if she has some on hand, or bread and jam. In the late afternoon, she may also offer the female visitor some sweet liqueur. Men will fetch the wine bottle (always red), at all times of day for a male visitor, and offer him a drink.

There are five times, each named, when food is served for the family members themselves. This pattern is particularly uniform among farm families. These meals include (1) a light breakfast (*petit déjeuner*) before milking in the morning, (2) a snack (*le casse-croûte*) at mid-morning, (3) a largish cooked noonday meal (*le dîner*), (4) another snack (*quatre-heures*) in the late afternoon, and (5) a light dinner (*la soupe* or *le souper*) after the evening milking. It is generally only at noontime and in the evening that all family members assemble together for a meal. Children most often have their breakfast and snacks with their mothers or grandmothers, while their fathers are in the barn or fields. Most school-children in Lavialle eat lunch at school five times each week, joining their families for a meal in the evening. At supper, they have a chance to tell about their experiences at school that day and, for older children, to pass on gossip they have heard about the teachers or other families to their parents.

Although everyone eats the same food, both age and gender divisions are marked by beverage consumption in Lavialle. Bread and jam are served to everyone for breakfast, but men will drink coffee, women coffee or tea, and children hot chocolate.[5] At snack times, bread, cheese, and sometimes sausage are eaten. Men will have either wine or coffee, women will usually drink coffee, and children will have hot chocolate. At lunchtime, a typical meal would include some cooked meat, mashed potatoes, salad, cheese, bread, and a dessert or fruit. Men will drink red wine full-strength at lunch, whereas women will dilute theirs with water. Children have either plain water, or water mixed with a bit of wine or syrup at meal times. As a boy gets older, his water glass becomes redder and redder with wine. The evening meal usually includes some leftovers, soup, a salad, bread, and cheese – with the same beverages as those for lunch. Later, many of the women drink an herbal tea in the evening before going to bed, as, they told me, an aide to digestion. Gender and age distinctions are displayed and reinforced for children through this code of drinking.

Gender is also made explicit at meals in other ways. The authority of the head of household over the family is made clear when all are seated at table. At lunchtime, the most formalized meal in Lavialle households, the head of the household, usually the male farmer who is in charge of the farm (even if he has an elderly father who lives in the household), usually presides over the meal and sits at the head. Men always bring their own pocket knives to the table, while women and children use tableware. It is usually the father who slices the bread with his pocket knife and serves it to the others. The wife of the household head takes charge of preparing the meal, and serves it before sitting down to join the others. Children are not expected to sit at the table for long periods of time until they reach school age, and young children often run around the table during meals, or get up and down from their mother's laps. In households with young children, the atmosphere at mealtimes is fairly jovial, and the men and women will tease the children.

Although clear gender role distinctions are explicit, middle-class standards of appropriate "manners" at meal are rarely visible and verbally scoffed at. The table is not set in a uniform pattern, and little attention is paid to noise or posture at the table. This inattention to "manners" is not out of ignorance of proper etiquette, but, rather, part of the Laviallois identity as people who are "simple" and do not put on airs. Once when I was eating with a Lavialle family and refused a second helping of potatoes and carrots, the farm wife teasingly said to me: "What is it? Is this food too *paysan* for you, for the 'mademoiselle'?" At another family meal, the farm wife told me "We don't worry about manners here. Me, I don't know anything about manners."

There is a recognition among parents and grandparents that children need to learn manners, because these are expected in other social contexts – outside of Lavialle. Parents expect teachers to teach children manners at school, but do not teach these explicitly at home. The aunt of one young schoolchild in Lavialle told me that she was so pleased that the little girl was learning to say "please" and "thank you" at school, and that she was now using these terms at home. A farmer remarked to his three-year-old son during a meal that he hoped he'd learn some manners when he began school in the fall. The families of artisans are more attentive to their children's manners, for the most part, than are those of farmers. For most families, however, behavior at home in Lavialle should not mirror the "social airs" of the middle-classes. Such "distinctions" have been aptly illustrated by Bourdieu (1984).

A typical meal was one that I observed on a summer day in the kitchen of a farmhouse in the southern portion of the *commune*. Present at the noon meal were the farmer and his wife, both around 50 years of age, their unmarried daughter visiting from Clermont-Ferrand, in her early twenties, and a grandson who was spending a few weeks with them. He lived with his parents, who were not farmers, in a hamlet in the northern section of the *commune*. This grandson and nephew, who was three, was treated like a treasured "pet." He was coaxed into eating, and allowed to drift to and from the table, or from chair to chair. This lack of attention to "manners" was common among farm families.

More importantly learned than manners at Lavialle tables, are the important gender distinctions between males and females, the need to enjoy one's food, and the special role of children in the family. Auvergnat identity is expressed for children every day at mealtime through the regional foods prepared and served by their mothers and through the appearances and behaviors of their fathers. When they see their fathers enter for lunch or supper from the barn or fields, with their dirty, calloused hands, shaking the mud from their boots and removing them before sitting down, and then taking out their knives, cutting bread and gulping some red wine, children are reminded that these are Auvergnat *paysans*. Their mothers cook a regional cuisine of local foods – from their own gardens or from local shops. Children are served *clafoutis* – an Auvergnat cherry cake,

Auvergnat cheeses like Cantal and St. Nectaire, Auvergnat sausage, and Auvergnat stews. Although their mothers and grandmothers have also learned to cook "new" recipes from cooking lessons offered through the French agricultural extension service or, earlier, from teaching nuns, they continue to remind the children when a typical regional food is offered. Mealtime is a daily ritual expression of important aspects of local identity in which families socialize their children.

Although younger children are expected to be "wild" and indulged at meals, older children are expected to behave in a more sober manner and to begin to mimic the gender roles of their parents. Boys will begin to have their own pocket knives when they are teenagers, and girls will help in food preparation and serving.

Middle childhood: *les gamins*

By the time children are about age seven, they have come to the period of "middle childhood." It is during this phase that children attend the primary school class in Lavialle. They are now expected to exhibit more controlled behaviors. I asked seven- and eight-year-old children what they considered to be the qualities of *sage* (well-behaved) and *pas sage* (ill-mannered) children. (These are terms used by children and adults in Lavialle to describe children.) Their responses reflect adult values, and show that they have begun to learn to repeat these. In general, the children could more easily define the naughty child by his or her negative qualities, than the well-behaved child by positive qualities. Here are some of their responses (verbatim), collected during school recess:

A *sage* child is one:
"qui fait pas des bêtises" (who doesn't do silly things)
"qui fait pas de bruit" (who doesn't make noise)
"qui aide à sa maman (à la maison)" (who helps his mother in the house)
"qui fait pas mal aux autres" (who doesn't hurt others)
"qui écoute le maître et la maîtresse" (who listens to the schoolmaster and schoolmistress)
"qui est poli; qui dit 'merci'" (who is polite, says "thank you")

A child who is *pas sage* is one:
"qui est vilain – fait mal aux autres" (who is bad and hurts others)
"qui fait du bruit" (who makes noise)
"qui tappe; qui donne des coups de poing" (who hits others)
"qui écoute pas" (who doesn't listen)
"qui n'aide pas ses parents" (who doesn't help his parents)
"qui n'est pas gentil avec les autres" (who isn't nice to the others)
"qui fait tomber les autres" (who knocks others down)

Against the grain? School promotes 1 identity,
the home another. No enforcement
at home?

It is, perhaps, significant that these responses were collected at school, rather than in the home environment, as they reflect many school values. Parents and teachers share several of the values expressed, and children have learned them both in school and at home. However, some of them are more important at school: such as listening, being polite, and not making noise. Although parents would agree that these behaviors are appropriate at school, they do not reinforce them at home for the most part. When children enter school, they learn that there are two different behavioral codes – at home and at school; and, more generally, that different social situations in life may call for different types of behaviors.

Most children in Lavialle live in extended family households; in all cases, close relatives lived nearby. Over half of the children who attended Lavialle's school had fathers who were farmers, and all but two of the 44 parents (22 couples) who had children attending the school were themselves the sons or daughters of farmers. There were only six (out of twenty-eight) children at the school who did not have intimate everyday contact with farm life, either on their own farm or on that of their grandparents.

Even children who did not live on a farm or next door to farmer grandparents, however, are well acquainted with an agricultural way of life, since they all live in farm hamlets. Fathers who are not farmers are locally employed, and most are self-employed. A few mothers in non-farm households work outside of the home. One, for instance, worked as an accountant in a nearby nursing home; another labored on the assembly line in a chicken processing plant.

During primary school, children's lives outside of school are characterized by the same kind of rhythm as the rest of village and farm life – a loosely structured routine organized around the requirements and exigencies of daily farm and/or household tasks. Especially in farm households, children come to expect the unexpected at home. Their play may suddenly be interrupted as everyone is enlisted to go off and help round up some young calves who have broken out of their grazing field. In the morning, a child may wake up to find no one in the kitchen because a cow had a difficult birth during the night and his or her parents are in the barn caring for baby and mother.

Children learn early that animals are worth money, either as potential milk-producers or as marketable animals for slaughter, and that their parents must direct considerable attention toward these investments. As a result, children develop a sense of caring and responsibility for the cows and other animals on the farm. They are particularly encouraged to take an interest in young animals and, if the family can afford it, are given a young goat or other pet to care for themselves. The group effort towards survival of the family farm is instilled early in the farm children. Young children's lives, like those of their parents, are primarily centered around the farm.

Although their labor is no longer necessary to the farm as it was earlier in the century, children continue to have their social lives focused on the household, since small family size, hamlet residence patterns, and population decline have meant that they have few playmates living close by. Children in Lavialle's primary school were spread out into thirteen hamlets, including the village of Lavialle, and six of these children were the only young children in their hamlets. Since many of the older children attend school as boarders during the week, there were few playmates around. When the population of Lavialle was larger (until about 20 years ago), such peer isolation was not the case. Informants remembered that, until quite recently, there were groups of children in each hamlet who regularly played with each other. While there have always been some isolated farms in Lavialle, the child population in most hamlets was higher in the past. For instance, while there were 18 children under the age of 14 living in the village of Lavialle in 1936, by 1981 there were only 8.

Not only are children isolated from age-mates in their hamlets, but many have few siblings within their own household. Most of the children in Lavialle's school have only one sibling, and five were the only children in their households. Their parents may eventually have more children, since it is not uncommon for couples in Lavialle to space the births of children over several years. It is difficult to predict whether or not the younger families in Lavialle will, indeed, have as many children (3–4) as their elders. Many young mothers with toddlers voiced their preference for two children, and intended to wait to have another baby until the first was at least two years old. One young couple in their late twenties (husband an artisan) had four children, aged two to six. This mother told me that she wanted a girl, and had kept trying until she had one – her fourth. She didn't intend to have any more children. Other young mothers felt that she was foolish to have so many, and expressed a mixture of criticism and sympathy for her "plight."

Several children told me that, because they have few playmates nearby, life at home is sometimes boring for them. This has the effect of increasing the importance of peer relationships formed at school, and helps make school attractive as a place to see friends. Many of the friendships that

→ Friendship are only in the public sphere.

arise for children at this age, therefore, do so almost solely in the context of school (during recess and after-school playtime), or of religious instruction (which involves the same children who are at school). Some mothers have enabled their children to entertain their school friends from other hamlets at home by inviting them to visit during weekends and vacations, but such occasions are rare.

I asked children how they spent their time after school on schooldays. For the children in farm households, the pattern was basically the same, and did not differ among girls and boys. Listed below are, first, two responses from children in farm households and, second, that of a child whose father works in the wood mill.

First child (farm household):
1. Je m'amuse un peu. (I play awhile)
2. quatre-heures (I take a snack)
3. Je fais mes devoirs. (I do my homework)
4. Après, c'est la traite. Je vais à l'étable. Je m'amuse.
   (Then it's milking time. I go to the barn. I play)
5. Je mets la cloture pour les vaches. (I fasten the gate for the cows)
6. Je mange. (I eat)
7. On regarde la télé: les films. (We watch movies on TV)
8. Je me couche. (I go to bed)

Second child (farm household):
1. Je mange. (I eat)
2. Je fait mes devoirs. (I do my homework)
3. Je soigne les animaux avec Maman. (I feed the animals with Mommy)
4. Je vais à l'étable avec mon papa. (I go to the barn with my father)
5. On regarde la télé. (We watch TV)
6. Je me couche. (I go to bed)

Third child (non-farm household):
1. Je pose ma cartable. (I put down my book bag)
2. Je prends du cafe. (I drink some coffee)
3. Je fais mes devoirs. Maman m'appelle pour faire mes devoirs. (I do my homework. Mom calls me to do my homework)
4. Je m'amuse avec ma soeur. (I play with my sister)
5. Mon père et ma mère regardent un peu la télé. (My father and mother watch a little TV)

6. On mange. (We eat)
7. On regarde la télé. (We watch TV)
8. Je me couche. (I go to bed)

The children's descriptions reflect the pattern that I observed while visiting families. The children arrive home at about five o'clock (depending on the distance from the school to their hamlet and the number of stops along the route), and then take the small meal called *quatre-heures*. I did not observe that children always did homework after school (as the children claim so diligently), but when it was done, it was done at this time. At around seven o'clock in the evening, the men start the milking of the cows. Supper is not eaten until afterwards, usually around 8:00 or 8:30. Children usually help their parents with work in the barn. Supper is eaten either before or during the evening movie shown on TV. Almost every night, there is a film on French television from about eight to ten or eleven o'clock. The children usually watch this with the whole family. After the film, the children go to bed. Some children went to bed at around 9:30 p.m., but most of those aged seven or older were allowed to stay up until the movie was over.

The children whose parents are not farmers, and who do not live in farm households, follow roughly the same pattern. However, they have no farm tasks, and watch more television. The teachers complained to me that both farm and non-farm children went to bed too late and were often tired at school. They did not share the parents' attitude that the children should be allowed to join in with the family activity of watching TV together in the evenings. The timetable of farm work causes the fathers to finish their work late, and so mealtime takes place when the teachers would like to see children in bed.

When left alone to play, which was most of the time, the children inhabited immense imaginative worlds at home. There were few store-bought toys. The children were, consequently, amazing little *bricoleurs*, who accumulated all sorts of objects to incorporate into their games. Their parents allowed them free rein in establishing play sites and in appropriating things for their use. One ten-year-old girl, who was the only child in her small hamlet during the week, had set up a schoolroom in a shed on her farm, where she played at teacher. Two brothers had turned half of their parents' attic into a vast play world, full of small plastic people (soldiers and other figurines) and a makeshift farm. On another farm, a brother and sister had turned a junked van into a little house – furnished with discarded furniture, cans, containers from their mother's kitchen, and other found objects.

Imagining reality

Children's play at home in Lavialle was almost exclusively cooperative and non-competitive in nature; it involved imagining and acting out settings much like those of adult life in Lavialle. Children played together as partners in these games, and if one child were older, it was deemed natural that this "big kid" should take the lead.

Absent in Lavialle was the children's festival, or *fête des enfants*, so common in other, less agricultural *communes* in the Puy-de-Dôme (and other regions). These school-sponsored events involve a parade of primary school-age children through the streets of the community, costumes, dances and plays performed by the children, puppet shows, etc.[6] Such ritual celebrations of middle childhood reflect a stronger identification with the school's aims among local families, and a different attitude toward childhood, than is found in Lavialle.

Late childhood: *les jeunes*

When children are promoted from primary school to middle school (Collège d'Enseignement Générale – CEG) in Lavialle, at age 11 or 12, there is *no* ceremonial marking of the transition, either at school or at home. Since all children now continue their schooling in either the public or Catholic middle school, completing the first phase of schooling does not receive much attention. Up until the 1960s, when most children completed their entire education in Lavialle's primary school, a certificate was awarded to those who had achieved a certain level of instruction and took a special exam (the *certificat d'études*). Those who did so enjoyed an elevated social status, and could be employed in civil service jobs. But now, the end of primary school is just the end of the first phase of education for all children.

Although there are no festive markings of the transition to middle school from primary school, there are some real changes associated with it. First, many children who attend the public middle school do so as boarders during the week, as do all of those who attend the Catholic school. This system arose due to the difficulty of transportation in an area of scattered hamlets and harsh winters. Its persistence, now that everyone has a car and roads are completely impassable only a few days of the year due to snow, is less easy to explain. One factor, that of cost, is taken care of for many families by state subsidies for room and board. Since there is no organized transport system for the two middle schools, parents are responsible for transporting their children to and from school. Some parents say that this is too much of a burden to do on a daily basis, due to farm tasks. A car pool among some parents has enabled their children to live at home, with the parents taking turns driving the children to and from the CEG in Grosbourg, which is about 10 minutes by car from the village of Lavialle (but farther from some hamlets). The Catholic middle school, run by an order of Brothers, is about 40 minutes by car, and considered much too far for daily commuting. This separation of children from their families while they attend middle school is encouraged by the school and accepted by parents. → Ecoraging independence + "civilizing"?

First communion (*la première communion* or *communion solenelle*)

An important ritual that coincides with entrance to middle school expresses and reinforces family ties and the child's role in the kindred. This balances the separation occurring between the child and his or her family through schooling. When children are promoted to the CEG, they also begin preparations for the religious ceremony of the first communion, which occurs in May after their first or second year of middle school. Children attend weekly sessions with the priest, and at around age thirteen (usually at the end of the first year of middle school), all children in the parish go through this ceremony with their age-mates. In the past, this ceremony coincided with the end of primary schooling, at age fourteen. Today, it is an important ritual marker of the transition from middle to late childhood (or adolescence) for the youth of Lavialle.

The precise sacred meaning of *la première communion* is unclear to most of the participants and their families, and it is not a Church sacrament, since the actual receiving of the eucharist for the first time occurs much earlier, at around age seven. However, this literal "*first* communion" receives scant attention by families, and is done in private during Mass. The local priest told me that he would actually prefer to abolish the more elaborate "second" first communion, since it has come to signal the end of all religious instruction or participation for most children.[7] He retains this ritual because he is aware of the opposition that would meet any proposal for its abolition. Here, the priest is in a similar position to that of the teachers in their efforts to change teaching methods. Despite its ambiguous role in the Church, first communion has deep meaning and significance for the families of participating children. It also has important social meanings for Lavialle as a community.

The ceremony itself is rather simple. The children attend a special Mass dressed in ritual white robes, looking somewhat like little monks (Plate 6). The girls wear the same costume as the boys, with the addition of small, short veils. Up until quite recently (before the 1970s), the children were dressed more like brides and grooms – with the girls in frilly, white full-

Plate 6 *Children dressed for the communion solennelle.* A group of Lavialle youth stand in front of the church after the ceremony, and before the family meals to celebrate the occasion. The girls wear veils over their heads. Boys and girls wear the same white robe, with a cross. This ceremony marks an important stage in the life course for Lavialle children, and also expresses the importance of the kindred.

length dresses and long veils, and the boys in suits. The new costume represents efforts by the Church to downplay both the expense of the costume and gender differences. *[handwritten: Importance of religious event @ home]* The important event of this ceremony is not, however, what occurs at *[handwritten: instead of @ church]* the church, but, rather, the celebration afterwards at the home of the parents of each participating child. Each household hosts its close friends and kin in a huge display of hospitality. The expense of each party is quite great. The communion child receives gifts (of money and objects, such as a watch) from the guests, and this is the main attraction of the whole party for the children. The displays of wealth and effort that occur in each household in this context are richly symbolic.

Some families remodel entire rooms of their homes for the celebration. One prosperous farm family had an addition built, which was used as a storage room in anticipation of the communion of their next oldest child. New clothes are also purchased. I accompanied the mother of one participating child to a regional outdoor market at which it became apparent through her purchases that each member of the family was to be newly outfitted for the occasion. She bought a new sweater to go with her mother-in-law's new dress, looked for new shoes for herself, and searched for just the right suit for her two-year-old grandson (the one she bought, in blue velvet, cost more than $75.00 at the time).

The ceremony of the first communion which takes place at home is called *le repas* (the meal). These ritual feasts are highly unusual in the *commune* for their degree of lavishness and display. In their everyday lives, the Laviallois dress unassumingly (women in housecoats, and men in overalls) and try not to be showy in any manner. Laviallois do not spend money freely, and carefully weigh most purchase decisions. The extravagance characteristic of the first communion is barely rivalled by weddings. In contrast to the norms of everyday life, where prudence and modesty (*être simple*) are most highly valued, first communion features lavish display. On the other hand, it carries another local value, that of showing hospitality to visitors (in this case, one's kindred), to an extreme. It is considered important to share one's best food and drink with guests. This is expressed with the phrase "la maison du bon dieu" (the house of the good Lord), used to compliment those houses that always offer good hospitality.

This conspicuous behavior reflects the ceremony's meaning for childhood in terms of both the kin group (*les nôtres*) and the *commune* in general. The solidarity of the kindred is strengthened through this celebration of the addition of a new quasi-adult member. For the child passing into adolescence, the emotional and material support received at this time furthers his or her identification with this group. Whereas this ceremony has always marked the end of "childhood," it now has meaning in relation to a new definition of "childhood" (see also Zonabend 1980). Before, the period of childhood coincided with the period of formal schooling: at the end of schooling, came the end of childhood. Now, childhood means the passing into adolescence or late childhood, which has become a more important period in the life cycle than it was when individuals fulfilled "adult" roles upon the completion of primary schooling.

The persistence of this ceremony, despite the priest's disapproval and its loss of synchronization with the end of formal schooling (due to educational reforms), attests to the resolve of families to maintain the kindred and their children's ties to it. At just that moment when young people are being separated from the family through educational experiences outside of the *commune* (through the institution of boarding at the CEG), the family expresses and tries to reinforce its hold on this member through the celebration of the first communion.

There is a further meaning of this ceremony in Lavialle which also expresses the importance of the kindred. The feasts of the first communion celebrated by households and their kin (*les nôtres*) are measures for status ranking in the community of the various households. The amount of money and effort that each family expends is a signal of its wealth and prestige. The day-to-day conservatism and norms against conspicuous behavior in Lavialle generally mask the economic differences among households. Through the first communion celebration, status is made overt. The ranking and pitting against each other of the various family groups involved further solidifies boundaries between each group, intensifying the importance of the household and its kindred. Rumors circulate widely about the lavish food, gifts, and clothing at these meals. They are, thus, important occasions for impression management in Lavialle.

The first communion and accompanying ritual meals also relate to potential alliances among households, and not simply to the maintenance of boundaries between them. The displays of wealth and status during these ceremonies communicate to other families the material contributions that a communion child could eventually bring to a marriage alliance. The first communion coincides with the onset of puberty, and signals the burgeoning sexuality of the communion child. It celebrates not just the addition of a new quasi-adult member of the kindred, but the potential intensification of the wealth of the patrimony that this person may bring to the kindred through marriage. The dress of the communion participants, in its continued similarity to wedding garb (despite the downplaying of this costume by the priest), makes most explicit this aspect of the ceremony.[8]

After the first communion, a child will become a member of *les jeunes* (the youth). He or she will no longer be referred to as a *gosse* or *gamin(e)* (kid). This age group roughly corresponds to the notion of adolescence, although it also includes unmarried, or married but still childless, young adults. *Jeune* (literally, "young" or "youth") refers to anyone who is not yet a parent or head of household. Becoming an adult in Lavialle is a gradual process, which one assumes through the stages of adolescence, marriage, parenthood, and then full adult status as head of household (and wife of head of household).

Many Laviallois say that the youth used to be more cohesive than they are today, and that they would hang around together in *bandes* (cliques or gangs). Parents of the children in school spoke of their participation in a youth clique in their teens. Since there are fewer young people in Lavialle now, and friendships are increasingly formed across communal boundaries, the youth of Lavialle participate in cliques which draw from several neighboring *communes*. These groups go to dances and have parties together, and often girls and boys in them date each other.

Many young people complete their formal education at the middle school by age sixteen, mostly as a result of being kept back a year or two at this stage (a common phenomenon for students in rural schools). Others pass on to technical schools at age fourteen, where they study until age sixteen. Very few children from Lavialle attend high school bound for university training. If they continue beyond this educational level, children must travel even farther to technical schools or *lycées*, and will most certainly live apart from their families during the week. Many of these young people return home each weekend, however, to assist with farm work and see their friends. Those who are able to find work locally, either with their parents or in nearby dairies or in trades, will return to live with their families after completing their schooling until, or even after, marriage. Those who are not, will, as they did in school, live and work in the city (usually Clermont-Ferrand) during the week, returning home on the weekends.

Early adulthood: the communal festival (*la fête communal*)

An important ritual associated with the transition from childhood to adulthood in Lavialle is the communal festival. At age eighteen, the youth of Lavialle form a group known as *les conscrits* and organize the communal festival in midsummer. This festival ritually marks their transition from late childhood into early adulthood (including preparation for marriage). In contrast to the first communion, which entails an extravagant party given in honor of the communion child by relatives and close friends, the communal festival is organized by the *conscrits* themselves for the benefit of the entire *commune*.

The term *conscrits* literally refers to draftees (conscripts) in French, and eighteen is the age at which young men enter France's mandatory military service. However, Laviallois girls (who do not participate in such mandatory service) are also members of *les conscrits*. In Lavialle, there is no direct relationship between departure for military service and the youth festival, but in some parts of France there are rituals specifically associated with the days preceding a young man's departure for service.

The main task of the *conscrits* is to organize the annual communal festival (*la fête communale*). In 1981, there were eight youths of age eighteen who participated, six of whom were the only eighteen-year-olds in

Conscrits

Lavialle. The other two youths, both male, lived in Clermont-Ferrand but were members of Lavialle kindreds: one was the grandson of a farm widow living in the village of Lavialle, and the other was the nephew of farmers in one of the more remote hamlets. Each of these boys had one parent who was a Lavialle native, and both were frequent visitors to Lavialle on weekends and during vacations. Of the Lavialle natives, two were boys and four were girls. Two of the girls were considered to be "special" participants because they did not fit the norm: one was mentally retarded, living with her parents on their farm; the other was the recently married daughter of farmers, with whom she lived with her husband and their infant son.

Only one of the *conscrits* was still in school; she attended an agricultural high school and hoped to become a farmer. One of the boys from Lavialle and one of the girls worked on their parents' farms full-time. The young mother was not working at the time. The other four youths worked in artisanal and semi-skilled occupations that did not require any further education. Except for the two boys from Clermont-Ferrand, all of the *conscrits* were the children of farmers in Lavialle. However, membership in Lavialle kindreds, combined with frequent visits to Lavialle, allowed these boys to be considered rightful participants in the group.

For *les conscrits*, the festival constitutes a classic *rite de passage* (Turner 1969; Van Gennep 1909) from late childhood to early adulthood. There are three distinct stages to their participation which correspond to the three phases of: separation or detachment from the social group, liminality, and aggregation or reincorporation. At the end of the festival, *les conscrits* return to daily life with a new status as young adults ready to leave their households (*ménage*) for employment, military service, and/or marriage. The participation of the youths in the festival takes place within the space of about one week, after they have spent months of planning. The three stages to their participation are marked by (1) the "selling of the *brioche*," (2) the festival proper (carnival games and dances), and (3) the day after the festival.

During the weekend before the festival itself begins, the *conscrits* decorate a tractor with fir trees and paper flowers left over from spring and early summer weddings. (Such trees trimmed with paper flowers are placed at the church, the mayor's office, and in the hamlets of residence of the wedding party.) In a carnival spirit of gaiety, the youths pass from household to household in each hamlet, selling *brioche*[9] from their tractor in order to raise money for the festival. The youths make the pretence of "offering" the bread as a gift to the household (rather than selling it out-

Why is this not in the text?

right), for which the recipient makes a "donation" to the festival, the amount of which varies. Heavy drinking on the part of both male and female *conscrits* is part of this procession from hamlet to hamlet, since they are invited for a drink at each stop. This selling of the *brioche* and its accompanying carnival atmosphere marks the separation of the *conscrits* from daily life and the beginning of a "liminal" phase (Turner 1969) which lasts until the Monday morning following the festival, when the youths return to jobs and family. After the *brioche* procession, the youths stay together as a group, often acting in a reckless manner, drinking, and keeping irregular hours, until the end of the festival.

Perceived as Folklore

The festival proper lasts from Thursday until Sunday, and, in 1981, included carnival games, kiddie rides, and two dances. Sangria, beer, and soft drinks were sold at the dances, for which a small entrance fee was also required. A *bal musette*, with traditional-style dancing for both young and old, was held on Friday night. A dance with rock music for younger people was held on Saturday night. The *conscrits* handled the ticket collection and bar at the dances, while the games and rides were run by a concession. The festival was attended by the Laviallois, their relatives who live in the region, people from nearby *communes*, and some "outsiders" (tourists or urbanites who came from Clermont-Ferrand). Most of the participants in 1981 came from the local district or were family members from the city.[10]

From Thursday night, when a few of the rides opened, to Saturday night, the *conscrits* became increasingly worn out from the all-night partying and drinking. They stayed at Lavialle's community center (formally a Catholic girls' school, sometimes called the youth house – *la maison des jeunes*) and most slept there. Rumor had it that the youths didn't sleep at all on Saturday night. However, they all appeared promptly (if somewhat haggard) for Mass on Sunday morning at 9 a.m., sitting together in the front row. The lay readings from the gospels that day were their responsibility, and they each appeared to have prepared for, and to take seriously, this duty. After Mass, the *conscrits* visited Lavialle's graveyard and then put a wreath on the communal war memorial. These activities express a symbolic conflation of Church, nation, and local community – symbolized by Mass, war memorial, and graveyard; as well as symbolic homage to ancestors.

By Sunday afternoon, adults in Lavialle (particularly but not exclusively women) were expressing concern about the lack of sleep and proper nutrition suffered by the *conscrits*. Mothers carried meals to them at the community center. There was an attitude of gentle tolerance for their behavior, devoid of criticism, and suggestions were made that they were not really responsible for their reckless behavior. By Monday morning, the *conscrits* had returned to their households and resumed either jobs, studies, or farm work. Their "liminal" status during the festival had ended, and they were re-integrated into daily life. They emerged from the festival with a new status, that of young adults approaching marriage (which usually occurs in one's early twenties in Lavialle). After age eighteen, young men fulfill their military service. Both males and females of this age begin, on a regular basis, to attend Saturday night dances in the local region – at which most courtship behavior occurs. The spirit of drinking and gaiety characteristic of their festival behavior would now be part of their Saturday night festivities at rock dances, when girls as well as boys drink heavily and travel in cliques or gangs of youth. During the week, however, these youths would be expected to prepare for adult roles and responsibilities with a greater degree of seriousness and prudence than before.

The communal festival has important meanings for local identity and socialization in Lavialle. The behavior of the *conscrits* expresses the value for reciprocity characteristic of Laviallois social life. Generosity and hospitality are highly valued in Lavialle, but only within a context of reciprocity. A desire not to keep an outstanding social debt is striking in Lavialle, whether it be in the form of a meal, labor, or a gift. The overt economic nature of gifts is evident in the behavior of Laviallois women who, when offering a cup of coffee to a visitor will say that they will "pay for it": "Je vais te payer un cafe." This term is used to express any offerings of food or drink, whether actually purchased in a cafe or served in the home of the giver. Reciprocity is also evident in the common practice of entertaining neighbors in order to celebrate the first of the year in Lavialle. In one cycle of which I was a participant, three households took turns serving meals to each other in the space of one week, so that none would owe a meal to another. An economic metaphor is also used by men at Easter, who say that they have "earned" communion on that day.

Through their participation in the festival, the *conscrits* are symbolically repaying their "debt" to the *commune*. They have been indulged, cared for, and protected by family, friends, and neighbors in Lavialle throughout their childhood and youth. Children are the recipients of many gifts for which they cannot reciprocate directly. During the first communion, each child receives a great deal of material and social wealth. The communal festival marks the emergence of the youth from childhood through a large "paying off," through the organization of the festival, of the debts of childhood to family and friends. This is a ritual accounting, however, since the festival is literally funded by donations from the adults of the

Repaying the debt of caretaking + upbringing by family + kindred

commune. Nevertheless, the *conscrits'* participation in the festival represents a rehearsal of the time when they will assume full adult status (gradually through marriage and childbearing), and begin to contribute as parents and members of local kindreds to the community. The communal festival, through the role of the youth, celebrates a new generation of adults and a renewal of local social life. In their obligation to organize the festival, the youths are reminded of their debts and responsibilities to both their elders and the younger generation.

A paradoxical aspect of the behavior of the *conscrits* is that, at least at first glance, it appears that at the same time that they are taking on a large amount of responsibility in planning and running the festival, their conduct is marked by recklessness and irresponsibility. The *conscrits* drink heavily, keep odd hours, and generally separate themselves off from the rest of the community. Although no harm comes to them, and their unruly behavior takes place within the context of the *commune* and under its watchful eye, the behavior of the *conscrits* is associated with a certain amount of danger. Concern for them is expressed throughout the festival.

This apparent recklessness, and its tolerance by the Laviallois during the festival, represents a ritualized, "what if" acting out of the fear that this new generation *will* squander the patrimony, *will* be lax in its duties in adulthood. These are important concerns in a land-based farming community, precarious in that the farms are family-run and depend upon the knowledge and accountability of responsible adults if they are to be successful. Even those adults who do not work full-time in farming continue to be members of local kindreds and often have rights to land and buildings in Lavialle. It is, therefore, with great relief on the part of the adults of the *commune* that the festival ends and the *conscrits* actually do return to normal daily life. The festival represents the best hopes and worst fears of the populace concerning the next generation of adults.

As in other facets of social life in Lavialle, belonging and "insider" status is expressed for the *conscrits* through membership in a local kindred in addition to, or in the absence of, residence in the *commune*. Social life in Lavialle, particularly since the immense out-migration of the 1950s and 1960s to urban areas, is being carried on with the aid and participation of kin who live elsewhere but return for such ceremonial occasions as the communal festival (see also Rapp 1986). Those youth from outside of Lavialle who participate in the communal festival are encouraged to continue to support their own kin living there, but, more generally, the social and ceremonial life of the *commune*.

Lavialle's communal festival displays similar themes of social change and transformation to those described for such festivals by Rogers (1991:4–5) for an Aveyronnais *commune* and Rapp (1986) for a community in Haute Provence. Rapp stresses the significance of the festival in Montagnac for returning urbanites who are native to the community, for whom it represents a "ritual of reversion" (to traditional life). Although I have chosen to focus here on the significance of the communal festival in Lavialle for the youths who participate in it, such wider meanings are closely linked to the meanings for individuals. Ritual events like French rural communal festivals are "symbolic expressions of cultural meanings and learning environments for children and adults who become socialized and resocialized in the ways of their culture" (Neville 1984:163). By organizing and staging the communal festival, the youth of Lavialle are not only experiencing their own *rite de passage*, but are also active participants in the recreation and perpetuation of meanings about the importance of cultural life in Lavialle.

Socialization and the life cycle

The major public ritual events in Lavialle coincide with life cycle transitions. Three of these that deal with childhood and the transition to early adulthood have been touched upon here: baptism, first communion, and the communal festival. Two others, weddings and funerals, continue to express themes of the attachment of individuals to their kindreds and to the wider collectivity of the *commune* and region. The scope of the social sphere incorporated in each ceremony widens with the stages in the life of the individual. Baptism occurs within the context of the household and close kin, first communion includes a wider group of kin and neighbors, and the *conscrits* of the communal festival encompass the youth of the entire *commune* and emphasize the solidarity of peer as well as kin relationships. Weddings incorporate the joining of two different families and their respective webs of kin and friends from the region. Funerals in Lavialle, in contrast to weddings, are open to all, and constitute the largest social gatherings, attracting people from the entire region and beyond who know the deceased and his or her kin.

A notable feature of the transitions of childhood emphasized in Lavialle is the absence of school-related events. Religious ceremonies dominate the phrasing of the life cycle at the local level. Baptism, first communion, and the communal festival (as well as the later events of weddings and funerals) while important social events, also have clear religious components. The school experiences of children, and the transitions associated with them, are not marked by ceremonial means in Lavialle. This does not mean that school is peripheral to experience or to values: children's lives are increasingly dominated by schooling. The ritual expressions of childhood in Lavialle are, rather, strategies for controlling the effects of school. The important values of family ties and loyalty to the local social sphere are sometimes emphasized at the expense of educational achievement. During the very important first year of middle school, a difficult transition both emotionally and scholastically, children are encouraged to concentrate on preparations for their first communion, whether or not this causes their schooling to suffer (a concern expressed to me by the Director of the public middle school).

In Lavialle, it is late, rather than early, childhood that receives most ritual attention. This reflects an interest in children as future adults, members of local family groups, and participants in the local socio-cultural system. Childhood rituals serve as a collective counter-narrative to the school's emphasis on the development of the child as an individual. A not unfounded fear among the Laviallois is that schooling encourages distance from social origins and attachment to the values of dominant French culture.[11]

Family-based socialization in Lavialle is geared toward the perpetuation of an agricultural way of life, and of the family farm as a socio-economic and kinship unit. Getting a good basic level of instruction is important, since modern farms require people who have the skills to deal with modern techniques and bureaucratic procedures. In general, however, the aim of family-based socialization in Lavialle is to encourage children (even those who will not pursue farming careers) to become responsible members of local families with strong ties to the community – the success of which is eventually measured by the number of people who attend one's funeral!

Family-based socialization in Lavialle is very much related to the *commune*'s historical and on-going inclusion in a modern state, and must not be viewed as a "survival" of traditions. Childhood rituals, such as first communion, are part of a defensive strategy of resistance to the state's efforts to control socialization. They constitute one aspect of the family's defense against the "interventionist" state (see Donzelot 1979). By intensifying their children's emotional and material links to the family and local collectivity through ritual, even those children who will not become farmers, the Laviallois are pursuing a strategy that, they hope, will ensure the social reproduction of farm life. Families in Lavialle have not let the school be the sole orchestrator of childhood, and have used rituals of both the Catholic Church and the family to provide alternative phrasings of the transition from child to adult to those of the school. Children still pass through the school's levels and stages, and adults identify age-grades on the basis of schooling, but important links to family and peers are also forged through work, through family meals, and through the rituals of first communion and the communal festival.

6

Schooling the Laviallois: historical perspectives

Not necessarily conversation or discussion

Two important cultural themes have dominated discourse surrounding the history of French education: issues of secular vs. religious control over schooling, and issues of social and educational stratification. The rural village school plays a role as "key symbol" in thinking about the formation of a unified, secular, French nation. The history of French education is often phrased in terms of the spread of a specifically "French" identity and set of values, radiating out from Paris into the innermost depths of each peasant village. Jacques Ozouf has written that "in every village, there was at least one schoolteacher and one school, a uniform patterning, reassuring or threatening depending upon one's perspective, but never neutral" (1967:7; my translation). It was in such schools that, supposedly, the French language and secular morality of the bourgeoisie was spread to the provincial masses. The history of French education, and in particular, the history of the village schools, has taken on the trappings of an "origin myth" of the nation. The titles of two books capture this – Weber's *Peasants into Frenchmen* (1976) and Baker and Harrigan's edited volume *The Making of Frenchmen* (1980). In Lavialle, the school and teachers are still trying to turn peasants into Frenchmen over one hundred years after the institution of mandatory state education. The historical and ongoing struggle between families and the school in Lavialle indicates that local populations must be viewed as taking a very active role in the history of education, but that this role can vary according to regional circumstances.

Regional, active role in history of ed.

Peasants into Frenchmen?

obtain forcefully

The French state took its final step in wresting the ancient monopoly of primary education away from the Catholic Church during the Third Republic, with the Ferry laws of 1881 and 1882. Jules Ferry, known as the architect of the French primary educational system and its spread

110

throughout the provinces, also orchestrated the great colonial expansion of France overseas during the 1880s.[1] His laws made primary education in France a public, secular, and obligatory experience for all children. With these laws, the village school and its teacher became linked to a centralized national system promoting French language, culture, and civic values. The Ferry laws advocated the importance of a secular moral education influenced by the positivism of Comte and Durkheim (Stock-Morton 1988). They represented a great victory for supporters of secular education and set forth the general pattern of primary schooling that exists today.

French primary education during the Third Republic (1870–1940), especially as embodied in the Ferry Laws, is a vital part of nationalist ideology, and is often used to symbolize the unification of the nation (M. Ozouf 1985).[2] Nineteenth-century French primary school teachers, inspired with Republican visions of society that followed closely on the heels of French defeat in the Franco-Prussian war,[3] saw themselves as secular missionaries, spreading French moral and civic values throughout the provinces (M. Ozouf 1963; Singer 1983; Weber 1976).

Universal French primary education was an "invented tradition" (Hobsbawm 1983: 271) of the French Third Republic, which competed with other educational institutions and with the family for control over children and their futures. Although a public primary school was eventually established in each French *commune*, the role and meaning of schooling depended to a great degree upon the local context.

Throughout the nineteenth and early twentieth centuries, the French state gained increasing control over its primary schools and their pupils. France was not alone in this trend, through which education became a tool for nation-building. All Western nation-states developed systems of education intended to spread literacy, official languages, and notions of citizenship to "the masses" (Boli, Ramirez, and Meyer 1985; Green 1990; Weber 1976). Hobsbawm, tracing the "mass-production" of traditions by the state in Europe during the nineteenth century, notes that "the standardization of administration and law within it, and, in particular, state education, transformed people into citizens of a specific country . . ." (1983:264). The French model was one of state control through a centralized bureaucratic structure. The architects of this system wanted, as Mendras writes, "to transform backward conservative peasants into educated citizens, dedicated to the defense of the republic" (1991:91).

Most historians agree that rural education eventually came to be accepted, as measured primarily by the fact that people learned to speak and write French, and that parents sent their children to schools. There is, however, a great deal of disagreement among educational historians regarding the extent and nature of popular demand for schooling. A wave of studies of French schooling carried out during the 1970s and 1980s, influenced by social history and close attention to the local level, argued that peasant families did not initially accept schooling (Strumingher 1983 and 1985; Maynes 1985a and 1985b; Thabault 1971; Weber 1976; Zeldin 1980). Another strand of research on schooling and state power has argued that in France, as in other nations, universal schooling is associated with the growth of the state (Green 1990). These studies suggest that if and when peasants came to accept schooling, this was a result of their own changing perceptions and conditions. Eugen Weber thus declares that "people went to school not because school was offered or imposed, but because it was useful. The world had to change before this came about" (1976:303; see also Thabault 1971).

Two recent trends in the history of French education, since the 1980s, have attempted to challenge previous assumptions. First, a growing literature on mass schooling in a worldwide perspective questions the role of the state in the proliferation of schools. John Meyer and colleagues (Meyer 1977; Boli *et al.* 1985; Boli and Ramirez 1986) argue that mass schooling had a momentum of its own that predates the rise of the state, but which was then coopted by political leaders in state societies. The fact that schooling looks so similar in different national settings, with different types of state system, helps to bolster this position.

Another trend concerns French education more specifically. Here, recent work by Grew and Harrigan (1991) challenges the established view that the French state imposed mandatory education upon a reluctant peasantry – a view espoused by such historians as Eugen Weber. Grew and Harrigan present statistics at the national and departmental levels to suggest that schooling was widespread long before the leaders of the Third Republic, such as Jules Ferry, institutionalized the centralized primary education system. They conclude that "the demand for education was greater than the supply" in rural France by the late nineteenth century (1991:236).

There is supporting evidence for Grew and Harrigan's statistical research from local histories which suggest that, in some parts of France, peasants welcomed state schooling and maybe even national culture. Two studies of peasants in southeastern France (Lehning 1980; Rosenberg 1988) indicate a strong interest in education and high literacy rates among the populations they studied going back to the early part of the 19th century. These studies from the Alps region challenge the view of French education as simply imposed on French peasants. They indicate that universal schooling may have been a response to a growing demand for literacy, so that the Ferry laws of the early 1880s were not necessarily as instrumental to changes in French society as previously assumed; rather, they were the result of changes already occurring. Maryon McDonald's (1989) recent anthropological study of the language question in Brittany, to which I will turn in greater detail in chapter 7, concludes that it is Breton militants, not Breton peasants, who reject French education. She argues that residents of a mountainous *commune* in northern Brittany actually welcomed French language instruction and schools, challenging influential views that French education was always "imposed" on unwitting populations. Brittany, particularly in the north, has, like the Alps region of France studied by Harriet Rosenberg, historically demonstrated high levels of both education and literacy (Prost 1968; Henriot-Van Zanten 1990). This makes it quite different from the region of the Auvergne, in which Lavialle is located, where public schooling was not uniformly welcomed and literacy rates were low.

Despite recent evidence that schooling was desired by many inhabitants of rural France, the goal of instituting a national educational system faced many obstacles. Schooling in most rural French *communes* during the 19th century was uneven, surrounded by conflict, and in many instances, met with a reluctant peasantry (Gildea 1982; Heywood 1988; Maynes 1985a; Strumingher 1985; Thabault 1971). School attendance was low and irregular throughout rural France during the mid-nineteenth century, but especially in mountainous communities such as Lavialle. In earlier centuries, the need for child labor was so great that even the incentive of free education would not have been sufficient for many peasant families to educate their children (Gildea 1982:253). Educational experiences were uneven, and varied among children. In addition, many other instructional settings (legal and illegal) competed with the official, state schools for students.

Although the myth of French education implies that such obstacles were eventually overcome by the triumphant Third Republic, leading to the transformation of "peasants into Frenchmen," the story is not so straightforward. It is important to bear in mind, however, that the history of schooling in rural France is the history of a particular social form involving deliberate means of inculcation and control. Guy Vincent (1980) usefully draws attention to important features of the school-as-institution with the term "school form," reminding us that formal schooling embodies a particular type of instructional content and method. This is not necessarily synonymous with the history of instruction or literacy (Furet and Ozouf 1982; Maynes 1985a). Many peasants in France appear to have desired literacy skills, but not necessarily the system of social control embodied in schooling.

There is, indeed, an important distinction to be made between valuing literacy skills and valuing the school as an institution. François Furet and Jacques Ozouf (1982) found in their detailed history of French literacy that it is important to go beyond the history of schooling itself in order to understand the history of literacy. Citing Jack Goody's work, Furet and Ozouf show that the relationship between oral culture and written culture, and the transformation from the former to the latter, had to do with much larger changes in French society than the development of schools. They argue that the claim of a causal relationship between literacy and schooling, and its self-evident nature in Western culture, has been used for political purposes to foster certain educational policies and myths about schools and their efficacy (see also Graff 1979). Their work suggests that the issue of whether or not peasants considered schooling "useful" should not be taken to gauge also their attitudes toward the acquisition of literacy skills. Peasants could object to certain aspects of schooling without rejecting literacy altogether.

Several historians of rural France have attempted to go beyond global statistics and literacy rates in order to understand the cultural meaning of education for families (Maynes 1985a; Strumingher 1983). In many cases, as Laura Strumingher points out, ". . . peasant parents were not opposed to learning as such; they were opposed to sending their children to schools brought in by authorities from outside the community, whose values and purposes, and in some cases even language, were different and suspect" (1983:35). According to Theodore Zeldin, French education came from an impetus outside of local communities and was then "enforced on them" (1980:147). Zeldin notes that even though literacy made huge gains in France during the 19th century, this was not necessarily a result of schooling having spread, since less formal means of instruction were also available. It was not until much later, in the mid-20th century, when family allowances were tied to school attendance, that universal enrollment in French primary schools was achieved (Zeldin 1980:203).

The moral component of nineteenth-century French education was explicit in textbooks, educational policy, and discourse (Stock-Morton 1988). Peasants and the urban poor were constructed as "the other" by educational reformers (Lynch 1988). They were illiterate, which was viewed as a threat to an orderly and productive industrial society, and did

[handwritten margin note: Belief in schooling]

not share the moral values believed necessary to create a loyal and unified citizenry. Schooling, it was hoped, would change this. Recent analyses of textbooks used in rural France during this time show how bourgeois gender images were deliberately used by the French educational system in order to impose dominant values on working-class and peasant children (Struminger 1983; Clark 1984).

In her study of schoolbooks written for rural children in nineteenth-century France, Laura Struminger shows how educational reformers increasingly viewed rural mothers as the best vehicle for the transmission of middle-class values to peasant children, and, consequently, de-emphasized the role of fathers in their children's daily lives. Stories in these readers portrayed domestic scenes, and painted "Mother" as a source of moral and emotional support, while father was portrayed as affectionate but distant. Struminger argues that there were deep contradictions between these images and the actual sex roles and relationships between peasant men and women. She writes that "these ideas which emphasized the dichotomy between family and work, between men's and women's roles, were alien to the rural way of life. Though peasants knew gender role differentiations, they were not based on a middle class division of labor and myths of the perfect mother and father" (1983:33; see also Segalen 1983).

[handwritten margin note: Textbooks]

It is important to bear in mind that schooling involved much more than instruction in literacy skills, or even in citizenship. Gender has played a large role in the history of rural French education, both in terms of different educational experiences for boys and girls, and in terms of the idealized images of gender roles within the family promoted by teachers and schools. Opposition between teachers and families in Lavialle, as subsequent chapters will show, has often been expressed through a discourse of values concerning gender role behaviors. Both teachers and parents ascribed inappropriate gender behaviors to each other when launching criticisms. *[handwritten: Misconceptions of the "other"]*

Any public demand for schooling among French peasants did not necessarily reflect a desire for the acquisition of bourgeois codes of morality and national French "culture." The demand was, primarily, for basic literacy skills – reading, writing, and arithmetic. This is an important distinction that continues to guide the educational strategies of families in Lavialle today, who seek a basic education for their children, but encourage them to value local cultural identity. They exhibit a selectivity in their acceptance of schooling, and resist those aspects of it that undermine or challenge local cultural meanings and values.

Puy-de-Dôme: mid-nineteenth century

The department of Puy-de-Dôme, in which Lavialle is located, serves as a useful example of a highly rural department far from Paris in which educational reforms took a long time to be implemented. The Guizot Law of 1833 was the first major educational reform of primary education since the French Revolution (Stock-Morton 1988:30). It asserted that each *commune* with 500 inhabitants or more had to maintain a school for boys and subsidize the schoolteacher's salary (hitherto based mainly on tuition payments). Although schools were run on a tuition basis, the law required that poorer students be admitted for free. Guizot also placed primary schools under the authority of a local committee composed of the mayor, the parish priest, and other elites (*les notables*). This intensified the already precarious position of the teacher between the authority of the mayor and the priest. Even in state-run schools, teachers were still required to be Roman Catholic, and the teacher was often perceived as "the pawn of the priest" (Singer 1983:73) in rural communities.

The Guizot Law arose partly in response to the belief of national elites that "the absence of education promotes political instability" (Schnerb 1937:10, my translation). Guizot, then Minister of Education under Victor Cousin, was a Protestant from southern France who, nonetheless, enlisted the aid of the Catholic Church in organizing schools for the purpose of instructing the masses. At the time of this law, the focus of educational policy was primarily on urban schools, since it was in cities that the fears of social unrest were most keenly felt (Lynch 1988). The value of political control through a literate peasantry was, however, becoming evident. Following the Guizot law were several other reforms, such as the Falloux Law of 1850, aimed at increasing state control at the local level. Nevertheless, school attendance continued to be voluntary and education was greatly influenced by the Church and its clergy (Grew and Harrigan 1991; Stock-Morton 1988).

In 1837, less than one-half of the *communes* in the department of Puy-de-Dôme had a school, which placed this region, along with Finistère in Brittany, well behind the rest of France (Mayeur 1981:16). A history of education in the Puy-de-Dôme at mid-nineteenth century by M. Schnerb (1937) provides a glimpse into the precarious situation of a very locally-controlled system, despite the state's efforts to control education from above. In 1833, the Department of Puy-de-Dôme had a large rural population, making it difficult to implement the Guizot Law. Financial obstacles, low school attendance, problems in attracting good teachers to remote areas, and the strength of competing religious education, all plagued the village schools.

Schnerb reports that after the Guizot Law was passed, there were three types of school operating in the region: (1) *l'école communale* – public schools run by the *commune*, according to Guizot's plan, which were either coeducational or sex-segregated (although public schools for girls were still rare at this time); (2) *l'école privée autorisée* – private, religious schools authorized by the state to teach, and usually run by nuns for instruction to girls; and (3) *l'école clandestine* – illegal schools (not sanctioned by the state), which were often cheaper than the other two, and taught by unauthorized teaching personnel, such as itinerant teachers, local inhabitants, or the parish priest.[4] Competition among these three types of school was sometimes fierce, and poorer parents often preferred to send their children to the cheaper, clandestine schools. The official state school was, therefore, just one among several places that offered instruction to children during this period.

Local attitudes, including those of elites, did not always support the "official" schools. Schnerb gives an example of this in the town of Grosbourg, near to Lavialle:

Unfortunately, certain municipalities which (having received the state subsidies) agreed to spend the money on a school, channelled the funds for another use: (Grosbourg) and V. each made a rectory . . . the schoolteacher was left to lodge at an inn and the prefet found himself powerless in the face of the force of inertia of the town of (Grosbourg) . . .   *(Schnerb, 1937:20, my translation)*

As this account shows, funds for state schools were sabotaged and redirected, and, in the case of Grosbourg, delivered over to the clergy (for a rectory). Local elites also interfered with the Guizot mandate that free schooling be offered to poorer students. Communal authorities obeyed the law in granting these children a free education, but presented obstacles by not furnishing them with the proper materials (such as books and paper) with which to acquire literacy skills. Moreover, local elites often managed to get their own children on the list of non-paying pupils (Schnerb 1937:22).

The low esteem that families held for teachers at this time is a common feature of French rural history. According to Pierre Goubert, in the seventeenth century "not every village had a schoolmaster, and they must have seemed less useful members of the community than the miller or the tavern-keeper. Often they had the reputation of being weak or deformed, and therefore ill-suited to the heavy work of the countryside" (1986:140). Education was explicitly viewed as a commodity, and it was "sold" as such. Schnerb notes that "a teacher who didn't manage quickly enough to teach reading would find his school empty at the end of the year" (1937:25). Weber (1976) and Zeldin (1980) point out that many of the early schoolteachers were really "peddlers" of sorts, selling their wares, in this case, literacy skills, just as did other tradesmen.[5] The low status of teachers – as – "peddlers" in this period of French history stands in marked contrast to the exaggerated, mythic accounts of the late-nineteenth-century schoolteachers – as – "secular missionaries."

Teacher as Peddlers

Lavialle in the nineteenth century

The case of Lavialle shows that local context was crucial in determining the development of schooling, despite the centralized mission of the state educational system. Family strategies for the education of children in Lavialle are apparent in the evidence from nineteenth-century schooling, even though peasant voices leave no direct record. For farmer-owners, such strategies have been part of overall decisions concerning the reproduction of the family and farm as a viable unit, but can also be seen as responses to state efforts at inculcating dominant values among peasant populations through education. The historical record in Lavialle indicates that the aims and values of parents have modified the effects of the national educational system in ways that permitted the continued strength of local and regional attachments.

Lavialle's school was built in 1881, at the time of the Ferry Laws which made French primary education mandatory and free for all children. It is a massive concrete building, whose architecture and imposing presence in the village of Lavialle serve as a metaphor for the state's attempts to secure permanent control over the education of children in rural France. There were schools in Lavialle long before the current school was built and before schooling became mandatory, but from how early a time is not entirely certain.[6] In earlier centuries, the dispersal of village settlements in Lavialle, harsh winters, and, above all, the poverty of the region and consequent need for child labor at home on the farm were important deterrents to schooling. Reports of abject poverty and even starvation among the population of Lavialle during the early nineteenth century (Manry 1987) help to explain the reluctance of families to send their children to school when they could work. Before schooling was compulsory, Lavialle families most likely viewed the school as a place where children could gain certain basic skills, particularly during those times when they were not needed on the farm. Attendance at early schools was sporadic, but there was schooling in Lavialle during the 18th and 19th centuries – especially

[handwritten annotation: Info from a ruling, literate source]

for boys. Although the need for farm labor was a deterrent to the acceptance of schooling among rural families in Lavialle as throughout rural France, this factor alone is not sufficient for an understanding of educational history. As the need for child labor on the family farm decreased during the twentieth century, families in Lavialle did not automatically embrace schooling wholeheartedly. Schooling represents more than a place for children to acquire an education; it represents a place where regional identity, language, and ties to family and farm have often come into conflict with French bourgeois values and dominant language use. *[handwritten annotation: Conflict w/ French elite.]*

Information on schooling in Lavialle during the mid-nineteenth century and earlier comes primarily from census reports. The 1836 census shows that there were two schoolteachers living in Lavialle. Since there was one male and one female teacher (not a married couple), there were probably two schools, or, at least, two classes (one for boys and one for girls). These were lay teachers, and I found no record of religious schools in Lavialle at the time – although such schools were most likely situated in nearby Grosbourg. That there were only two teachers for a population of 1,125 indicates that school attendance was not very high. Some instruction was, however, probably offered in unofficial schools, for which there is, unfortunately, no record.

A fuller picture of schooling in Lavialle emerges in the 1870s. Tension between families and the school is quite evident in the portrait of Lavialle provided by a local schoolteacher, Monsieur Brun, in his reports to educational authorities during the 1870s which I found in Lavialle's communal archives. Before turning to the teacher's reports, a brief overview of social life in Lavialle during this period will set the stage.

Lavialle's population lived in 18 settlements, as is the case today – including the *bourg*, or village, of Lavialle. This village, with about 70 residents at the time, was not, however, the largest settlement in 1876. Six hamlets surpassed it in population and one had as many as 137 inhabitants. There were 1,118 people living in Lavialle in 1876 – about one-third of whom were children under the age of 14. Lavialle was a highly endogamous community, a trend which continues today. Only 26 inhabitants were not native to Lavialle, and of these, only nine were born outside of the department of Puy-de-Dôme. Many of these "outsiders" (probably the nine mentioned) appear to have been only temporarily lodged in Lavialle while working in a surface mine in one of the hamlets. They were not listed in the next census.

The adult population (over age 14) of 785 included only 84 persons who listed an occupation other than farmer-owner: many of these, however, were laborers who worked on the farms and in households (the census category *doméstique*). Women not mentioned specifically by an occupation were most likely farm women. A breakdown of the non-farmer/owner population by occupation is listed in Table 2 for the entire *commune*, and then for the village of Lavialle. These occupations, along with farming, include the usual cast of characters for rural *communes* in the Monts Dore region of Auvergne at this time (Fel 1962). The agricultural base depended on a mixed subsistence economy of cereals, sheepherding, livestock raising, and some cheese production. Farming was not mechanized, and horses and/or mules were kept, in addition to cows.

Lavialle was, like other *communes* in its region, an agricultural community of fairly poor, small farmers, who, for the most part, owned their own farms (Fel 1962; Moulin 1991:110). The household was the major economic, as well as social, unit. The population was remaining steady, and even rising a bit, indicating that the society was at least replicating itself and that children were not leaving in great numbers to seek their fortunes elsewhere. It was a more or less self-contained unit, with some socio-economic ties to the larger *commune* of Grosbourg. In many ways, Lavialle was a Redfieldian "cradle-to-grave arrangement." A diverse array of services necessary for day-to-day living was available there, many more than would be found a century later.

The absence of any commercial occupations, such as "shopkeeper" (to appear in later years), is noteworthy. At this time, country fairs and markets were still the most important locations for trading, buying, and selling. These were found in larger centers, such as Grosbourg – which had a market each Tuesday and a fair once a month. It was on market day that the goods produced in Lavialle were brought to Grosbourg to be sold, and there that most goods not available in the *commune* were bought. Activities such as baking and weaving were not specialized and listed as "occupations." Although these tasks were being carried out, they were still part of the household economy. Large baking ovens were, for example, owned jointly and shared by households in each hamlet.

The village of Lavialle (the *commune*'s major center) contained the most diverse population. Here resided the usual triad of mayor, priest, and teacher, and the largest concentration of artisans. There were nineteen households in the village of Lavialle in 1872. Most of these households were composed of non-farmers, but everyone had a garden. Even the parish priest maintained his own little plot of land and kept some cows and sheep for his own consumption. The Laviallois are always amused to

Everyone's a Farmer

Table 2. *Occupation of non-farmer/owner inhabitants of Lavialle (1876)*

Occupation	Commune of Lavialle	Village only
Mayor	1	1
Nun	1	1
Farm/household help	28	5
Parish priest	1	1
Vicar	1	1
Male schoolteacher	2	1
Female schoolteacher	1	1
Shepherd	2	1
Carpenter	5	1
Blacksmith	4	0
Road laborer	3	1
Garde-champêtre[7]	1	1
Miller	2	0
Female servant	1	1
Sawyer	1	0
Mason	1	0
Stenciler	1	0
Foreman	1	0
Tenant farmer	1	0
Diggers (in mine)	15	0
TOTAL	73	16
TOTAL POPULATION	1,118	70

tell the tale of a priest in the early twentieth century who used to house his animals in the church during the week!

The difference between the farmer and the non-farmer in nineteenth-century Lavialle did not depend as much on involvement in agricultural tasks, since everyone engaged in some subsistence farming, as it did on the amount of time and energy spent on them. The need for child labor was greater in farm families, however, and the first families to send children regularly to school in rural France were those of the artisans (Thabault 1971; Weber 1976). It is safe to assume that this was also the case in Lavialle.

Portrait of a school in the 1870s

The first detailed mention of schooling available in Lavialle's archives comes from the reports of a schoolteacher in the village of Lavialle to the departmental inspector of primary education in the years 1871–75. This teacher, Monsieur Brun, taught in the public boys' school. His reports provide a good portrait of the schooling situation in Lavialle, at least for boys, and also show the resistance and reluctance he encountered from families.

Monsieur Brun was twenty-nine years old in 1871. He was born in a village about 20 km from Lavialle, but must have permanently settled in Lavialle, for he is buried in the cemetery. As is still the case for the schoolteacher in Lavialle, Brun worked as the town clerk (*secrétaire du maire*).[8] Although he had not attended a teacher's college (*Ecole Normale*), he did hold the brevet diploma, the minimum requirement at the time for all lay teachers. The building which housed Brun's school is still standing and located right in the center of the village of Lavialle, across from the church. The old school was identified to me by informants as a combined dwelling/barn structure which is one of the oldest buildings in Lavialle, dating from the early eighteenth century. At the time of my fieldwork, it housed the lodgings and shop of one of Lavialle's grocers, but this building has served many functions, and was a blacksmith's shop before being converted into a store.

Many of the same conditions described by Brun in his report are portrayed by Jean Anglade (1971), a regional Auvergnat author, in an essay on the travails of a new schoolmaster in Lozère in 1878. Anglade writes ironically of the sparse conditions of the school, the emptying of the classroom throughout the agricultural season, and the dominant role played by the local priest. His description of the Lozère school as the schoolmaster first saw it upon his arrival in the village, where conditions were similar to those in Lavialle, helps contextualize Monsieur Brun's report. Anglade describes the "sad air" to the building "under its mop of gray thatch." The first floor, which served as a combination kitchen/bedroom/living room for the teacher and his wife, was underneath the classroom, which pupils noisily entered by way of a ladder (1971:213–14).

Although living conditions have improved, this link between the primary school teacher's family and his school, reinforced through the family's residence in the school building, persists in Lavialle and other French rural *communes* today. In many ways, this mirrors the connection between a family and its farm, and reproduces the model of the family economy for teachers as well as farmers. The rural school modelled, therefore, not the industrial pattern of increasing separation between work and home, but that of the agricultural pattern of connection between the two. However, while the farmer produced food, the teacher produced pupils and tried to transform them into French citizens.

In 1872, Monsieur Brun had a total of 52 students, all of whom were male. One can assume that most of the pupils were the sons of artisans or farmers since, apart from the clergy, there were no elites, other than the mayor, living in Lavialle (Census 1876). According to Brun's report, only one student attended his school during the full nine months in which it was in session, and fourteen students were only in class during two months of the school year. Brun writes that six children between the ages of seven and thirteen in the village of Lavialle did not attend school and had no formal instruction at all, and that only eight of his pupils knew how to read and write. Twenty-two students were between the ages of seven and thirteen, and sixteen were older than thirteen years of age. Tuition was paid by thirty-eight out of the fifty-two students. Brun laments that there were no books or other instructional materials in the classroom, and that the classroom and building were, in his opinion, "unsatisfactory in every way."

Brun's reports are in the form of an annual questionnaire pre-printed by the Departmental Inspector's office on which teachers were asked to respond to a variety of questions about their schools. These questions addressed both the technical and moral aspects of education. There was room for further commentary in essay form at the end of each questionnaire. An extensive quotation from Brun's 1871 essay conveys his attitudes toward, and especially dissatisfactions with, his position. It also reveals the reactions of local families to his efforts. Brun repeatedly uses the third person when referring to himself, objectifying his conditions through bureaucratic language.

In winter, the communal school for boys in [Lavialle] assembles from forty to fifty students, in summer from ten to twenty. In order to raise this number, the administration would have to close all the clandestine schools which have existed for several years in the *commune*; the population desiring free instruction. As for visits from the district delegates, they are rare. The local authorities take great pleasure in visiting the school and animating the students' zeal by their presence; their relationship with the teacher is very good. The teacher of [Lavialle] has a class of adults six days a week for four hours a day. This is completely free, even the materials are given for nothing. The teacher of [Lavialle] is not one of the richest men; he is head of a family and until this year earned only 600 francs, so that he is obliged to go into debt in order to raise his family. He desires a raise. The simultaneous method is used in the school and the students do fairly well in their lessons but the parents are indifferent. The teacher of [Lavialle] has not yet introduced singing into the school since the parents maintain that it is a waste of time for the students to make them sing.   (*Communal archives; my translation*)

In 1875, Brun's essay is shorter, but the tone is more distressed. Some excerpts:

. . . the population does not want to instruct its children . . . the teacher desires that he be provided with another house, since his has become uninhabitable . . . most parents are indifferent . . .   (*Communal archives*)

A great deal can be learned from these texts, especially when they are placed alongside of the statistics supplied by Brun in his reports. Brun emphasizes the irregular and seasonal attendance of students, and especially the emptying of the school in the warmer months, when farm labor was most needed. For those students who did attend school, then, it was viewed as a seasonal activity, as were many agricultural tasks. Brun writes of the existence of "clandestine" schools in Lavialle, which competed with the public school for students. The presence of such schools in Lavialle suggests that there was demand for free literacy instruction among local inhabitants. Brun's solution to the problem of these unofficial schools was not, however, to recommend free public instruction, as would come with the Ferry laws just a few years later, but, rather, to suppress the schools.

Local, rather than regional, authorities took the most interest in this school, according to Brun. These would have included the mayor and town council members, along with the priest. Brun writes that delegates from the district of Grosbourg rarely visited, whereas the communal committee (presumably that established with the Guizot law) had established a good relationship with him. One wonders, however, why the school was so badly equipped if the local authorities did, indeed, maintain a strong interest in the school. Like other teachers, Brun was an employee of the *commune*, although this too would change after the Ferry Laws. His school was locally financed. Perhaps Lavialle's educational authorities looked toward the department for subsidies, which were not forthcoming, and this is why Brun complains of such bad conditions. Perhaps the mayor and town council members in Lavialle were more supportive of the school than was the general population. Or, perhaps Brun's comments were rhetorical, and aimed at improving his stature with the communal committee.

Lavialle's school offered adult classes, Brun reports, and these were free

– in contrast to schooling for most of the children. Such adult classes were encouraged by the state, in its efforts to increase literacy. Schooling during this period was not viewed as an activity exclusively for children. The business of Brun's school was instruction in the skills of reading and writing, as well as in civic morality, and it took men and boys of all ages.[9]

Brun's reference to the "simultaneous" method shows that he used one of three teaching methods in vogue during this period. The "simultaneous" method consisted of dividing the class into sections according to ability and of having one section work on an assignment, while the other was being taught directly by the teacher. This method was invented and advocated by the Frères des Ecoles Chrétiennes, a teaching order of religious Brothers that ran many early primary schools. This was the most popular method in the Puy-de-Dôme at the time (Schnerb 1937:26–27) and was the basic method still used by Lavialle's teacher in a multi-age classroom in 1981.

At the close of Brun's report, he describes parents as "indifferent" to their children's lessons, a common refrain among educators of this epoch. Furthermore, he writes, he cannot include singing in his curriculum because parents see it as a "waste of time." Brun's comments suggest that families in Lavialle, like other peasants during this period, had a very practical aim in mind for their children's instruction and saw education as a "commodity." They wanted some literacy for their children (boys at least) and they were paying this teacher for the acquisition of such skills, even though they preferred that schooling be free.

Missing from Brun's report is any reference to problems with the clergy. He remarks that he had good relations with the local authorities, and the parish priest was, presumably, one of these. Schooling at this time, before the Ferry laws, was still closely supervised by the church, and religion was part of the curriculum. We cannot know if the "clandestine" schools were run by clergy, although many in France were at this time, or if Brun was as staunchly anti-clerical as later schoolteachers would be. On the basis of the strong religious participation of the Laviallois today, it seems likely that before the state mandated secular education in Lavialle, schooling was, as in many communities, under the thumb of the priest.

Monsieur Brun was *l'homme de la commune* (the *commune*'s man; Schnerb 1937:31), in the sense that the local community wielded considerable power over his school and his position – through its control of his salary, his facilities, and the number of students who attended his school. All of this official local control over the teacher was to erode when schooling became obligatory and teachers were paid directly by the state.

Interestingly, however, the teachers whom I knew in Lavialle, over one hundred years after Brun, would probably have listed similar grievances against local families! Instead of leading to compliance, increased state control has met with continued forms of resistance to the teachers in Lavialle, as families still try to influence their children's education.

In the 1870s, Laviallois families could choose whether or not to send their children to school (if they could afford to do so in the first place), and had several schools from which to choose. Schooling was not mandatory, although all *communes* were required to offer it. Moreover, many of those parents who did send their children to public school resisted aspects of the teacher's instruction that they found offensive or irrelevant, such as singing. Lavialle's public boys' school had not yet fully established itself as a local institution in Lavialle by the 1870s, despite the forty-year-old Guizot Law mandating its presence. This school was still gathering its "clients" and increasing its importance. Monsieur Brun was not only trying to attract more students, but also seeking to improve the material aspects of school – such as the building, instructional materials, and his own salary.

By the end of the 19th century, as the educational system and its bureaucracy grew, schooling became more established in Lavialle, as did the record-keeping of schooling. A survey of French *communes* published in 1899 gives a brief snapshot of Lavialle and its schools at that time (Joanne 1899). The population had remained steady, and was now 1,101. A fourth public school had been established, probably in one of the outlying villages. Sawmills and cheese fabrication were noted as means of income alongside of farming, and there was a social welfare office in Lavialle. Grosbourg, a larger *commune* nearby, had, in comparison, a population of 1,434, three public schools, and two Catholic schools. The growing importance of Grosbourg's town as an urban center for surrounding *communes* such as Lavialle is evident in this portrait, and reflects the trend toward urbanization in rural France at the time. Lavialle had no private school at the turn of the century, whereas Grosbourg, as district capital, had two. It is most likely, however, that, as they did during the twentieth century, families in Lavialle who wished for their girls to receive a Catholic education sent them to Grosbourg.

M. Brun's reports date back to the eve of crucial legislation in the history of French education – the Ferry laws. By that time, education was established in most *communes* in France. However, national debates on education have continued. Before turning to more recent periods of education in the Puy-de-Dôme and in Lavialle, I will briefly review two major themes that have informed French education. More contemporary issues will be taken up in chapter 7.[10]

Cultural themes in French education

Church and state

The Ferry Laws did not settle the differences between the state and the Catholic Church over educational control, and conflict between secular and religious education has continued to be a major theme. The debate about the proper extent of state involvement in religious education and religious involvement in state education has long been an explosive issue in French national politics. Opinions among proponents of both secular (*laïc*) and religious (*libre*) education have varied, but this debate has been a contentious one at least since the French Revolution. It continues today, most notably with the controversy over public education and Muslim students – particularly those girls who wear veils to school. Before the Ferry Laws, the Catholic Church still controlled primary education. The state's victory over the Church was clear in a 1904 law which prohibited any religious personnel from teaching in public schools. Many clergy subsequently left their orders so that they could teach as lay teachers. The financial situation of Catholic schools worsened, with funding based exclusively on their fees, and many critics decried that their standards were inferior to those of public schools (Prost 1981:417–18). A deep animosity intensified in many rural communities between the public school and the private Catholic school, between the public schoolteacher and the village priest. Such animosity prevails in many *communes* today, most notably in the region of Brittany.

During World War II, these secular reforms were temporarily altered. The reactionary Vichy Regime, contending that an intellectual and moral laxity in the nation had to remedied, lent renewed support to religious education (Halls 1976:12–14; Prost 1968). The state re-introduced aid to religious schools, and the secular teacher training schools were abolished – with the rationale that they espoused the same anti-clerical ideas which had led to the reforms of the Third Republic. Jews and freemasons were prohibited from teaching school, and the crucifix reappeared on classroom walls. Most of these changes introduced by Marshall Pétain and his government were short-lived and rescinded at Liberation.

The issue of Church vs. state control over education was again in the forefront of national debate in the 1950s. The Debré Law of 1959 instituted two types of state aid to religious schools. This law was opposed by the most vehement members of each side, and led to a great deal of controversy before its implementation in 1960. Under the Debré Law, each religious primary school could get state aid if it entered into either a *contrat simple* with the state (which would pay teacher salaries if the school would comply with certain minimum standards), or the more binding *contrat d'association*. The latter stipulated that if a Catholic school agreed to follow most of the same guidelines applying to public schools, including the abolishment of fees, then the state would pay teachers, and local *communes* would assume the costs of building maintenance. This law was supplemented by increased grants to private schools in 1977.

The church–state issue became less visible in national politics during the 1960s and 1970s, which led W.D. Halls to write in 1976 that "it is doubtful . . . that the mass of the French population . . . feels passionately any longer about 'the religious question'" (1976:240). This perception was misleading, however, and during the French Presidential campaign in the years 1980–81, the issue of religious education was again raised by the Socialist platform of François Mitterand, which proposed the nationalization of all private schools. This platform was eventually abandoned.

Stratification: l'école unique

Rural primary schools have been on the lower rung of a two-tiered, class-based system of education during most of their history. Beginning with the Guizot Law in 1833, a dual system of primary education existed in France. Schools separated, on the one hand, the children of agricultural and urban workers, and, on the other hand, the children of the bourgeoisie and the upper classes. This was accomplished through the establishment of two types of primary school: schools attended by the children of workers and peasants that did not lead to secondary education, and primary school classes for the bourgeoisie attached to high schools (*lycées*), which provided the only access to the tuition-based secondary system. It was not until 1933 that fees were abolished for high school (Prost 1968:415), and not until the early 1960s that access to secondary education was granted (at least in theory) to the entire population. Even today, the costs associated with boarding a child who is attending high school (since these are usually located in cities and, therefore, not within daily commuting distance), are prohibitive for many farmers.

The effort to establish a so-called *école unique* (that is, a unified, unstratified, system) began after World War II. It was not until the Berthoin Reforms of 1959 that real changes were legislated in order to establish a common curriculum for all primary schools (Lewis 1985; Prost

Different family strategies
for kids...

1968:422–26). These reforms also abolished the high school entrance exam and established a common phase of "orientation" between the ages of 11 and 13, after which time children would enter one of four avenues in the tracking system. This reform delayed the tracking of students until after primary school, but did not abolish educational stratification.

Also in 1959, middle schools (Collèges d'Enseignement Générale – CEG) were established in rural regions of France in order to house the new orientation phase. After leaving primary school, students now had the option of attending either a CEG or a high school. At the same time, the school-leaving age was raised from 14 to 16 for entering children, who would turn 16 in the late 1960s. In 1963, a second type of middle school (Collèges d'Enseignement Secondaire – CES) was created in order to house all lower secondary education. These schools were established to initiate the gradual phasing out of both the CEGs and the primary school classes attached to high schools. The *école unique* was believed by some to be fully realized by the creation of the CES. However, the establishment of these schools was not immediate, and a tracking system within their institutional structure perpetuated educational differences between social classes (Lewis 1985:36). The first CESs were built in urban and densely populated areas, although they were slated eventually to replace the CEGs in rural regions.

At the time of the 1959 Berthoin Reform, "three times as many of the children in the higher social categories went to lycées than went to CEGs" (Lewis 1985:35). The curriculum and methods of rural primary schools were not subject to much change from 1890 to 1940 (when some temporary changes were introduced by the Vichy government), and were not changed substantially until the late 1960s, when a new *tiers-temps* curriculum was introduced.[11]

Many of the reforms associated with eliminating stratification in education and creating the *école unique* were aimed at the middle schools and secondary system. An overall neglect of primary education among both educational policy makers and politicians in France (see Halls 1976) was characteristic of the French educational system for a long time after the Ferry laws. This was to change with the Haby Reforms of 1975, which reflected a renewed interest in primary education. These will be discussed in chapters 8 and 9, in light of more recent events in Lavialle.

Puy-de-Dôme: mid-twentieth century
A report written in 1945 by the Inspector of Primary Education in the Department of Puy-de-Dôme to evaluate the post-war educational situa-

tion, helps to characterize Lavialle's regional context during that period (Rapport sur la situation . . . 1945). Attendance statistics were, by this period in French educational history, carefully recorded by teachers and monitored by the educational bureaucracy. Differences in school attendance rates between urban and rural primary schools were still marked. Winter was the only time that attendance levels for urban and rural children were similar – with 88% of urban, and 87% of rural, children attending school in the department. In fall and spring, however, older children in rural primary schools attended sporadically, if at all, due to seasonal farming requirements. Attendance levels for urban children during these months were around 90%, whereas for all rural children, they were near 80%. The Inspector wrote that children in mountainous *communes* (such Lavialle) only attended school from November to March or early April – "All Saints' Day to Easter" (Rapport sur la situation . . . 1945). These are important dates on the traditional agricultural calendar in Auvergne for both cultivation and animal grazing, marking the beginning and end of the long, harsh winter months. Animals were grazed in the mountains from Easter to All Saints' Day, and it was often children who guarded animals.

The report also noted that the vast majority of teachers were native to Puy-de-Dôme (only 12 were from outside of the department), and that most were women (2 to 1). Teaching has always been a common profession in France for the non-inheriting son or daughter of a farm family. Because of the lack of industrial jobs in Puy-de-Dôme before World War II, teaching was a popular alternative to farming, especially since there were so many small farms in this region, always pushing some children out. Many Auvergnats were itinerant teachers in earlier centuries (Fel 1977). There was, therefore, no shortage of teachers in the Puy-de-Dôme, and pupils were taught by fellow Auvergnats, even if they did not explicitly reinforce regional and ethnic identifications.[12] This was also true for priests in this region, the vast majority of whom have been native to the diocese of Clermont (Poitrineau 1979).

The 1945 Report also gave statistics on attendance in Catholic vs. public primary schools in the Puy-de-Dôme. There were 41,860 children attending public primary schools, compared to only 16,516 attending private (mostly Catholic) schools. Important gender differences are evident in this report. More than half of all school-age girls attended private schools, compared to less than one-third of all boys.

Public schooling was, thus, much more common than private schooling at the primary level in the Puy-de-Dôme at mid-century, but girls were much more likely to receive a religious education than were boys. Fewer boys than girls attended either type of school, however, and had a higher drop-out rate. By the mid-sixties, despite the spread of public education, the region of Auvergne had a higher percentage of children attending parochial elementary schools than did most of France. In Puy-de-Dôme, about one-fifth of primary school-age children attended private school, compared to less than 15% in many regions to the north and south. This is, however, much lower than private school enrollment levels in the southern Auvergne, which were closer to one-third of all children, and in the region of Brittany, where over half of the children attended Catholic schools in the mid-sixties (Prost 1968:479). This pattern remained essentially the same in the mid-seventies (Prost 1981:436).

Up until the late 1960s, the system of schooling which had been set in place at the turn of the century had remained fairly constant in Lavialle. Most children attended primary school until age 14 (raised from 13 in 1936), at which time they completed all of their formal education. Schooling in Lavialle was not significantly changed by the reforms of 1959, since the "orientation phase" could take place in existing primary schools, and 14 was still the effective school-leaving age. Those classes already established in some village schools to give optional advanced training until age 16 (*le cours complémentaire*) were simply incorporated into the new system. School records from Lavialle indicate, however, that there were no advanced primary classes there. And, moreover, a CEG was not built in the region until the 1960s. It was still very difficult for a child to enter high school if he or she had not attended a primary school class attached to one beginning at age 11. The CEGs were not created to provide the same type of academic training that pre-high school students received, and thereby perpetuated a two-tiered system prohibiting access to secondary education for most children in remote rural regions (Grignon 1968 and 1975; Jegouzo and Brangeon 1976).

In the early 1980s, twenty years after the creation of the CES (middle schools), children from Lavialle were still attending a lower secondary school (CEG) built in the 1960s. The educational reforms of the late 1950s were felt in Lavialle a decade later, when the *commune*'s primary school ceased to provide all schooling for most children. When the school-leaving age of 16 became effective in 1968, all students began to spend some time in the CEG located in Grosbourg, or in either a technical or Catholic secondary school.

It is important to view the private vs. public (or church/state) education issue in Lavialle from a local perspective, rather than purely in terms of national debates. The tradition of religious education for girls and secular education for boys seems to have allowed the co-existence of both types in Lavialle, and steady support for the public school. Boys in Lavialle have generally attended public primary schools, but religious education for girls after the early primary level was a common practice in many Lavialle families until the school operated by nuns in Grosbourg was closed in the 1960s. As evidenced by contemporary religious participation in Lavialle (see chapter 3), there is a strong gender division in religious practice. Women are much more active in the Church than are men, and this reflects the history of religious education in Lavialle.

A religious school for girls opened by an order of Alsatian nuns was located in the village of Lavialle for several years before World War II, and it offered instruction in domestic skills to older girls. Elderly women in Lavialle who attended this school remember a more contentious climate surrounding the issue of public vs. private school during this period. Girls who went to school *chez les soeurs* (with the nuns) were taunted by those who did not. When middle schools became the norm during the 1970s, and children continued their education after primary school, many parents in Lavialle sent their children to religious secondary schools. In the early 1980s, almost all children in Lavialle attended the communal primary school. For middle school, however, half of them attended a Catholic school run by an order of Brothers, and the other half attended the CEG in Grosbourg.

A look at the history of schooling in Lavialle and its surrounding region shows that there has been a great deal of continuity in the family strategies of farm families as they have responded to the imposition of the "social form" of the school. Resistance to education in Lavialle has rarely been expressed as outright rejection of schooling – both because this made no sense when schooling became legally compulsory and because there has long been a recognition on the part of families that literacy skills are necessary. As the above statistics show, families in Lavialle sent their children to school – and they developed a mixed strategy of both secular and religious education for boys and girls. Rather than exhibiting a total rejection of education, families in Lavialle have articulated resistance in the form of small-scale, "everyday," informal modes of influence, non-compliance, and subversion of the schooling process. We see evidence of this in the case of parental "indifference" to many of M. Brun's efforts at the school in the mid-19th century. These practices of everyday resistance intensified as state control over education grew, and become more apparent during the twentieth century. The major term used by Lavialle teachers to describe parental attitudes in the nineteenth century was "indifference," but this changed to "mistrust" by mid-twentieth century. This linguistic turn captures teachers' perceptions of a shift in parental attitudes from reluctance toward schooling to a defensive posture of resistance – which grew as schooling became more established.

7

Families and schools

For most of the nineteenth century, as chapter 6 illustrated, schooling was neither available to, nor considered necessary by, all families in Lavialle. The school was not a given, with which one *had* to develop means to interact, as it came to be in the twentieth century, but, rather, a new social form that only gradually came to have meaning and value (either positive or negative). Lavialle families interacted in diverse ways with the social form of the school after it had become established during the first half of the twentieth century.

There were no dramatic transformations of the local population in Lavialle from the late nineteenth century until the years following World War II. Until the mid-1960s, farming remained unmechanized for the most part, and farmers in Lavialle continued to rely on a mixed economy of cereals, cows, and cheese production, with some sheep farming. The switch to a specialization in dairy farming was not accomplished until the late 1960s and early 1970s. Schooling levels were fairly stable during this period, as well. The national mandate for primary education that was established at the turn of the century remained in place, and educational policy did not change significantly until the 1960s and 1970s.[1]

A closer look at educational disparities and population differences within Lavialle shows, however, that schooling during this period was not free from conflict and was profoundly influenced by the educational strategies of families in different sections of the *commune*. In addition, the educational experiences of males and females differed significantly. The educational strategies of families affected the types of changes that occurred in the *commune* during this period. After an historical analysis of the social context of Lavialle's elementary schools during the first half of the century, I will end this chapter with regional comparisons in school-community relationships.

Three schools, three histories

Three public schools operated in Lavialle up until the 1960s, each of which was embedded in a different social context and had different relationships with families. There were variations in the educational strategies of local families at each school, ranging from accommodation and cooperation with teachers to conflict and resistance. As would happen again in the 1980s, schooling became the arena for local political conflict in Lavialle, indicating that schooling is not only a process involving the formal education of children, but is a social space that reflects the interplay between changing local and national meanings.

By the late 1960s, there was only one primary school remaining in Lavialle, located in the village. The *commune* has gone through an educational cycle that began with few schools, then burgeoned into several schools, and has most recently dropped back to one school. The diversity of schooling choices available to families in the *commune* in earlier years eventually disappeared, and the state's control over primary education became concentrated in one site. For a period of over fifty years, however, from the early 20th century up until the mid-sixties, Lavialle had three public schools. In addition to the school in the village which is still open today, there were two schools established for children in outlying hamlets. Lavialle was divided into three educational districts associated with clusters of hamlets: the northern hamlets, the southern hamlets, and the village of Lavialle. The relationship between these schools and their surrounding local settings varied, with families most cooperative with teachers in the southern hamlets and least cooperative in the northern hamlets. The more established village school fell in between these two extremes.

Because the village school was the largest school in Lavialle and is still in existence, records for its history are more complete than are those for the hamlet schools. To neglect the history of the hamlet schools would, however, only tell part of the story of the relationship between families and schooling in Lavialle. Although the historical record for the hamlet schools is less complete than for the village school, when combined with oral history, it does provide some clues about the educational strategies of families whose children attended them. This history shows that there were significant educational variations within the same *commune*.

The two hamlet schools in Lavialle were both closed in the mid-sixties due to diminished enrollments. Their buildings are still standing, and each is owned by the *commune* and rented out as a residence. When these schools closed, their students transferred to the school in the village, which now represents a merging of the previous schools. The hamlet schools were administratively and socially independent from the village school, in keeping with the centralized school system. Former teachers from both types of school told me that contact was minimal, and that each school reported directly to the Departmental Inspector of schools. There was a definite hierarchy between teachers in the two-room village school (of higher status) and those in the one-room hamlet schools.[2] It did not occur to any teachers to participate or cooperate jointly in educational or other activities, and they did not socialize with one another.

Schooling in the hamlet schools contrasted in many ways with that in the larger, more established, village school. These were small, badly equipped, one-room schools, taught by a succession of teachers, none of whom stayed for long periods of time. Most of the teachers were young and ambitious single women, eager to secure a teaching post in the city eventually; for them, Lavialle was only a stepping stone to a better job. In contrast, husband-wife teaching teams have been the norm in the village school throughout the twentieth century. Male teachers in the village are also town clerks, linked to the state bureaucracy, and have often projected a stern masculine *persona*. Because of the strong authority role adopted by male teachers, in particular, there was more social distance between teachers and families at the village school than in the hamlets, and it was not as immersed in its setting. Teachers at the village school participated less in local life, and the larger school building was more forbidding. Whereas the hamlets' schools mainly taught the children of farmers, the village school served a larger, more heterogeneous population of both artisans and farmers. Even though most of the earlier village teachers were of rural background, they worked to maintain strong boundaries between themselves and their clients – through both language use and class-based social behaviors.

There were some important structural similarities, however, between the three schools. Like teachers in the village, teachers in the hamlet schools were hired by the same regional authorities in Clermont-Ferrand. Likewise, they followed a uniform curriculum set by the national educational system. The two hamlet school buildings were, as in the case of the village school, under the jurisdiction of the mayor and town council of Lavialle, which was responsible for each school's material upkeep. I will now turn in more detail to each school and its history, beginning in the village.

The village school

The current village school was built in 1881, and is the direct descendent of Monsieur Brun's old communal school which occupied another building. The village of Lavialle had a diverse population of farmers and artisans in the early 20th century, which is reflected in the school records. This sets it apart from the population of the *commune* as a whole, which was overwhelmingly agricultural throughout the century. The teachers at the village school taught children from small farm and artisanal households who would eventually leave the *commune*, but also had children whose families encouraged them to stay in Lavialle and the nearby region.

In keeping with educational policies in France, Lavialle's teachers have kept good records of the enrollment levels for children attending this school. School records indicate that in the early 1900s there was a great disparity in the attendance levels of girls and boys, who were taught by same-sex teachers in separate classrooms. The school year ran from October to June. In 1915, only about 15 boys attended this school, and only during a period of six months, from November to April. Those who did attend came fairly regularly, with an attendance rate of 88% in the fall and 79% in the winter. In contrast, 30 girls attended this school, at least 15 of whom came steadily from October to July. School attendance for girls was 91% in the fall, 79% in winter, and 82% during the spring. Boys were dropping out of school earlier than girls in 1915, probably in order to help on their family's farms or obtain work on other farms. This was, of course, during World War I, when many of their fathers were absent, and their labor was greatly needed. Low enrollments in winter months for both boys and girls were most likely exacerbated by difficulties in getting to school during times of severe weather conditions.

By 1926, more boys attended Lavialle's school than did girls, since a religious primary school had opened in Grosbourg which accepted only girls. Lavialle's school had 33 students enrolled in that year: 20 boys and 13 girls. Attendance rates are not given according to gender for this period, but 92% of all students came to school in the fall, 81% in the winter, and 86% in the spring. After leaving school, many youths worked either on their own farms or for other families (*chez les autres*) for a small wage.

Until quite recently, children in Lavialle travelled great distances by foot in order to attend the village school. There were two households in Lavialle which took in children from far-flung hamlets as boarders during the week while they attended school. Elderly informants told me that children who were preparing for their first communion would often attend the village school, rather than one closer to their hamlet, so that they could be near the church and priest. A few households in the village provided a place for children to eat their lunch, which was not taken at school. Children would bring a noon meal that was packed at home and ready to be reheated. Informants remembered that this usually consisted of potatoes, bread, and wine[3] – reflecting the poverty of the region before World War II.

Twenty years later, in 1948, enrollment in the village school was little changed from levels in 1926. It was attended by 21 boys and 11 girls. In an annual report for this period, teachers recorded that no children attended the village school after age 14, and that there were no students in advanced (*cours complémentaires*) classes. Age 14 remained the cut-off point for formal education in Lavialle, and most people received a minimal level of instruction.

Following World War II, Lavialle underwent a period of social and economic decline, due to outmigration (the "rural exodus" that touched all of rural France) and its consequent slowing of social life. The Laviallois today remember a general drop in morale in the *commune* during this period, which lasted until the mid-1970s. Many people feared that the old agricultural way of life was in danger of dying out completely. Teacher attitudes to these changes and their effect on education reveal their own views of farm life and the values they were encouraging in the school. These were evident in interviews with former teachers. The husband–wife teaching team who taught in the village of Lavialle during the years from 1949 to 1964 explained to me that few young people were staying on the farms, and that social life was "really dying." The teachers, Monsieur and Madame Plante, stressed to me that they did not blame the youth for wanting to leave, and offered a multitude of reasons for the exodus (reflected in demographic losses) from Lavialle. They pointed to the economic boom in Clermont-Ferrand caused by the growth of Michelin, which, they felt, pulled youth to the city. Also important, they felt, were forces pushing the youth out – the lack of "interesting" things to do in Lavialle, the drudgery of farm life, and the harsh mountain climate. Girls left first, the Plantes reported, which created a glut of bachelors in Lavialle.[4]

Monsieur and Madame Plante were themselves from a rural *commune* not far from Lavialle, which they had left for teaching careers in the late 1930s. Monsieur Plante told me that life in this region during the 1930s resembled the "Middle Ages," and that a real revolution had occurred with World War II. Having themselves left agricultural life, these teachers viewed Lavialle as backward, and as an unattractive place for what they referred to as "bright" individuals. Their comments reflect a negative image of rural life that was part of an overall trend during the post-war period in France of devaluing "peasant" society (Moulin 1991:191; Rogers 1987). This was to change during the 1970s with the "back to nature" (post-1968) movement, with which Henri and Liliane Juillard, who taught in the early 1980s, most closely identified. Disparaged in the 1950s, rural life was to be romanticized by urbanites in the 1980s.

According to the Plantes, the Laviallois were "mistrustful" people, reluctant to accept changes – such as the state family subsidies instituted after the war to encourage fertility. They complained that school funds had to be raised by passing around the hat at weddings, but noted that the Barange Law of 1951 had helped assure a more stable financial situation through a national subsidy per child to the school. Parents did not send their children to school when the weather was bad, Madame Plante told me, although rarely did agricultural duties interfere with schooling. Her observation is in keeping with the statistics cited above for lower enrollments in winter than in spring or fall. Monsieur Plante explained that children did not help their parents very much with farm work, because dealing with dairy cows was too delicate a task for children. He suggested that the introduction of electric fences in grazing areas made a crucial difference in children's lives, and this sentiment was also expressed by farmers in Lavialle. Before, children were needed in the fields to stand watch over animals during long periods of time. After the electric fences were introduced, however, children were freed from a large part of their labor.

In their conversations with me, Monsieur and Madame Plante downplayed the language issue in schooling, and remarked that the children who entered their school were bilingual in French and *patois*.[5] Many middle-aged Laviallois who attended school in the 1940s and early 1950s remember differently, however, and said that they did not know French when they arrived at the school. Luckily, one woman told me, the schoolmistress knew the *patois* and helped the younger children, but her husband was less tolerant.

The Plantes continued to visit Lavialle on occasion for many years after leaving the school, and kept in touch with a few former students and their parents. Madame Plante was remembered by many Laviallois as a kind and generous woman, and her manner during my interviews with her bore out this claim. Monsieur Plante, on the other hand, was remembered as a harsh disciplinarian, and a man more interested in his job as town clerk than in his duties at the school. Several parents of school-aged children during my fieldwork told stories full of resentment, of having been kept after school and punished by him for fairly small offenses. One woman remembered that her parents had been very angry when she had been kept after school for what they considered an insignificant infraction of school rules. She added that they had not hesitated to let Monsieur Plante know of their dissatisfaction.

The Plantes were approvingly remembered as people who kept to themselves and did not try to introduce any changes in the school. This feature of their behavior was often noted in contrast to the innovative attempts of the newer teachers in 1980. As one former student of theirs put it: "They didn't want to upset anyone." I once asked the Plantes about the state of the school building during their stay. Madame Plante started to complain a little bit about the facilities, but her husband quickly spoke up, asking: "What could we do, it wasn't possible to change everything overnight!"

In many of the stories that the Laviallois tell about teaching couples in the school, gender plays a large role. The Laviallois generally portray male teachers, like Monsieur Plante, as harsh disciplinarians, while their wives, as in the case of Madame Plante, are described as more gentle. An overt dislike for the male teacher who taught during the period from 1936 to 1948 is voiced by most of his former students. One man told me the story of a hunting party in which this teacher had participated several years ago. When a hare was caught, someone suggested that it be given to the teacher, to honor him, since it had been traditional to share a part of the catch with the schoolmaster in Lavialle. Someone else spoke up, however, saying that this man had been such a "bastard" to them at school, that he wasn't going to let him have any of it. The man who told this story ended it by saying that he had very "bad memories" of school in Lavialle because of this teacher. The teacher in this story and his wife were, like the Plantes who came after them, from a rural *commune* near to Lavialle. They were remembered as being particularly anti-clerical, but, nevertheless, as having maintained cordial face-to-face relations with the local priest.

One elderly man whose son was in the school of an even earlier teacher recalled that he had been engaged in conversation with this teacher when church bells began to ring announcing Sunday mass. The teacher reminded him that he ought to be getting along to church. This incident had stuck in this man's memory, he told me, because it contrasted with the usual pattern of non-communication between teachers and the priest in Lavialle and neighboring *communes*. And yet, although he would always tip his hat to the priest, my informant told me, this teacher never set foot in the church. This elder of Lavialle also remembered that the teacher could see everything that happened in Lavialle from his apartment high in the school building, and surveyed the behavior of the children outside of school. He would later report to parents when he saw a child misbehave. (See also Zonabend 1979:499.) My informant's attitude to this surveillance was ambivalent, and his story served more as a comment on the teacher's authority role than on any close association between him and local families.

The period during which these teachers taught, from the 1920s to 1964, was characterized by a relatively stable script for the relationship between families and the village school. A strong authority role on the part of the male teacher, in particular, was an expected feature of teacher–student, and parent–teacher, interaction. Parents and teachers in the village maintained formal, overtly cordial relationships, and there was a clear boundary between their roles – parents did not enter the classroom and teachers rarely visited homes. For most children, schooling was viewed as something to be tolerated until age 14, before they entered the labor force full-time. There were exceptions to this among some girls in Lavialle. One farm wife remembered that she had to hide books from her parents, who disapproved of her studies.

The relationship between families and the school in the village of Lavialle up until the 1960s appears, if not identical, at least similar to that described by Wylie (1975) for a southern French village in the 1950s, and by Zonabend (1979) for the years prior to the 1950s in a Burgundian village. In each case, there was a lack of overt conflict between families and the school. Despite the absence of obvious and explicit expressions of conflict, however, the Laviallois were not wholly accepting of the school and teachers, as illustrated in the examples above. What Monsieur and Madame Plante describe as mistrust among the families of Lavialle may also be read as subtle resistance to school, and a refusal to accept the "social form" of schooling completely.

The southern hamlet school

When it closed, this school had only six students, who ranged in age from 6 to 13. Between 1945 and 1964, during the period that the Plantes were teaching in the village, 45 students from 21 different families were taught in the southern hamlet school. All of the children, with the exception of the son of one of the teachers, were from farm families. Two fathers were agricultural workers, but the rest owned and worked their own farms. Eleven different teachers taught in the southern hamlet school during this period of twenty years, eight of whom only stayed one year or less. This is in dramatic contrast to the average stay of fifteen years for teaching couples at the village school. The teachers in this hamlet school were all from towns or large cities in the Puy-de-Dôme, and thus were more urban than the teachers in the village. Also unlike the case in the village, where at least half of the teachers were male, only three out of the eleven teachers at the southern hamlet school were male.

I interviewed two female teachers from this school. The first taught there from 1929 to 1936, and still lived near Lavialle in 1981. The other, who taught from 1951 to 1959, maintained a summer residence in Lavialle. Both spoke of a harmonious relationship with the parents and town council. Former students of this school generally have positive memories of the teachers there, in contrast to memories of harsh male teachers in Lavialle. Mme Monet, the teacher during the earlier period, said that she had often been invited to First Communion meals in people's homes, and had spent many evenings playing cards with local families during the long winters. She received many gifts from families and students and, although these were mainly farm products, there were enough other small gifts to fill several display cases at her house, which she proudly showed me. Certain families were described by Mme Monet as "plus près du maître"; that is, closer to the teacher. These families treated her well and their children were her favorites. They were employing a common strategy in rural France, especially among wealthier farm families, of offering gifts to teachers in return for special attention to their children at school – a form of social manipulation and influence on education. This was particularly effective in the case of smaller schools where young, single teachers were more vulnerable and had lower salaries. This social manipulation exerted subtle parental authority over the teacher, and allowed some control over children's futures.

Mme Tulle, who taught later, also remembered that she visited homes often during her tenure at the school. She made a point of stressing that she felt there had been many good students among those she taught in Lavialle. There had been, she said, interest in schooling among many of her pupils, some of whom were now teachers themselves. Mme Tulle lamented, however, that many families nevertheless discouraged their children from continuing their studies beyond primary school.

In the southern hamlet school, relationships between families and the teacher were relatively free from overt conflict, despite the frequent turnover of teachers and lack of good facilities. The female teachers who taught there were not perceived to be harsh disciplinarians, as were the male teachers in the village of Lavialle, and escaped the sharp critiques of families. Some of this goodwill may be attributed to the less authoritarian approaches of the teachers, and to their gender. But the overall socio-economic context of the southern hamlet school also played a role in school-family relationships.

The hamlets served by this school were located in the mountain valley close to Grosbourg and, consequently, had always been more in touch with social life outside of the purely agricultural realm of the hamlets. The terrain is hilly in this part of Lavialle, which borders on the surrounding mountains, and is, therefore, difficult to cultivate. The southern hamlet section lost over half of its population between 1954 and 1975, in contrast to a loss during the same period of only one fifth in the village section. There were only 63 people living there in 1980, compared to 251 for the hamlets in the village section.

That many children's parents had developed a relatively favorable attitude toward schooling, reflected in their gifts and hospitality to the teacher, while others discouraged education, reflects the mixed strategies of farm families. On the one hand, favorable attitudes to schooling can be explained in terms of this section's on-going contact with, and proximity to, the town of Grosbourg. This would have brought its inhabitants into greater familiarity with positive strategies for dealing with teachers. Most families in this section, however, faced a weak economic future as farmers. It seems likely that many of the families in this section wanted their children to do well in school in order to secure work elsewhere, and were not encouraging them to stay in farming. It thus made sense for these families to adopt a good working relationship with the teachers, so as to ensure favorable treatment for their children. But there was also always a need for some children to stay, and, thus, to be discouraged from an interest in education. As in the case of Lavialle families today, described in chapter 4, a family might encourage schooling in some of its children, but not in the one who is expected to continue in farming. The child who was being groomed for farming, either the eldest or the one chosen for that role (as in "faire l'aîné"), would not likely also be the child viewed by the teacher as "plus près du maître."

The northern hamlet school

Records for this school are not as complete as those for the other two schools, and detailed information on either enrollments or former teachers is no longer available. A longstanding dispute over this school among neighboring hamlets, which involved the teacher, is, however, documented in correspondence on file in the regional educational archives in Clermont-

Ferrand. This dispute gives a more vivid picture of school–community relationships than can be gleaned from enrollment statistics.

Social relations surrounding the northern hamlet school were full of strife, in contrast to the situation at the southern hamlet school. From 1903 until 1946, a series of letters circulated between the prefecture of the Puy-de-Dôme, the school administration in Clermont-Ferrand (L'Inspection Primaire), and inhabitants of Lavialle (parents and town council members). This correspondence reveals a series of disputed attempts to relocate the school to different hamlets within the northern section of Lavialle.

Hamlet rivalry is very evident in this correspondence. First one faction of hamlets, then another, claimed that the school would be better located in one of their hamlets. In 1903, after letters indicating that differences in population justified the school's relocation to a more populated hamlet, the school was moved from one hamlet to another in the northern section. Later, in the 1920s, another factional dispute arose about the location of the school, with claims that it should again be moved. Although the town council was in favor of this move, the Departmental School Inspector rejected it on the basis of cost. Other letters, asking for repairs to the existing school, also appear in this correspondence, and indicate that the mayor of Lavialle was cooperative neither with the teacher of this school, nor with the inhabitants of the hamlet in which it was located. There was talk of closing the school at one point, then of building a new school in the same hamlet. Finally, both the prefect of Puy-de-Dôme and a member of the Chamber of Deputies wrote to the Inspector of Primary Schools urging him to keep this school open. The Inspector agreed to this under pressure, but refused funds for the construction of a new school.

In the early 1930s, there arose a renewed dispute over the location of the northern hamlet school. This time, all of the hamlets in this section, except the one in which the school was located, came together to oppose the school and to request that a new school be built in another hamlet. Continued correspondence about this issue, as well as about the poor state of the school building, did not, however, result in the construction of a new school.

The next and last mention of this almost half-century-long issue was in 1946, when a fire destroyed the school building![6] There were still rumors concerning its origins during my fieldwork, and the topic aroused intense emotions. After the fire, the town council member who represented the hamlet in which the school had been located started the construction of a new school on his own initiative, without going through the proper channels. This resulted in a dispute between the teacher and this council member over the construction of the new school, and the teacher eventually resigned, with the official excuse that she wanted to move nearer to her husband's work (in nearby Grosbourg). A settlement was finally reached, and a new building was eventually constructed for the school, which stayed open for another 15 years, apparently without much further incident.

Given the continued hamlet rivalry that I observed in Lavialle during the 1980s, this series of disputes over the location of the school appears to reflect rivalry among families and hamlets more than either educational resistance or enthusiasm. It illustrates the ways in which local politics can envelope primary schooling in a system even as centralized as that of France. Although local government in Lavialle has no formal say in the content or methods of education, the mayor and town council do have some control over the building itself. The northern hamlet school became the arena for factional disputes among Laviallois families, who fought for the establishment of a school in their own hamlets. At the time of my fieldwork, people from the northern hamlets were still reticent to speak about this dispute, but some inhabitants of the village expressed their continued disapproval of the town council member who had caused trouble in the 1940s, and said that he was dishonest. Rivalry between the village and the northern hamlet section is still evident in the negative comments of villagers.

The school became a pawn in factional politics between families in the northern hamlets and in the village. The ability to locate the school in one's hamlet was a symbol of political strength for the posturing town council members. Although this case suggests that the school was a vital resource, given that it became the object of dispute, it is important to consider the role and meaning of education and of the school in order to understand fully disputes over the school's location. This fight over the location of the school did not emerge from a climate of cooperation with and acceptance of the school and teachers, but, rather, from one of resistance and manipulation. The school, not education *per se*, was evidently a symbol of status, and the disputes over its location reflected inhabitants' attempts to exert power and authority within the *commune* over education by relocating the school.

Like the village, this section of Lavialle lost only one fifth of its population between 1954 and 1975. It had a population of 134 in 1980 – twice that of the southern section. Its households enjoy a substantially larger income from timber than those in other sections. Residents of the village of Lavialle consider people from the northern hamlets to be a bit "wild" and more rustic than themselves. A large number of homes and farms in this section are indeed less "modern" than those in the rest of the *commune*, with fewer renovations and appliances, even though many of the wealthier farms in Lavialle are located there. Farm families in this section have retained a more "traditional" culture, and have been able to support a larger population than those in the southern hamlets. This situation did not lead them to encourage good educational performances among their children until quite recently, since so many could be absorbed into farming. They came to see the value of schooling (in terms described by Thabault 1971 and Weber 1976) later than families in the other two sections of Lavialle.

Relationships between families and teachers in this hamlet are described in negative terms by families.[7] Former students say that teachers were mean (*malin*) and did not like children. These teachers, like those in the southern hamlet school, were mostly single women who did not stay long at their posts. Farm families in the northern hamlets adopted a different approach to teachers and schooling from that of the rest of Lavialle, and surrounded the school in local controversy and dispute.

Disputes about the location of the northern school tell as much about local rivalries as they do about attitudes toward education among the Laviallois. However, it was precisely because public education was not wholly accepted by families that it became an arena for conflict among hamlets. These disputes over the school most likely masked other, economic and political disputes, among the households and farms of the northern hamlets, and also show conflicts between this section and the village. Families who hoped to encourage their children's educational future, such as those in the southern hamlets, would be more likely to influence schooling through gifts and cooperation than through threats and disputes. It was families living in this northern section who led opposition to Lavialle's teachers in the early 1980s, and a knowledge of their contentious history helps to understand current disputes better.

Accommodation and resistance

The three schools located in Lavialle during the mid-twentieth century display, as their stories show, three different models of relationships between schools and families. This illustrates the workings of different educational strategies within the same *commune*. Teachers and families at the southern hamlet school got along fairly well with each other, while, at the opposite extreme, the northern hamlet school was surrounded for many years by outright controversy and conflict. In the village, relationships between teachers and families were more formal than in the southern section, but cordial in comparison with those in the northern section. This suggests that generalizations about education, even in so tiny a place as Lavialle, must not be overstated. It also suggests that families can exert important influences upon education – both through positive strategies of manipulation and through negative strategies of resistance.

How can we account for these differences? All three schools were in the same *commune*, during the same time period, and operated within the same overall institutional and ecological framework. The differences in the type of relationship that each school had with local families belies the notion of the *commune* of Lavialle as a homogeneous "community" of farmers. The varying relationships that these three hamlet sections had with their respective schools underscores the importance of hamlet and kin identity for social relations in Lavialle. It was on the basis of the "family economy" (Tilly and Scott 1978; Maynes 1985a and 1985b) and hamlet residence that families interacted with the schools and teachers. Moreover, families in the three sections of Lavialle did not have equal resources – either in terms of the type of education offered or in terms of their own economic and cultural capital. The state's imposition of a homogeneous model of schooling and citizenship in rural Lavialle was necessarily tempered by the educational strategies of Lavialle families.

Lavialle's population declined during the period examined in this chapter, and this decline accelerated after World War II. Even though many farms did not survive, the depopulation of the region and new agricultural adaptations led to economic growth for those families that remained. The strategies adopted in each hamlet section significantly affected the type of role that the school could play in socio-economic change. Families in the southern section, where farming was least viable and alternatives more visible (due to proximity to Grosbourg), maintained good relations with the teachers in the school (in order to enhance their children's chances). They encouraged some children to complete their primary schooling and discouraged others from continuing. In this case, the families' use of the school clearly helped along the process of demographic loss and decline. There was a greater perceived need for schooling among southern hamlet families, who, therefore, were hospitable to teachers.

A different type of strategy was developed in the northern section, where factionalism and hamlet rivalry overshadowed educational goals. Families were hostile toward the school and teachers, and used the issue of

the school's location as a vehicle for the expression of local political conflicts. This reflects the values of farm families most invested in the "traditional" way of life, who were ambivalent about the need for formally
educating their children. The conflict over the location of the school hindered its influence on children, given the unstable context in which it operated, and constrained its ability to promote social and cultural changes.
This section of Lavialle has changed more slowly than other sections, in
part due to the constraints its families placed on education. Although the
disputes may reflect some genuine concern for children among the players,
and a desire to place the school within walking distance of individual
farms, the shifting alliances and the longstanding nature of this battle also
suggest that local political maneuvering was greatly at stake.

In the village section, there was a more complicated situation, arising
both from the more "established" nature of schooling there, and from the
more heterogenous character of the local population. Significantly, the
teachers at the village school were better adept at keeping families "at bay"
than were the village teachers. This is an important factor since the workings of more direct influences (both positive and negative) are so evident in
the hamlets. The village school was associated with a large, imposing
building, and with authoritarian male teachers who also served as town
clerks. Parents had less direct access to the school and its teachers, and role
relationships between families and teachers were more rigidly defined than
they were in the less formal settings of the hamlet schools. Avenues for
direct expression of conflict were, therefore, fewer there, and resistance was
expressed as mistrust. This school taught the children of artisans and
shopkeepers, well as those of farmers. Their families were, for the most
part, more favorable to schooling than were most farming families in the
commune. While parents maintained superficially cordial relationships
with the teachers at this school, in order to ensure a stable environment for
their children's education, they were not wholly supportive of the teachers,
and harbored resentment and hostility toward them, as the stories they tell
about schooling experiences show.

An emphasis on families' influences upon education in Lavialle must not
overshadow the very real power of the state. The institutional and social
constraints present in the French educational system are as important in
understanding schooling in Lavialle as are the economic and cultural
interests of families. It is not really possible to discuss one without the
other. Rural schools in France have not always been intended as places
providing unlimited opportunities for children. For a long time, the presence of a dual system of education, separating elites and non-elites, hin-

dered whatever educational aspirations French peasants might have had for their children. The negative comments about former teachers, described as "mean," heard so often in Lavialle are a vital means of expressing frustration over the imposition of national forms of power and authority at the local level through schooling.

Family strategies are very much connected to the perpetuation of the patrimony and of the kindred. Relationships between parents and teachers are, thus, filtered through the wider social meaning of property and kinship in Lavialle. Modes of cooperation and conflict surrounding schooling reflect the interests of individual families as well as the overall relationships among families. The forms of influence upon education that Lavialle families developed in the three different school contexts reflected a divergence of strategies and responses to an educational system which was taking on new meanings both as a national institution and as a local institution.

Gender, schooling, and farming

Families in Lavialle do not educate their sons and daughters in the same manner, and an understanding of their socialization strategies must not ignore these important gender differences. The educational strategies of families in Lavialle have resulted in low educational achievements for most children, male or female, from the *commune*. In this, Lavialle is not dissimilar to other rural and working-class populations, since farmers and workers have always trailed the rest of the French population in level of education. Few adults in Lavialle have post-secondary degrees, but this is not out of keeping with the majority of the French population. A far more significant feature of education in Lavialle is the growing disparity between the educational levels of males and females, with girls now receiving much higher levels of schooling.

The population of Lavialle has become increasingly "schooled" throughout the twentieth century. This is mostly as a result of educational reforms that prolonged the period of mandatory education, but is also due to the increased desire of families to have their children learn skills necessary to run profitable farms. Hardly any resident of Lavialle who was born in the early part of the century continued his or her schooling past primary school. This is not surprising, given both the isolated and predominantly subsistence-oriented nature of Lavialle during this period, as well as the highly stratified educational system that offered few opportunities to Lavialle's children.

Those born later in the century have had higher schooling levels.

However, changes in educational attainment during the twentieth century for those Laviallois who remained in the *commune* have differed a great deal for men and women. Males led the initial trend for increased schooling levels, but females caught up in the post-World War II period. For those Laviallois aged 35–55 in the mid-1970s, 20% of all men had some formal training beyond the primary level, compared to only 2% of the women. A reversal of this situation began with the post-war generation, however. Women's educational levels increased dramatically, bringing them close to men's levels – which also increased, threefold.

Higher overall levels of schooling for the post-war generation are partly due to the extension of the school-leaving age to 16, which took effect in 1967. For the total population of adults in 1975 over 17 and not in school, 55% of the men and 49% of the women had the primary school certificate (CEP). By the mid-1970s, young women in Lavialle surpassed young men in educational attainment. At this time, two-thirds of all youth in Lavialle continued their education beyond the required 16 years of age. Of the 22 youths in the age group of 17–19 in 1975, 13 were still in school; and for the 20–24 age group, 3 were in school. Whereas three-quarters of all girls aged 17–19 were in school in 1975, however, this was only true for less than half of the boys.

The trend for increased levels of schooling for girls has occurred throughout France (Terrail 1992), as well as in the region of Auvergne. In the Auvergne as a whole, the children of farmer-owners are less likely than all but the children of blue collar workers and service personnel to continue their education beyond the obligatory 16 years. However, in all occupational categories (except for that of "other"), females in Auvergne have significantly higher levels of schooling than do males.

In Lavialle, gender differences in schooling are more extreme than they are for the region as a whole. Males have schooling levels far below the average for the children of farmer-owners in the Auvergne, as well as below that for any other category. In contrast, females in Lavialle have levels much higher than the average for farmer-owner children, and trail only the three categories of industrial and commercial managers, liberal professions, and management (the highest categories). Whereas boys from Lavialle have much *lower* levels of formal education than boys from all occupational categories in the region combined, girls from Lavialle have higher levels than most girls in the Auvergne region. The educational gender gap in Lavialle is, indeed, wide. Several factors in the family strategies of Lavialle farmers help to explain this.

Most studies of gender and schooling in peasant societies focus on the unequal educational chances of boys and girls (Kelly and Elliott 1982). The French educational system as a whole does tend to favor male achievement. As Bourdieu and Passeron (1964; 1990) have shown, selection occurs in French secondary and higher education according to both gender and social class. However, Frederic Charles has recently found that, in primary and lower secondary school, French girls generally do better than boys, and "are less likely than boys to be eliminated from the competitive school system at any point" (1991:69; see also Terrail 1992). Sirota has suggested that this is because girls in French primary school classrooms tend to behave more like "model" pupils than do boys (1988:84–5).

In Lavialle, girls tend to like school more and to want to continue their training longer than boys. This both reflects and reinforces family attitudes toward the education of girls. Families in Lavialle are more apt to encourage advanced schooling among their daughters for two major reasons. First, good accounting skills are considered important for a farm wife to have, and many Laviallois girls pursue this type of training after leaving middle school. Secondly, whereas girls are encouraged to work outside of the farm before marriage, and to gain training for employment, boys tend to live and work at home before marriage (even if they are not inheriting sons). One young woman in Lavialle told me that she felt she had three choices: to stay at home with her parents, to get married, or to leave Lavialle and work in Clermont-Ferrand. Although she had many friends who had pursued the last option, she hoped to stay in Lavialle.

Underlying the differential education of sons and daughters in Lavialle are fundamental attitudes toward gender roles. The Laviallois view male teachers as being "different" from other men, and view education as something which sets a man apart from farmers and artisans. This reflects ambivalent attitudes toward male teachers that go back to earlier centuries. One elderly farmer in Lavialle remarked to me that it takes a "special" kind of person to become a schoolmaster, cooped up all day in the school with children. Teaching behavior seems more "natural" in the Lavialle scheme of things for women, the usual caregivers of young animals and children, than for men. For the Laviallois, among whom Auvergnat masculine identity is strongly associated with cunning, subversive behavior, the norms of conformity and civility associated with schooling conflict with dominant concepts of manhood.

As Willis (1981a) and, more recently, Holland and Eisenhart (1990) have shown, gender ideologies play a much more important role in education than has usually been granted. The manual/mental division of labor in European society, and its link to masculinity, often causes young working-class and rural males to reject schooling because it conflicts with their cultural definitions of masculinity. For Lavialle males, schooling conflicts in important ways with masculine gender roles. For females in the primary grades, this is not the case. Although the families of Lavialle do not encourage their daughters to become so schooled that they cut themselves off from the family, their educational strategies have entailed growing support for the education of girls. Girls have, thus, more readily accepted schooling than have boys because it does not conflict with valued gender behavior.

Bourdieu and his colleagues (1962; 1972; Bourdieu *et al.* 1973) have blamed the higher levels of education among rural girls in France for the decline of the peasantry. They suggest that when girls are encouraged to pursue advanced education, they then leave farming and eventually marry non-farmers. The symbolic devaluation of farm life that occurs through their daughters' rejection of farmers as husbands, Bourdieu argues, is a way in which farm families participate in their own destruction (1973:103–6). This is part of the "deculturation" of the farm child who learns to be a "pupil" and, thus, breaks away from the rest of peasant society (Bourdieu *et al.* 1973: 106). It is connected to the spread of schools to rural areas and the rising age of mandatory schooling.

For the decades of the 1950s and 1960s in Lavialle, Bourdieu's characterization seems to carry some weight. Farm children, and especially girls, reacting to the devaluation of peasant life in the wider society, but also drawn to promising economic opportunities in Clermont-Ferrand, did leave Lavialle in large numbers. In Lavialle, as in other parts of rural France, there were quite a few bachelors unable to find a farm wife. Beginning in the late 1970s, however, there has been a renewal of interest in farming among the youth of Lavialle, and many girls have married farm boys. Girls can inherit land in Lavialle, and receive sizeable dowries from their families that can be applied to a new household. Although levels of education for girls have remained higher than those for boys, most of the instruction girls receive is in accounting or other secretarial skills. These are viewed as useful skills for the wife of a farmer or artisan, enabling her to "keep the books." Education for girls is part of a strategy to perpetuate farm life, as they learn skills helpful to farm management, rather than one leading to its dissolution.

Rather than seeing the educational strategies of families in Lavialle as playing completely into the hands of the dominant classes in France, as Bourdieu seems to do, it makes more sense to view their uses of education in terms of family strategies aimed not simply at "reproduction" but also at adaptation in the face of changing circumstances. The role that education has played in the depopulation of Lavialle can then be seen to depend upon changing family strategies and changing economic opportunities both within and outside of the community. Increased levels of education, especially for girls, are best interpreted in terms of wider cultural meanings both of gender and of farm life.

Regional variation: Auvergne, Brittany, and Touraine

This analysis of schooling in Lavialle stresses the role of Auvergnat regional identity in the educational strategies of Lavialle families. Their resistance to certain aspects of schooling is very much informed, I have argued, by their self-identity as Auvergnat "paysans" through which they define themselves in opposition to refined, French-identified urban dwellers. The Laviallois do not reject French identity outright, and their socialization strategies are aimed at teaching children to juggle both an Auvergnat and a French identity. The Laviallois are, however, ambivalent about French identity and about the school as "social form." As the historical portrait which I have painted in this and the previous chapter shows, they have never wholly embraced the French language or the Republican ideals which accompanied schooling over local values and language use. It is important to recognize that the Laviallois are not necessarily representative of all French peasants, and that their case is unique in several respects. Two contrasting ethnographic examples of rural schooling help to show the ways in which regional variation in the role and meaning of schooling exhibits itself in France.

Maryon McDonald's (1989) anthropological study of the language question in education in Brittany concludes that it is Breton militants, not Breton peasants, who reject French education. Although McDonald's study is mainly focused on the Breton language movement, she presents evidence from a rural *commune* called Plouneour which has long accepted French nationalism, language, culture, and education. She writes that "while enthusiasts in the towns have been imagining their 'Breton' world tucked away in the mountains, the people in the Arée mountains have themselves been actively espousing, within their own structures of identity and aspiration, the ideas and politics of the French Republic" (1989:222–3). Although McDonald's book is entitled, "We are not French," it is Breton militants, not peasants, whose voices are reflected in this phrase. There are some very important contrasts between the *communes* of Plouneour and Lavialle, which help to explain their different reactions to schooling and to French national identity. In both cases, however, reactions to schooling seem to be connected to forms of resistance to what is perceived as the dominant culture by the social actors involved. Both Plouneour and Lavialle are mountainous communities which have forged an identity in reaction to outsiders and in response to national stereotypes of regional identity.

In Brittany, a highly Catholic region where the clergy is strong, the discourse of red (left-wing and anti-clerical) vs. white (right-wing and church-supporting) has been a salient shaper of identity and political behavior. As McDonald indicates, the residents of Plouneour define themselves as defiantly "red" in contrast to the "whites" of the nearby valley. Therefore, they support French nationalism and Republican schools as a mode of opposition to neighboring peoples who were associated with the church. As urban, bourgeois militants increasingly celebrate Breton language and culture, this identification with France intensified among the peasants of Plouneour. I interpret this process as a form of resistance to bourgeois values.

Lavialle does not exist within the sharp contrast of red and white that has long dominated Breton cultural discourse, nor has discourse about its regional identity been dominated by a militant regionalist movement. Lavialle is situated in a mountainous part of the wider region of Auvergne which has forged an identity in terms of an opposition between the Auvergnat peasant and the person who is urban, refined, and French-identified. Although Church vs. state battles are not absent in this region, this is not the discourse which most shapes identity and behavior. Plouneour is a community in which less than half of the workforce is engaged in agriculture (McDonald 1989:247), and in which the rural exodus of young women, in particular, has led to a dramatic population loss in recent decades. Lavialle has a much higher percentage of its population engaged in agriculture, on family farms, which reinforces local and regional identity in opposition to state power and bourgeois values. Bourgeois values in the Auvergne criticize what are viewed as crude and backward peasant lifestyles; there are no Auvergnat militants who champion regional identity in the same way as do Breton militants.

Perhaps one of the most striking elements in the case of the two *communes* has to do with gender identity and its connection to regional identity. This has played itself out very differently in the two contexts. Whereas Brittany is associated with a romanticized femininity in the popular national imagination (McDonald 1989: 244), the Auvergne is associated with a more brutish, masculine image. In the case of both Lavialle and Plouneour, however, at the local level, education and the speaking of

French are associated with femininity and contrasted with regional language use, which is associated with masculinity. In Lavialle, as I have shown in the previous section of this chapter, the dominant masculine image of the Auvergnat peasant has informed the widespread rejection of schooling among males in Lavialle in part because of the school's association with feminine values. Females in Lavialle have much higher levels of education. Whereas the same gender dichotomy exists in Plouneour, however, it is associated there with a higher rejection of Breton language and culture among that population than in Lavialle.

In Lavialle, Auvergnat regional identity and its masculine associations are used in the service of family strategies that are fundamentally economic strategies aimed at perpetuating the family-owned and -run dairy farm. The case of Plouneour indicates that in a regional context where land ownership has been less widespread and wage-earning occupations were more common, appeals to regional identity were less salient. It probably made more sense for the Plouneour residents to identify with national culture and educate their children in French language. They had much less at stake than did the Laviallois in losing their children to jobs in the city. Whereas Plouneour women and girls were encouraged to express their femininity in using French and adopting "refined" modes of behavior and discourse (McDonald 1989: 247–9), females in Lavialle participate in a system which values rough, Auvergnat masculinity and provides sanctions against those who "put on airs" (Reed-Danahay 1987b).

A second ethnographic example, which is at the opposite end of a pole of French vs. regional identity, comes from a village in Touraine. Touraine contrasts sharply with Brittany in that it is a region in which the French language has historically been dominant, and where the Catholic Church has had a minimal influence over education. Sanda Jo Spiegel's study of Villay, an agricultural community in Touraine, in west-central France, indicates that there can be conflict between families and schooling even when cultural identity is shared. Spiegel reports that for Villay "the values and beliefs of its people are not dissimilar to those of the individuals who make up the rules and regulations" (Spiegel 1978:91). In Villay, there is no *patois* and no strong regional identity. However, she found that there was "ambivalence in their attitudes" toward schooling and teachers. Spiegel cites several cases of disputes over schooling that occurred in Villay over its history. She attributes this to the centralized nature of the educational system, which leaves little power to the local community. Residents of Villay react toward the school with ambivalent and passive attitudes, she concludes, due to the long history of exclusion from educational decision-making characteristic of French education. Nevertheless, when the residents of Villay cannot get the results they want through formal channels, she writes, they resort to informal means of influencing the school and teachers. Spiegel argues that in the absence of regional distinction, the explanation for conflict between school and community must lie with the system itself, rather than with cultural difference.

The case of Villay presents an interesting contrast to that of both Plouneour and Lavialle. It suggests that identification with French culture, which McDonald posits as contributing to positive attitudes toward French education among the Breton peasants of Plouneour, does not necessarily result in such attitudes. There can be school-community conflict even in the absence of cultural difference. It also indicates that the conflict between families and the school in Lavialle is not wholly dependent upon cultural differences between French schools and Auvergnat families. Spiegel's study supports my claims that the behaviors and attitudes of Lavialle families toward schooling constitute responses to a centralized, hierarchical system of education as much as they reflect local cultural values. When compared with the case of Lavialle, these other two examples show that the French educational system is manifested very differently in different local contexts, despite its centralized and supposedly homogeneous nature. Economic, religious, and cultural factors play a large role in the types of educational strategies adopted by families. Lavialle represents but one constellation of these factors.

8

The politics of schooling

In this chapter, I turn to Lavialle's school in the most recent period considered in this book, that of the early 1980s. Because of the centralized nature of French education, parents in Lavialle have been constrained in their ability to influence schooling directly. They have, nevertheless, adopted effective ways to influence the education of their children. Both positive and negative forms of influence have been used by families, which can be considered as forms of accommodation and forms of resistance. As was seen in the previous chapter, the strategies which families adopt in order to influence schooling vary according to their own perceived needs and the avenues for influence available to them. During the period under consideration here, forms of resistance to the school and teachers were striking. These were, for the most part, responses to changing circumstances and reflect the overall stance of conservatism in Lavialle that has, paradoxically, helped it to survive as a viable community. These educational strategies did not reflect a total resistance to learning, or to all aspects of schooling. Rather, they were forms of influence on the schooling that children experienced.

My fieldwork in Lavialle coincided with several important events at both national and local levels. First, 1981 marked the beginning of the celebration of the centennial of the Ferry laws establishing universal public primary education in France. This was also the year of the landmark 1981 French presidential elections, in which a Socialist president was elected for the first time in fifty years. In Lavialle, I observed the first election of a representative Parent Committee at Lavialle's school; and there were two new teachers, only in their second year at the school.

The first occasion, the Ferry Law centennial, played little role in relationships between families and the school. There was no explicit mention

157

of the centennial by either teachers or parents in Lavialle, although it enjoyed a great deal of rhetoric and remembrance at the national level. On the other hand, François Mitterand's election, and the events which preceded and followed it, played a major role in the politics of schooling in Lavialle during 1981. There were also changes at the school that year. As part of the ongoing implementation of the 1975 Haby reforms, a new institutionalized form of parent participation in French elementary schools was put into place during the fall of 1980. In addition, the teachers in Lavialle were only in their second year at the school during 1980–81, and their presence was having an effect on school-community relationships. Partly as a direct result of these changes, Lavialle's school became a volatile arena for the maneuvering of local and national politics during the period of my fieldwork. The school and the events which surrounded it during the early 1980s serve as an instructive setting in which to look at the intricacies of power at the local level in rural France.

By the early 1980s, education had become well established in Lavialle. Several generations of Laviallois had attended the communal school, the entire population could speak French, and almost all adults were literate. Conflicts between families and teachers were no longer shaped by "indifference" to education (as Monsieur Brun characterized parental attitudes in the nineteenth century) or even primarily by "mistrust" of schooling (as teachers during the mid-twentieth century labelled parental resistance). Contemporary teachers attribute what opposition they encounter among families as due to rural "backwardness" or parochialism.[1] It is common for educated, urban-oriented French people to attach labels to the perceived traditionalism of rural dwellers, and to describe them as backward, or "closed in." Anthropologists, for their part, frequently question assumptions that rural traditionalism is a given (Rosenberg 1988:1–3; see also Henriot-Van Zanten 1990:143). Fabian (1983) has usefully shown that the labelling of subordinate groups as "the other" through distance in time (that is, calling them "backward" or "behind the times") is a common device by means of which dominant groups have attempted to secure their own power. The seeming traditionalism of the Laviallois is best understood as the result of active strategies of keeping certain kinds of changes "at bay."

If schooling in Lavialle could be seen in terms of conflict between the state and the local community in earlier periods, the situation has grown more ambiguous. The teachers are still perceived as "outsiders" and agents of the state, but the school has taken on a great deal of local meaning and helps to shape local identity. The physical presence of the communal school enables the inhabitants of the *commune* to imagine Lavialle as a political and cultural unit, but the school also serves as an arena for the expression of local political divisions and social fragmentation. The politics of schooling is not just about state hegemony in Lavialle; it is also about local struggles and local meanings.

The school: architecture and power
The school building in Lavialle (Fig. 1) is a tangible symbol of the articulation of state and local forms of power. In chapter 1, I described the school, located in the center of the village, as a massive building rivalled only by the church in size. Although the Laviallois usually refer to this building as *l'école*, public education is not its sole function. The school is also the site of the teacher's apartment, the mayor's office (*la mairie*), and the communal archives. This multi-functional arrangement is common in rural French municipal buildings, especially those built in the first half of the 20th century. In larger towns, such as Grosbourg, the school is in a separate building from the town hall (*l'hôtel de ville*), and teachers have independent lodgings.

Within the walls of the school, four major functions are thus incorporated, but not entirely meshed. Schooling is conducted in the two classrooms on the first floor, and the school's lunchroom is located on the second floor. In a two-bedroom apartment on the left side of the second floor is the home of a young family – that of the teachers. Local government, the third function of the building, is housed in the mayor's office, centrally positioned at the top of the stairs on the second floor. Finally, the archives (official records for the state and *commune*) are located next to the mayor's office on the right side of the building.

Schooling in Lavialle is not, given its location in a multi-functional building, spatially set apart from other activities, as is often the case in urban French schools and in most American schools. The state's involvement in public education is very directly expressed through this arrangement. Children begin their formal education in the same building in which other state obligations are fulfilled: it is where people vote, get married (in the mandatory French civil ceremony), file official documents, and make local governmental decisions (since the town council meets in the mayor's office or school lunchroom). That teachers live and raise their families in this same space intensifies local perceptions of their close connection to the state.

The school building is imbued with a strong aura of power due to the concentration of state activities housed under its roof. This physical

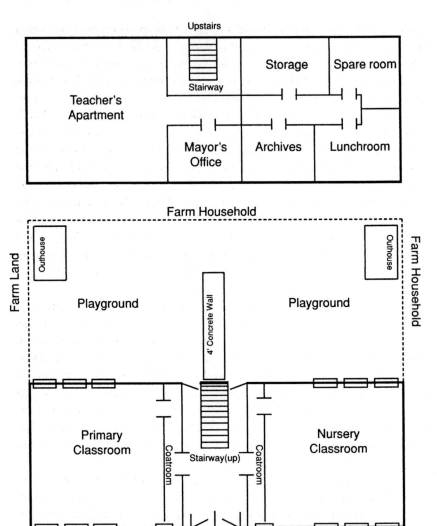

Fig. 1   School building, Lavialle

arrangement reinforces the distance between the decision-making bodies of education (in Clermont-Ferrand and Paris) and the families of children who attend the school. It also keeps the teachers very much set apart from local life, by both insulating and exposing them at the same time. On the one hand, they are somewhat protected by this seeming fortress from exposure to hostility on the part of the community; on the other hand, their place of residence locates them directly in the center of the public eye and causes their lives to be deeply enmeshed with official business. While personal contact with them is hindered by their physical location within the walls of an official building, their every action is closely scrutinized by the community due to the central location of the school building in the village of Lavialle. This was made particularly clear to me through my own experience of moving from my first lodgings in the school building to my own apartment in the village; my social interaction with neighbors increased dramatically when I lived among them and not set apart in the school.

The local government of Lavialle is totally responsible for the financial support and maintenance of the school building, through its own funds and any state subsidies it may obtain. Lavialle provides the teachers with free lodgings, although their salaries are paid directly by the national government. All heating, electrical, and janitorial expenses of the school are paid by the *commune*. Any improvements made to the school building are initiated and paid for by the town council, subject to the approval of educational authorities in Clermont-Ferrand. The town council also pays for school transportation and for the lunchroom (neither of which are mandated by national educational policy).

In general, the teachers who have taught and lived in Lavialle's school have considered the building and their own lodgings to be in fairly good condition. Monsieur and Madame Plante, who taught there between 1949 and 1964, told me that they were attracted to Lavialle in the first place because the school was in good shape compared to other schools in the region. When I arrived in Lavialle in the fall of 1980, the students still used outhouses located in the play area behind the school, but the teachers had indoor toilets in their own apartment. The teachers' apartment also had a modern kitchen, whereas the children's noonday meal was prepared in a lunchroom equipped with a wood stove and a sink with no hot water. The young woman who prepared the lunch used to arrive early in order to get the oven fire going before cooking, and she heated water for the dishes while we ate lunch. During the year that I lived in Lavialle, major renovations were initiated in the lunchroom, and indoor toilets were built for the children. A new gas stove was added to the lunchroom, which was repainted, and new kitchen utensils were purchased. All of these renovations were carried out by local artisans, who were also fathers of the children attending the school. Most of it was completed by the time I left.

Although the school building in Lavialle is certainly not ultra-modern in comparison with new schools in urban and suburban communities, it now has all of the facilities considered basic in modern rural society – indoor toilets, a telephone, and central heating. In comparison with most of the houses in Lavialle, lacking central plumbing and heating, the school is indeed "modern." This is an indication of both the community's willingness to put time and effort into maintaining a school and attracting teachers who will be happy living there *and* a view that teachers are urban, middle-class people, who require better facilities than those to which rural dwellers are accustomed. Major renovations to the school building since World War II have usually coincided with the arrival of a new teaching couple, as did the most recent improvements.

The school building embodies conflicting meanings of local identity and childhood socialization in Lavialle. Despite its statist architecture and apparent consolidation of state power, the school building has important local meanings. Its archives contain the official repository of Lavialle's history, and its classrooms have been inhabited by generations of Lavialle children. There are important contradictions between the ways in which the school symbolizes the power of the state and the ways in which it reproduces a culture of childhood in Lavialle (to be taken up in the next chapter) and helps to represent the *commune* physically as a social collectivity.

The teachers

Henri and Liliane Juillard,[2] a teaching couple in their early twenties, came to Lavialle in the fall of 1979, almost directly out of the regional teachers' college. They were both children of mid-level civil servants, and had grown up in the suburbs of Clermont-Ferrand. Lavialle had been high on their list of preferences for a teaching post. Influenced by the "green" movement in France (the back-to-nature trend of the 1970s), the Juillards very much wanted to get a position in a rural setting, where they expected to live a simple life in an environment of fresh air and nature. To their dismay, they arrived in Lavialle somewhat ill-prepared to deal with everyday life in a rural farming community, with its local conflicts, defenses against outside intrusion, and very different style of life. The teachers' college curriculum concentrates mostly on teaching methods and philosophy, and gives its students no sense of the social milieu in which they will teach if sent to a rural school.

The Juillards replaced another husband–wife team who had taught in Lavialle from 1965 to 1979, but had not, according to parents at the school, enjoyed a good relationship with the community. After their own difficulties in Lavialle, the Juillards eventually left Lavialle sooner than their predecessors, six years after their arrival, taking new jobs closer to the city of Clermont-Ferrand. Their shorter stay contrasts with the average fifteen-year stay for previous Lavialle teachers during the 20th century, but is close to the pattern in other rural French schools and in the old hamlet schools of Lavialle.

Henri Juillard was the director of the school and, following the pattern of previous male teachers in Lavialle, worked part-time as the town clerk. He was, therefore, both a state and local employee, since his teaching position was paid by the state and his job with the mayor's office was paid by the *commune*. He was responsible for maintaining the communal archives, doing the paperwork for local and administrative matters, and keeping the minutes of the town council meetings. Since all civil documents are filed at the level of the *commune* in France, the teacher's role as town clerk has important links to the state bureaucracy. The teacher/town clerk is, thus, a liaison between state and local bureaucratic functions.

The Juillards were Socialists, as are many primary school teachers in France. Henri was an active member of SNI-FEN, the largest union of primary school teachers, to which 70% of all such teachers belong (Lewis 1985:145). The SNI-FEN, leftist in orientation, takes a position of opposition to rightist reforms, especially at the national level. Although Liliane did not attend union meetings, in part because she cared for their young child while Henri went, she expressed support for her husband's involvement. Henri reported to me that the union meetings were poorly attended and that only a small core of teachers in this region were actively involved.[3]

Although they were residents of Lavialle, the teachers' participation in the everyday life of the *commune* was minimal. Strongly secular in approach (like their predecessors), the Juillards did not attend Mass and had no contact with the parish priest. They shopped mostly at urban malls and stores near to Clermont-Ferrand, rather than in local shops – for which they were criticized in Lavialle, particularly by local shopkeepers. Laviallois women interpreted Liliane Juillard's lack of participation in local marketing activities as a sign of her haughtiness and unwillingness to come into contact with her neighbors on an informal basis. The Juillards' distant style and urban-oriented frame of reference differed, people told me, from what they remembered as the more personal and paternalistic style of previous teachers.

Henri had contact with many Laviallois, not just the parents at the school, due to his job as town clerk and his honorary membership, as director of the school, in local associations. As town clerk, he had frequent dealings with the mayor, town council members, and residents of the *commune* visiting the mayor's office. Sometimes, parents with business at the mayor's office would engage Henri in a discussion of their child's progress in school, and an informal parent–teacher conference would take place. I was often present during Henri's office hours, working on archival and cadastral materials. He adopted a strictly formal manner while wearing his town clerk "hat," and did not try to engage people in friendly conversation. Town hall business was carried out in a bureaucratic, formal tone (similar to that used in classroom teaching).

Although Henri was present at most town council meetings, he was occasionally asked not to come when controversial issues were being discussed. In this way, he was excluded from much local political maneuvering. His job was to keep records of the meetings, and when he was not present, he was informed later of the essential (i.e., "official") issues by the mayor. Henri told me that town council members would also often speak in local dialect in his presence so that he could not understand conversations. In spite of these exclusions by town council members, Henri felt himself to be on good terms with the mayor, who was generally cooperative with his efforts at the school.

As director of the school, Henri Juillard was, like the parish priest and the mayor, invited to participate as an honorary member in local voluntary associations. His participation in most of these was limited to attendance at their annual banquets, but he was actively involved in the Youth Club. The demands of the various associations on Henri's leisure time were considered to be onerous by the Juillards. Sometimes these demands conflicted, and Henri was once strongly criticized by members of the Youth Club for attending the annual banquet of the fishermen (an older group) rather than their own meeting held at the same time. Since Henri was only an honorary member of most of these clubs, his contacts with their members were sporadic.

The Juillards' personal and professional lives, like those of farmers and artisans, did not have the clear-cut boundaries characteristic of most urban workers, since they lived where they worked. At least since the time of M. Brun in the 1870s, the school has presented a model of family-based labor which is familiar to families in Lavialle. A family is associated with the school just as a family is associated with a farm. The teachers' position in Lavialle is no longer widespread in France, where, in most urban contexts and in many rural settings, teachers do not live in the *commune*, and have personal lives divorced from their school. In such settings, parents and children only see teachers at school (see Anderson-Levitt 1989).

Despite their residence in the *commune*, shared Auvergnat origins, and family-based system of labor, Henri and Liliane were, however, defined as "outsiders" in Lavialle. The Juillards had little close contact with most parents, and had never, for instance, visited the homes of any of their students who lived outside of the village. During the summer, as do many middle-class French, the Juillards left for extended trips.

Because parents had little direct opportunity to learn about the teachers' private lives, but were curious about their activities, they relied upon their school-age children to report to them about the teachers. An impressive network of gossip concerning the teachers operated among Lavialle mothers. This informal, behind-the-scenes, mostly negative conjecturing and discussion about the Juillards reinforced a critical stance toward teachers, and contrasted with an atmosphere of polite formality that characterized most face-to-face encounters between teachers and parents.[4] I often observed dinner-table discussions in some families at which the teachers would be criticized. Some parents would encourage their children to talk about the teachers; in fact, this was much more common than the typical American question, "What did you do in school today?"

Parent participation
The French primary school system incorporated limited forms of parent participation with the Haby Reforms, while continuing to exclude parents from curricular decisions and teacher hiring. There is a division in the French educational system between the control given to the local *commune* over the material and financial aspects of schooling (apart from paying teacher salaries), and the total absence of local control over the content and structure of the schooling process itself. This system places the burden of maintaining the school building on the community without giving families much say in their children's education. Primary education in France was intentionally designed in this way to enable the teacher to operate in the classroom autonomously from local pressures (Prost 1968). As the history of education in Lavialle shows, however, parents generally find other means by which to influence the teachers.

In Lavialle, there has been a parent–teacher group (*La Coopérative scolaire* or School Cooperative), dedicated primarily to fundraising, for several years. A new type of parent participation in schooling was mandated by the Haby educational reform of 1975, which called for each French primary school to create an elected parent committee (*Le Comité de parents*). Lavialle's school elected its first parent committee in 1980. This group has had an uneven history ever since.

The school cooperative

The School Cooperative in Lavialle is a loose coalition of teachers and all families that has periodic parent–teacher meetings. Three meetings, organized and chaired by Henri Juillard, were held during the 1980–81 school year. Well attended by parents, the meetings lasted from about 8:30 in the evening until at least 11:00 p.m. Henri consulted parents during the meetings about such matters as the installation of new indoor toilets for the children, the renovation of the lunchroom, the school transport system's route and schedule, and fundraising activities. The teachers were particularly interested in enlisting parental support for fundraising efforts to aid the school's extra-curricular activities, such as a film series, the school Christmas party, and an exchange trip to Normandy.

There were two major fundraisers during the 1980–81 school year: a bingo game and a dance. The bingo game netted the School Cooperative over 4,000 francs (equivalent to about $1,000 in 1981). Parent–teacher meetings were often taken up with discussions about the dates, times, and arrangements for these activities. A lengthy discussion took place, for instance, about the types of prizes to be awarded for the bingo game.

The tone of these meetings was often informal and jovial, with lots of joking, especially among men. As in most public discourse in Lavialle, an attempt was made to avoid overt conflict and to pass over possibly controversial topics with a witty remark. Henri worked to keep discussion focused on practical and material issues at hand, avoiding topics that were potentially disruptive, such as his methods of teaching or summer camps (which he wanted children to attend and was working hard to convince parents about in less formal settings).

During the first six months of my fieldwork, these meetings did not accurately reflect the tensions that I was observing in relationships between the teachers and local families in other contexts, nor did they deal with the most important concerns of parents about their children's education. They constituted gatherings in which teachers orchestrated the agenda according to their perception of what they could reasonably get parents to agree upon. Parents showed their support for their children and their education by attending the meetings and working together on a limited basis to raise funds for the school and influence decisions about areas in which they were permitted to have some formal control.

Because the teachers initiated the meetings and set the tone, these meetings acted as ritualized occasions for the expression of their authority at the school and reinforced the general lack of institutionalized control over education that parents had. Parents were seated at their children's desks, places where many of them had not too long ago sat as pupils themselves, reminding them of their own often traumatic and harsh schooling experiences. Despite the teachers' attempts to control the situation of the meetings, however, parents did not passively and unquestionably yield to them.

Parent–teacher meetings usually ended when they did because of time and fatigue, not necessarily because the discussion had been spent, and their length reflected the active participation of parents in the discussions. Sometimes, it took a great deal of skill on the part of Henri and other mediators in the group to reach a consensus on a particular matter. At one point in the first meeting I attended, a woman turned to me with a smile and said: "In France, it takes a long time to reach a decision!" That so many parents wanted to attend and put in their two centimes' worth indicated interest and concern for the school.

Parent participation was also reflected in the high attendance rate. During a typical meeting, there were 34 parents and children present: seven couples, six mothers who came alone, two fathers who came alone, and two children accompanying their parents. Those present represented all but one family of the children in the primary school class and a total of 16 families (out of 22 for the whole school). Both teachers and the school aide, Lucette, were also there. Someone from each family attended at least one meeting during my observations from fall of 1980 to late 1981, although a stable core of people attended each time. Participation by farm and non-farm families was proportionate: ten of the fourteen farm families had at least one member present at the April meeting, and six out of the eight non-farm families were represented.

While there was no strong pattern of variation in participation between the farm and non-farm families, there were gender differences. Two-thirds of the parents present at the meetings were mothers, and seating patterns at the meetings reflected trends of public gender segregation in Lavialle. The meetings took place in the classroom of the older children, and parents sat at children's desks, while the teachers sat on top of desks or stood. Men tended to cluster at the right side of the room, near Henri Juillard's desk, while women clustered towards the left side of the room.

Couples who attended did not sit together, but with their own gender group.[5] Despite such spatial segregation of the sexes, however, women participated on an equal footing with men in discussions, voicing opinions and engaging in decisions independently from their husbands or other males. Although I did not make a formal count of speech frequency, I noted that while men were more likely to speak up, women did regularly voice opinions.

The difference between gender patterns in parent meetings in Lavialle and those in more urban, middle-class milieu is illustrated by the experience of a couple, originally from Lavialle, who had moved to a depopulated village near a large town in another district. Their daughter attended nursery school in the town, since this was not offered in the village. I was staying with them for a brief visit when the school's first parent meeting was called, and the wife wanted her husband to accompany her to the meeting. Since I was there to babysit, there was no practical restraint on his attendance. But he resisted, saying that he knew the meeting would be dominated by women. I mentioned to him that in Lavialle, many men attended the parent-teacher meetings. He responded, half jokingly, "In Lavialle, it is the men who are more resourceful (*debrouillards*); here, it is the women!" He eventually accompanied his wife, at her urging. The next morning, he told me that there had indeed been only a few men present, and that a handful of women (wives of the most influential men in the town) had dominated the discussion. My friends spoke with resentment and sarcasm of these women, and told me of instances where school functions sometimes had to be changed so as to not interfere with what they perceived to be frivolous social activities – such as tennis lessons.

The discomfort of these Lavialle natives in a more stratified, urban environment in which parental influence in primary education had been "feminized" by the middle classes helps to highlight the strength of the kindred and its role in education in Lavialle. In the bourgeois model of family life (LeWita 1988), mothers show concern for the upbringing and care for young children while fathers provide the economic support – a model harking back to Strumingher's analysis of nineteenth-century French schoolbooks mentioned in chapter 6. In Lavialle, where men and women jointly operate farms and work together, but where men dominate in the "public" sphere of politics and women in the "domestic" sphere of the household, both mothers and fathers are involved with early schooling. Both attend parent meetings, and families publicly interact as a unit with the school.

Primary education is connected to family strategies in Lavialle – with the family defined primarily in terms of the household and wider kindred, rather than the nuclear family. Male heads of households take an interest in their children's early education because control over socialization experiences is an important element in the overall strategies for the reproduction of the household and its patrimony. Men's participation in the school also signals the important political meaning of education in Lavialle. Although women are by no means passive followers of their husbands' leads in Lavialle, their participation in schooling activities is not independent of their gender roles. Women in Lavialle, especially in public situations, are expected to behave in less overt, more "modest" ways than men. Their behaviors in the private sphere of the household do not, however, necessarily conform to this model.[6]

The labelling of men in Lavialle as *debrouillard* by the young father who had moved away from the *commune* shows the importance of this concept to parental dealings with the school. In Lavialle, it is highly admired to be *debrouillard*, which, in this instance, means to be able to "deal with" and manipulate the teachers and school to one's own advantage. The use of this term in relation to parent meetings indicates, however, that this is a stressful situation, in which one must be on his/her guard. As will be remembered from my discussion of this concept in chapter 3, resourcefulness and cunning are most often applied to threatening situations in which one tries to cope ("make do"), and, if possible, get the upper hand ("make out").

The parent committee

In late November 1980, the parents of pupils in Lavialle's school elected their first Parent Committee, as mandated by the Haby Reform of 1975. Similar parent groups had already been established by previous reforms in French secondary schools. Under the Haby law, parents at each primary school were to elect a committee of at least two members, with the total size dependent upon the school enrollment level. Each committee was to meet with the teachers and director of the school at least three times per year. The committees were to be consulted on such matters as school rules, communication between families and teachers, nature classes, school transport, day care, lunch programs, extracurricular activities, and school hygiene (Réforme du système educatif 1980). By carefully circumscribing those matters with which the parent committee could concern itself, the Haby Reform ruled out any formal parental influence on instruction, the form and content of curriculum, grading, or homework. The classroom itself remained untouched by the parent committees.

This was the first time that parent participation, albeit narrowly defined, was given a formal place in the French educational system at the local level. The debate over the Haby Reform was intense at the national level in the late 1970s and early 1980s, particularly between parent associations, teacher unions, and the Ministry of Education. The Giscardian government saw the reform as a big step in the "democratization" of education. But leftist primary school teachers (and most are "Socialist") opposed the Reform for various reasons – in large part simply because it was the product of a moderate administration, but also because it threatened their power in the schools. Many did not readily implement the law. Some teachers felt that the Reform had not gone far enough in the direction of parental input, others that it gone too far in giving a voice to parents. In contrast to the teacher unions, most parent groups organized at the national level supported the parent committees. (See discussions in Coombs 1978; Delwasse 1980; Duclaud-Williams 1983.)

The Haby Reform called for the first elections of parent committees to take place in the fall of 1977. Teachers in Lavialle were late in implementing this reform, however, and nominations for the first elected parent committee in Lavialle did not take place until a parent–teacher meeting in the fall of 1980. The Juillards had waited to hold these elections until the start of their second year in Lavialle because, as Henri told me, he feared that they would open a can of worms that he would not be able to deal with during his first year. He wanted to assert his authority as director of the school, before allowing the parents any leverage which might come with this committee. The tension between parents and teachers in primary education in France is well illustrated by the Lavialle teachers' expression of their fear of parents in this instance.

When Henri Juillard began to raise the matter of the elections for a parent committee at the November 1980 parent–teacher meeting, parents were a bit reticent, but willing to put forward nominations. Two parents were to be elected, with two alternates, so that four names in all had to be presented. As it turned out, those nominated ran uncontested. The two men nominated were both non-farmers: one was a salesman (originally from a nearby *commune* and the son of farmers), the other was a plasterer/painter (from the district but not a Lavialle native, and the son of an agricultural laborer). It was agreed, at Henri's suggestion, that the plasterer/painter (a Socialist) would be helpful in plans for renovations at the school. The salesman, a Communist, was nominated by a Communist farmer. The two alternate members of the committee nominated were both male and native Laviallois farmers in the moderate political camp.

This reflected the type of political coalition between left and center present in the town council, whose members were, however, all farmers (except for the mayor, who was a retired insurance salesman of peasant origin).[7] There was little discussion over the nominations, and no open dissent.

When Henri explained that formal elections would have to be held, despite the seeming agreement over the candidates, several parents protested, asking why they could not all just vote right then and there with a show of hands. The need for a bureaucratic procedure to validate the committee was not self-evident to many parents. The balloting procedure sent home with children later that week displayed typical "officializing" discourse, as can be seen in the translated ballot instructions below. This document shows concern over sabotage of the elections in some communities, which prompted many parents in Lavialle to express their resentment of such implications. Despite some initial opposition, the vote was eventually taken and the Parent Committee formed without open disruption. Soon after the elections, Henri Juillard and the new electees cooperated in the supervision of renovations to the school lunchroom and in the installation of indoor toilets for the children.

Ballot instructions: Parent Committee elections (Fall 1980)

The elections will take place at the school on Friday, the 28th of November from 9 to 12 o'clock a.m.
The procedures for voting are the following:
–the parents may have only one vote per family
–in order to permit the most widespread participation, absentee ballots are
   authorized. The ballot, having neither words erased nor crossed out and written over, must be inserted in the clean envelope displaying no inscription or identification mark. This sealed envelope is then slipped into another envelope, also sealed, on which are written on the front the address of the school and the label "Elections au Comité de Parents" and on the back the last and full name of the voter as well as his address and signature. All votes not carrying the above mentioned labels will be declared invalid.

–the ballots are to be mailed, with the correct postage or handed by the voter
   himself to the Director of the school before the time of vote counting. Those ballots received or handed in after the closure of the polls will be declared invalid.

The ballot as well as the envelopes are attached to this notice.

During the course of 1980–81 school year, a slow evolution took place during parent–teacher meetings, whereby parents became more outspoken in their views, usually rallying behind one of the elected Parent Committee members.

Events of 1980 and 1981

Schooling became entangled with both local and national politics in Lavialle during 1981. Parent-teacher relationships during this period had clear links to historically based educational strategies among local families, but were also bound up with contemporary socio-cultural and political changes. Conflict reflected a subtle mixture of resistance and accommodation to the teachers and school, but also expressed local political processes. Parents were trying to influence education, but were also trying to influence local politics. I will first give a brief chronology of this period, and then turn to specific cases of dispute between teachers and parents.

During their first year in Lavialle, as I have already indicated, the Juillards attempted to keep a low profile, in order to avoid hostility from the community. There were few areas of conflict surrounding the school that year, and both teachers and the families seem to have spent the time observing and assessing each other. During the fall of 1980, which marked the beginning of the teachers' second year, relationships were, on the surface, cordial between parents and teachers. Several fathers and a few mothers used the *tu* form of address with the teachers, which is a mark of familiarity in France. In late November 1980, the first elections of the Parent Committee were held, and, at first, all went smoothly.

During the spring of 1981, the teachers and parents worked together on fundraising projects and organized two exchange trips with a primary school in Normandy. A few disputes arose during the 1980–81 school year, but relations between teachers and parents remained overtly civil in public. By the fall of 1981, however, relations between the teachers and parents had markedly deteriorated, and one parent–teacher meeting became the scene for verbal attacks on Henri. Many of those who had been on a first-name basis and used the familiar *tu* form of address with the teachers when I arrived in Lavialle were by then using the formal *vous* form of address and referring to the teachers as Monsieur and Madame Juillard.

The most obvious root of conflict during this period was party politics. The impending presidential elections in the spring of 1981 contributed to an overall climate of discord and strain in Lavialle. Lavialle is not emphatically split along political lines in non-election times. People of differing political party affiliation marry, join voluntary associations together and participate jointly in various social activities. It is mostly during elections that political divisions surface.

The presidential elections were to be followed in the spring of 1982 by town council elections and the appointment of a new mayor in Lavialle, which intensified the local significance of the national elections. The incumbent mayor, a supporter of Valèry Giscard d'Estaing, had been mayor during most of the post-war period and was planning to retire from office. A new coalition had to be formed. Left and center-right divisions, which had not been highly visible in everyday life before, surfaced in the spring of 1981. People who usually had good relations stopped talking to each other because of political differences. Rumors circulated about closed-door maneuvering by political leaders in the region, and of bribes offered to supporters.

This volatile atmosphere changed after Mitterand was elected, and by the summer of 1980 everyday social relations among the Laviallois began to resume on a more normal basis. However, the victory by Socialist François Mitterand had not been easily accepted by the moderates who had supported Giscard d'Estaing. The majority vote in Lavialle had gone to Giscard (as he is referred to by the Laviallois), although Mitterand had received substantial support. Out of 338 voters in the final vote, 199 voted for Giscard and 128 for Mitterand. With the Socialists now in power at the national level, a complete turn around had occurred in the power structure of Lavialle. The Socialist and Communist *minority* in Lavialle was suddenly aligned with a Socialist national government (which in France means access to sources of state subsidies and other political favors), including the leadership of the centralized educational system.

During the elections, the teachers had exhibited what was criticized as partisan behavior among many Laviallois. The Juillards openly discussed their Socialist views with two young non-farmers, also Socialist, who then shared these with others in the *commune*. One of these men, in particular, was seen as irresponsible in Lavialle and not considered to be a model of discretion. Henri Juillard was seen by many inhabitants (including other Socialists and Communists) as having been very foolish in discussing his political views with these men. Later, when Mitterand won the election, the teachers openly celebrated his victory with a few leftists in the *commune*. This gesture, especially for schoolteachers (supposedly impartial civil servants), was viewed as a grave offense in Lavialle, and was frequently used later on to criticize Henri and Liliane by moderates. The Laviallois know that many French primary teachers adhere to the political Left in France, and it was not the views of teachers that parents resented so much as what they perceived to be their openly partisan behavior.

During the period under consideration here, subtle resistance of parents to the teachers turned to open confrontation, although cooperation in some matters accompanied resistance in others. The complexities involved in relationships of power and resistance are clearly illustrated through several incidents that occurred after the elections. These involved the school grounds, the lunchroom, and the classroom. The surface content of the disputes was, for the most part, of a seemingly trivial nature, but carried a heavy symbolic load. These incidents shed light on the contexts and ways in which "everyday" resistance can be transformed into open confrontation.

Cases of dispute
The school grounds
During the summer of 1981, after the election of Mitterand and before the explosion of outright confrontation between parents and teachers, an incident concerning the school grounds signalled the beginning of conflict. When the teachers were away on their month-long summer vacation, a group of fathers spent an entire day cleaning up the grounds surrounding the school. They were led by the two alternate Parent Committee members who were politically moderate. This gesture was accompanied by harsh rhetoric proclaiming that the teachers took no interest in the schoolyard and that it was very dirty. One of my neighbors, a middle-aged woman, expressed support for the parents, saying that "it really is very dirty around the school."

This highly visible act (since the school is located in the center of Lavialle) had important cultural meanings. The clean-up was undertaken without consulting the teachers, and clearly involved a very personal attack on them. At the same time, it reflected pride in the school as a local building, and as part of the community. The former teachers, so often criticized in other matters, were said to have taken good care of *l'école*, and had planted flowers in the schoolyard. The new teachers, it was claimed, did not respect the school building (and, by extension, the *commune*). The parents' action was a way of saying that the school belonged to Lavialle, not to the Socialist party or to the teachers.

This was in many ways a delayed response to the teachers for their overt support of Mitterand. By making their political views explicit during the election and at the time of Mitterand's victory, the teachers had violated local norms of modesty and prudence associated with keeping such beliefs to oneself. Moreover, because they were supposed to be impartial, objective "civil servants" who transcended national party politics, by making their political views so explicit the teachers undermined their own authority at the school.

The gesture of cleaning the grounds when the teachers were away represented an attempt by families to exert a claim over the school, in opposition to that of the state and the teachers. It reflected a fear of increased
loss of control over the school, particularly in light of the changing
national government and the teachers' overt identification with the
Socialist party and new President. That this challenge was carried out in
the teachers' absence indicates the parents' reticence to confront them
openly. That it was performed in a highly visible way for fellow Laviallois,
however, shows that it signalled an attempt by these fathers to garner
support for their opposition from other inhabitants of the *commune*. This
example illustrates the ways in which Lavialle's school had become a community symbol, with the Laviallois portraying themselves as its rightful
caretakers. This certainly is a long way from parental "indifference" to the
school in Lavialle a century before. It also, however, indicates that parents
still do not passively accept the authority of teachers.

The lunchroom

Overt parental opposition to the teachers moved within the walls of the
school by the fall of 1981, and was no longer confined to the outer
grounds. The lunchroom had been the arena for disputes between parents
and teachers before in Lavialle, and again became a source of tension at
this time. Party politics again played a role in the dispute.

The lunchroom is the sphere within the school over which parents have
the most direct control, since the hot lunch served there is supported by
parental fees. Lucette, a local young woman who prepared lunch, was
paid by the *commune*, although the meal plans and organization of the
lunchroom were supervised by the teachers. The lunchroom is an
ambiguous zone, since it was not under the jurisdiction of the national
system and there are no official directives for its operation. It differs in
this way from the classroom, officially considered to be completely out of
bounds to parents.

During an explosive parent–teacher meeting in the fall of 1981, some
parents voiced the opinion that children should no longer be asked to help
Lucette (whose father was an outspoken Communist in Lavialle) with the
dishes. They argued that she was paid for her labor and should not depend
on small children to help her. The usual routine at lunchtime was for children to stay behind and help Lucette clear the table on a rotating basis,
while the others went off to the playground. The teachers felt strongly that
this was a good system, which instilled a cooperative spirit and sense of
responsibility among the children. As I will show in chapter 9, it was also

an important time for the shaping of resistance to the culture of the school among children.

During the course of this discussion and debate, one of the alternate members of the elected Parent Committee (a political moderate) made the statement that François Mitterand wasn't going to come and wash the dishes! This remark, which provoked a great deal of laughter among all the parents, implied that Mitterand could not come to bail the teachers and Lucette out of this situation. The attitude that children should not help with dishes did not spring from an overly protective posture toward children and work in Lavialle, since children are encouraged to carry out chores at home and on the farm. It was, rather, an attack on the teachers and on Lucette and her family for their association with them. The parents stood by their refusal to have their children help Lucette, and the practice ended shortly thereafter.

Two other lunchroom issues were raised at this same meeting. First, some parents said that they felt older children should pay more than younger children, since they ate more. Bernard, the school van driver and a young farmer, countered this, saying that since the young ones would eat more when they got older, it would all even out in the end. This dispute had not been resolved when I left Lavialle.

Finally, the member of the elected Parent Committee who was a plasterer/painter led an attack on the tradition of giving potatoes to the school. This practice had a long history in Lavialle, since potatoes are plentiful and a staple in the local diet. Many parents who agreed with him said that the potatoes donated were rotting and not being used. Others voiced their suspicions and resentment that the teachers had used the potatoes for their own consumption. It was agreed by all parents that they would no longer donate potatoes to the school.

All of these examples from the lunchroom represent an attempt by the parents to express their opposition to the teachers, and to exert some control over events in the school, especially in that arena in which they already had some leverage. The ways in which washing dishes, lunch payment, and donating potatoes were phrased reflect a refusal on the part of parents to cooperate wholly with teachers. These issues used economic metaphors to express resistance. The refusal to donate children's labor to the school in the form of dish-washing, and parental farm labor in the form of potatoes, shows the important value of manual labor and its power among Lavialle families. The teachers' control over the mental labor of their children was not openly questioned, and discontent with schooling was voiced through more tangible issues of manual labor. In the issue of lunch payment, an economic metaphor is again used. This issue challenged the teachers through an overt discussion of money given to the school by Lavialle families that was threatened to be withheld.

In their attempts to stop children from helping Lucette in the lunchroom, parents were unaware of the ways in which contact with Lucette actually helped the children forge a local identity. For them, labor at school was labor for the teachers. During this time of political factions in Lavialle, made explicit because of the Presidential elections, Lucette, as the daughter of a left-wing farmer, was associated with the teachers, also left-wing, by more moderate parents. In this case, left–right political divisions were cutting across local–state divisions.

It should be noted, however, that almost all parents were involved in one of these disputes with the teachers. It was not only moderate or right-wing parents who challenged the teachers. Socialist and Communist parents also argued against giving potatoes to the school, and some also sided against the teachers in the case of the dishes. No parents openly supported or defended the teachers against other Laviallois, no matter what their political views.

The classroom

The classroom has rarely been the subject of public discussion between parents and teachers in Lavialle because, as I have repeatedly stressed, it falls under the jurisdiction of the national system and outside of local control in France. Parents privately criticized the teachers and some of their methods, and the teachers were aware of parental disapproval of certain aspects of the curriculum, but this was never openly expressed. In the same meeting at which the lunchroom became the focus of dispute, the classroom was also brought up by some parents. A few politically moderate parents remarked that they felt Socialist children were being treated better in school than were their own. This sparked a heated debate, and as one Socialist parent put it later, with some satisfaction, caused Henri Juillard's face to "turn completely white."

In addition to this direct display of tensions, several parents later acted outside of the meetings to express their concerns over the teachers' attempts to "hold back" their children from promotion to the next grade. Henri told me that the teacher before him had never flunked a student, but that he felt that this had been a mistake, and that the teacher had acted this way because he feared parental reprisals. Henri wanted to stand up to the parents. His position was that it was necessary to retain some children, since the former teacher had not prepared them to do well in middle school. Parents, however, interpreted Henri's flunking of children as due to his own failure to teach them. One mother placed her daughter in Catholic school when Henri refused to promote her to the next grade, and two other mothers threatened to do so, but never actually carried out their threats.

The threat to take children out of the school is one of the major weapons that parents can use against teachers. Lavialle's school is in a precarious position, and its existence is threatened unless the population remains stable and families continue to send children to public school. Families in Lavialle have some choice about where to send their children to school. They can, for instance, pay to send children to a Catholic school located forty miles away – attended by five primary school-age children from two Laviallois families in 1980 and 1981. Families who live in hamlets on the outskirts of Lavialle also have the option of sending children to public schools in neighboring *communes*, although none do so. Through these potential choices, parents wield some informal political leverage *vis-à-vis* the teachers, whose jobs are dependent upon a sufficient enrollment to keep both classes at Lavialle's school open. Parents have little say in what goes on in the school, but *can* choose whether or not to send their children to public school, especially if they have the financial means to board a child in private school. Threatening to withdraw their children from the school is an even greater form of influence over teachers for Lavialle families than the threat to withdraw their labor in the lunchroom.

Power and protest

Schooling has unquestionably come to be valued by families in Lavialle and is deeply entrenched in the life course. Because it has become such an important symbol of the *commune* as a collectivity, the Laviallois would immediately challenge any attempt to remove it. The educational strategies of local families do not entail a rejection of education, but, rather, are aimed at influencing the teachers in order to ensure that children have the types of educational experiences desired by parents. Parents want their children to acquire basic skills, especially in arithmetic, which are necessary to the operation of a modern farm. They generally shun modern, experimental methods, and want a curriculum that is "useful" and practical in day-to-day life. In this, they have retained a pragmatic approach to education reminiscent of earlier days of schooling in Lavialle.

Although the events of 1981 reflected continuity with past family strategies of influence over education, resistance to the school among families was intensified and came to the surface. This is due to several factors of change introduced during this period. In addition to the Presidential elections, already discussed, these include recent socio-economic changes in Lavialle and the arrival of a new teaching couple in the *commune*.

Lavialle was entering a period of re-adjustment during the early 1980's, having just emerged from the tremendous upheaval associated with the post-war period in terms of population loss and new farming technology. As has been described in earlier chapters, smaller farms have given way to larger farms, but an increasing number of young couples are enthusiastic about staying in the *commune* – due to early retirement incentives which give them more control over farms, the improved standard of living in farm households, and the decline in employment opportunities outside of Lavialle. Although there was a general spirit of optimism in Lavialle during the early 1980s in comparison with past decades, uncertainty about the future (with the acceleration of changes in agricultural technology and the increased role of the EEC) fueled parental anxiety about their children's education as well as the future of their own farms.

An added source of tension during this period was the arrival of two new teachers to the school. Not only were these teachers new, however, but they also brought a new "style" of teacher interaction with them, which vividly contrasted with that of the previous three sets of teachers. Whereas previous male teachers had adopted a stern yet "paternalistic" authority role, Henri used a more bureaucratic, impersonal style of authority, which was more diffident but less severe. Former female teachers took a "maternal" posture towards young children, but Liliane Juillard was less stereotypically "maternal" in her behavior. In contrast to the patron-client relationships previous teachers developed with families, the Juillards saw themselves as "specialists" who offered a service, that of education, to the *commune*. There was a striking contrast between their model of the role of teacher and that which the families of Lavialle had come to expect from previous teachers.

In addition, unlike their predecessors who, having themselves been raised in rural communities, felt pressures to maintain the "status quo," the Juillards were young suburbanites who adopted a relatively *innovative* style. They tried to introduce activities and programs of "enrichment" to Lavialle right from the start, and to project middle-class values. Their arrival in Lavialle coincided with the new educational reform, which they tried to implement, further fueling fears that they were trying to change schooling too rapidly. Former teachers did not try to introduce rapid changes, and had accepted what they called the *méfiance* (distrust or resistance) of the families as a fact of life.

Parental resistance to the school made use of ambiguities and subtleties hinging on shifting notions of insider–outsider relationships that are part of local social life. Parents appealed to various and shifting frames of reference in their confrontations with the teachers. The school grounds incident represented the manipulation of an opposition between the *commune* and the school by politically moderate fathers who wished to gather resistance to the Socialist teachers. In the lunchroom disputes, parents manipulated social divisions within Lavialle. The case of the dishes called upon both a local vs. national opposition (Mitterand and the national government vs. Lavialle), and internal political divisions associated with households. Lucette's family was, for instance, criticized for its alliance with the teachers. The cases of potatoes and payment for lunch made use of the local system of age grading (potentially pitting older and younger parents against each other) as well as opposition between parents as a group and the teachers. Internal political and kin divisions were also used in overt confrontations with the teachers concerning treatment of children in the classroom, and church–state opposition was manipulated by parents in order to pressure the teacher into promoting children to the next grade. These incidents show parents making use of a variety of group affiliations and ideological stances to pressure teachers and show their dissatisfaction with the school. At the same time, however, local tensions between competing factions in Lavialle were being expressed and worked out through the medium of the school.

That much of parental resistance to the school and new teachers was expressed in terms of national-level politics cannot be read primarily on the basis of ideological differences between the Left and the Right in Lavialle. The use of national politics in disputes surrounding the school is best understood when certain factors about local-level politics, local–national relationships, and schooling in Lavialle are taken into account. First of all, local politics in Lavialle is profoundly connected to kinship;[8] that is, people vote according to family traditions, and certain households are politically dominant in the town council. Husbands and wives do not, however, always vote in the same way. There is no direct connection between the ideological content of national-level politics and the uses and meanings of politics in Lavialle. When asked to articulate the policies of their own parties, for example, many of the Laviallois were at a loss. The political Left in Lavialle has, however, represented a party of the opposition at the local level for a long time, due to control of local government by the moderate and conservative majority. Its adherents defined themselves, before the elections, as particularly resistant to the state and its bureaucrats and politicians.

Neither does local educational politics in Lavialle reflect a strong division between secularism and religious affiliation, as it does in some parts of France. Everyone in Lavialle is Catholic and participates in religious rituals. In general, political moderates in Lavialle tend to send their children to the Catholic middle school more often than do others. However, the mother who took her children out of Lavialle's school and placed them in the Catholic school to avoid grade retention was leftist in political orientation. Given the importance of family farming and land ownership in Lavialle, and the strong history of secular education there, political struggles in Lavialle reflect competition and rivalry over land and family status more often than over religion.

In the cases of dispute described above, national elections became a vehicle for the expression of opposition to the school among local parents. Dissatisfaction with the school and new teachers was indirectly shown through the metaphor of politics. It is rare for parents to express opposition and hostility toward teachers openly. The climate of tension surrounding the presidential elections provided a license for open conflict that would not otherwise have occurred. Lavialle parents do not have a ready vocabulary for openly confronting the school concerning their lack of power, since the control of schooling has been so obviously in the hands of the state for over a century, regardless of the political party in power. For the most part, criticisms have been phrased through a gender idiom, as teachers were seen to exhibit foreign gender roles, and through a vocabulary of the individual personalities of teachers – that they were "mean," for example. The Presidential elections, which accelerated the open expression of conflicts in other matters, combined with the newly elected Parent Committee, provided parents with an easy handle with which to enter into open conflict with the teachers. "Everyday resistance" gave way to overt forms of conflict in this climate.

Through their direct confrontations with the teachers, the parents did not only show their resistance to the school, they also used the school as an arena for local political processes as had been the case for the northern hamlet school in previous decades. The Parent Committee and parent–teacher meetings became vehicles for the expression of local political conflict between the Left and the Right. Young men with political aspirations used issues surrounding schooling to begin to gather followings among other parents. This behavior was precipitated by the impending town council elections and facilitated by the formal leadership role for parents afforded by the elected Parent Committee. Like the Youth Club, the Parent Committee created a political field in which aspiring leaders could gather a following. Formal politics in Lavialle is dominated by middle-aged farmers, those who have assumed management of their families' farms. Younger men, like many of the fathers of children at the school, have traditionally tested their political expertise through informal associations, such as the Youth Club or JAC in Lavialle. The new Parent Committee became a vehicle for local political maneuvering in the wider context of the parent–teacher meetings.

The cases of dispute show that a vocabulary of national politics was used for local ends: both to oppose new teachers and to further local political goals. When a young plasterer (doubly excluded from local political power since he was neither a landowner nor farmer, and was young) took up the cause of potatoes in the lunchroom, he was not only helping to shape resistance to the school, but was also forwarding his own political aspirations. When Moderate parents claimed that the teachers were favoring Socialists' children, they were drawing the lines of party affiliation in anticipation of the upcoming town council meetings at the same time that they were opposing the teachers and school.[9]

The events of 1980–81 in Lavialle reflect the ways in which the Laviallois assert local cultural identity in the face of socio-cultural change. The resistance of the parents to the teachers reflected not total resistance either to change or to education, but, rather, an attempt to influence these in order to control the course of change and its effects on the *commune*. Parents no longer resist schooling altogether, but neither do they passively acquiesce to the teachers.

Although many of the issues that became objects of dispute had little to do with the formal aspects of the curriculum or with what goes on in the classroom, this does not mean that they had nothing to do with educational issues. These disputes demonstrate an attempt on the part of the parents to have some control over the discourse about power and identity in Lavialle. It was a way of flexing the collective muscles of the *commune* in order to show the teachers that there were local sources of power that could rise up to challenge state power. The parents have little voice in formal education, and, thus, express their power through a different medium.

The primary school in Lavialle is an arena for conflict, both between the *commune* and the state, and among local families. Despite their lack of official influence in educational decision-making at the local level, the families of Lavialle have adopted active strategies (both of resistance and of cooperation) with the school in order to secure their own goals and interests. Parents participated in several fundraising activities with the teachers at the same time that they were shaping resistance to them. They also willingly supported the renovations to the school building. Their behaviors show the operation of family strategies in Lavialle, and the ways in which educational strategies are diverse expressions of overall economic and social concerns regarding the perpetuation of the kindred and household.

Schooling in Lavialle is not just about the futures of individual children in nuclear families, with parents pressing for the educational advancement of their own children, as is often the case in middle-class settings (Lareau 1989; Allatt 1993; LeWita 1988). It is important to remember that the Laviallois see themselves primarily as members of kindreds and farm households, rather than as individuals. Therefore, the school is deeply entrenched in a system of local politics and the status ranking of households within the *commune*. This feature of schooling tempers the association of the school with state forms of power, and also tempers its hegemonic role in undermining local cultural meanings. These two processes – one of local power, the other of national power – co-exist, helping to shape the modes of compliance and resistance to the state adopted by Laviallois families and children.

The cases of dispute in Lavialle show that schools are not just about education; they are about power in a much more generalized sense. Classrooms usually form the bread and butter of educational analyses, but in this book the classroom has been relegated to a section of the final chapter and is viewed as but one site among many for the articulation of power and meaning about education. I will continue the theme of the school in Lavialle as an intersection of national and local sources of power in the next chapter.

9

Everyday life at school

Children in Lavialle must adjust to new rules, meanings, behavioral codes, and symbols of authority and power when they enter school. At home, they learn to be members of families. At school, they learn how to be both French and Laviallois – and begin to form a view of themselves in relation to people outside of the local region. Schooling has existed in Lavialle for over a century and, although the Laviallois do not wholly identify with the values of the school, it would be misleading to see home and school in purely antithetical terms. They are best seen in relation to each other. As Hope Leichter has emphasized, "it is not sufficient merely to look at the family's values as compared to the school's values at a given moment in time. One might rather look at the way in which communication between family and school serves to modify each" (1979:21).

Lavialle's school, like most schools, tacitly undermines local cultural meanings and works to reproduce forms of social stratification. Its teachers reinforce the chasm between urban middle-class life and rural life in Lavialle. Through subtle and not-so-subtle ways, they criticize Lavialle families and their mode of life, justifying their low status. At the same time, however, the families and children of Lavialle have developed modes of resisting these messages. The pupils in Lavialle's primary school undermine the "symbolic violence" (Bourdieu and Passeron 1990) of the school through active strategies of peer group solidarity and passive strategies of resistance to teachers.

Schoolchildren in Lavialle do not exhibit an outright rejection of schooling, and girls are more cooperative with the school than are boys. For all children, going to school has to do with growing up in Lavialle, and it is, in many ways, a part of local culture. Many of the pupils in Lavialle's school have parents and grandparents who went there when they were chil-

184

Rites of passage

dren, which instills an important sense of continuity. Children realize that schooling is an expected part of their lives, and an institution through which all members of the community have passed. Younger children look forward to the day when they will become "big kids," and be able to attend school. Many children live in isolated hamlets and enjoy being with friends at school, and children are also eager to learn to read and write at school. Even though it is part of a highly centralized educational system, Lavialle's school has important local meanings. But schooling is more than a place to meet friends and learn the three Rs. Lavialle's school is an important place for the negotiation of social and cultural identity, and the construction of relationships between family, community, and state. It is around these processes that relations of power and resistance are shaped in Lavialle.

Educational policy and practice

Lavialle's school is co-educational and has two classrooms. One is for preschool education, and the other is for the primary school. Henri and Liliane Juillard, introduced in the previous chapter, taught at the school during the year of my fieldwork. There were twenty-eight pupils enrolled in Lavialle's school during the 1980–81 school year, ranging in age from three to twelve.

Like all French primary schools at the time, Lavialle's school in 1980–81 had five levels (or grades), starting with CP (*cours préparatoire*), then CE1 and CE2 (the two levels of *cours élémentaire*), and, finally, CM1 and CM2 (the two levels of *cours moyen*). The primary school in Lavialle was housed in one classroom taught by Henri Juillard, who had 16 children in 1980–81 ranging in age from 6 to 12. Liliane Juillard taught the 12 youngest children (ages 3 to 5) in a combined nursery school/kindergarten class (*l'école maternelle* and *cours préparatoire*). The older children's class was referred to by both teachers and pupils as "the big kids' class" (*la classe des grands*); the younger children's as "the little kids' class" (*la classe des petits*). The teachers report directly to the office of the Departmental Inspection of primary schooling in Clermont-Ferrand, whose agents make periodic site visits to the school.

Many aspects of schooling are regulated by the national bureaucracy – with the intent of creating a uniform system. However, the myth of the French schoolchild studying the exact same thing at the exact same time as every other French schoolchild is definitely not true today. Teachers are given much leeway in their organization of the day, as long as they obey the general timetable of lessons each week. As W.D. Halls points out, "the many ministerial circulars they have theoretically to obey can be interpreted liberally, and often are" (1976:153).

The school year begins in mid-September and ends in late June.[1] School is in session each Monday through Friday from 9:00 a.m. until 4:30 p.m., except for Wednesday afternoons, which are set aside for those wishing to participate in religious instruction (given in the community center). Since only one van was used for school transportation at the time of my fieldwork, requiring three round-trips to transport all of the students, many children had to leave their houses earlier than 8:30 and returned after 5:00 p.m. All of the students who live in hamlets outside of the village of Lavialle spend their entire day in the school, and eat lunch in the school lunchroom; those in the village return home for ninety minutes at lunchtime. There were three breaks from the classroom during the school day: one twenty-minute recess in the morning, another one in the afternoon, and the lunch break which included a third recess period.

There was a definite rhythm and structure to the day at school, which children quickly learned. The children were not, however, "passive" recipients of discipline and control at school, and they devised ways of coping with the social form of schooling. The children's own educational strategies at school were an important component of the overall family strategies adopted in Lavialle to reinforce local identity and a commitment to local social life.

Social actors
The social actors in the everyday life of the school include the pupils, the teachers, the school van driver, and the school aide and cook. I have already profiled the teachers in chapter 8.

The pupils
Many families in Lavialle were introduced in chapter 4, and several of those mentioned had children in the school during my fieldwork. The pupils at Lavialle's school came from a variety of family situations, and their parents were from different age groups, political party affiliations, occupations, and kindreds. Nevertheless, they were all members of family groups with strong roots in the community. And they came from a fairly homogeneous population both culturally and economically, despite differences. Fourteen of the twenty-two families with children at the school were farmers. For a large part of the mid-twentieth century, there was a higher proportion (over 80%) of farm families represented at the school than is now the case. The rise of non-farmers in the general population of

Lavialle today returns the occupational diversity of the school population closer to its level at the turn of the century, which was 70%.

Except for five children who attended private Catholic schools, the children at Lavialle's primary school included all children of elementary-school age in Lavialle. Seventeen of the pupils were boys and eleven were girls, continuing the trend mentioned in chapter 7 for more boys than girls to attend the public school in Lavialle.

The van driver and school aide

Besides Henri and Liliane Juillard, two other adults worked at the school: a young man who drove the stationwagon transporting children to and from school, and a young woman who worked as cook and school aide. In 1980–81, they were both unmarried members of farm households in the village of Lavialle.

Bernard, the driver, was employed directly by the *commune*, since school transport is under its jurisdiction. He was about thirty years old in 1981, and a full-time farmer who lived with his parents on their farm. Well liked by parents and children, Bernard was getting to be known as a *vieux garçon* (a confirmed bachelor), since he was beyond the age at which most people marry.

Lucette, the school aide, was twenty years old in 1981. She had many duties during the day, which included preparing the noon meal for the children and teachers (for which she was paid by the parents), helping in the nursery-school class in the afternoons (paid by the state), and cleaning the school building after school (paid by the *commune*). Lucette's mother had worked in the lunchroom a few years earlier, and her sister-in-law cared for the Juillards' son during the day. Lucette was a hard worker who handled all of her responsibilities quite well. The children at the school were fond of her.

School culture: contexts for learning

An understanding of the experiences of Lavialle children at school cannot be confined to the classroom, since it represents only a partial view. There were three formal social settings in the school: the classrooms, the lunchroom, and the recess periods. There were also less formal, or liminal, contexts, such as the social and physical space in between the classroom and the lunchroom (i.e., the trip through the hallway leading to the lunchroom), and the time spent "hanging around" before and after school. Peer group interaction was most explicit and intense during recess and in the liminal contexts of schooling, and most controlled during lunchtime. The classroom provided a more mixed setting.

My participant-observation research in the school involved all of these contexts. In the classroom, I sat at the back and observed, usually taking notes. During recess and the free time before and after school, I attached myself to play groups and asked the children informal questions about their play. Because I lived at the school during the first few months of fieldwork, I had easy access to the children and their teachers, even on days when I did not observe in the classroom. During this time, I ate daily with the school in the lunchroom. After moving out of the school, I continued to return for periodic visits and observation.

The following description of the school is mostly concerned with its "hidden curriculum" – "the tacit teaching to students of norms, values, and dispositions that goes on simply by their being in and coping with the institutional expectations and routines of schools day in and day out for a number of years" (Apple 1979:14). This curriculum involves not only the tacit teaching associated with the aims of the school, however, but also peer socialization.

I start with the classrooms. Most of my classroom observations were carried out in the primary school classroom, since I was most interested during my fieldwork in the period of middle childhood. It is important, however, to frame the primary school class by looking at the children's previous experience in the nursery/kindergarten class.

The nursery/kindergarten class

The atmosphere in the nursery/kindergarten class, taught by Liliane Juillard, was much less structured, and discipline was more relaxed, than in the primary school class. A significant difference between the two classes was that peer group interaction was encouraged more consistently in the nursery/kindergarten. The children often did things as a group, and played together. In addition, Lucette, the school aide, was always present in the afternoons, representing a familiar local adult figure to the children. Activities included poetry recitation, painting, clay and beads. There was a small play house with a kitchen, dolls, etc., and group nature walks throughout the village were the norm when the weather was good. These activities were absent from the other class.

For the most part, Liliane's tone was gentle and positive when working with the children. There were exceptions to this, however, when she used ridicule and mockery to discipline. Once, when a three year old painted a picture using only black paint, Liliane tried to humiliate him in front of the rest of the class by saying that the picture was ugly. She admonished him with: "tu fait le clown" (you are being a clown) – an expression she often used to reprimand the children. She then ripped the picture up and threw it away, and the boy cried.

At other times, the influence of Lucette, the school aide, counteracted efforts to encourage "free expression" on Liliane's part. During another painting session, when children were asked to paint pictures of the sea, Lucette demonstrated to one little girl (her niece) the "proper" way to draw a stereotypical picture of the ocean, a ship, and the sun – most likely the way she learned to do so herself. Since little children in Lavialle had never seen the ocean, this was a particularly striking example of the social form of schooling – in this case, school art – being reproduced with little reference to local culture.

The transition from the nursery/kindergarten class to the primary school class marks an abrupt change in children's lives. During their first few years of schooling, children are exposed to various games and "fun" activities that are absent from home life, where there are few deliberate attempts to have "fun," since work and play are not clearly separated on a farm. Then, when the children enter the primary school class, they are placed in an atmosphere of serious learning, which depends upon self-control and obedience to a greater extent than before. They are evaluated according to standards which are often confusing to them. Moreover, they must adjust to a switch from a more gentle approach in the nursery/kindergarten class to Henri Juillard's more formal, impersonal, and critical teaching style. The contrast between nursery school and primary school is great throughout French education, but it is intensified in Lavialle since the two classes are conducted side by side in the same building.

Important lessons that socialize the child into the school form are imparted in nursery school, however. Children learn self-control, the role of the pupil, and peer relations. They also, however, begin to see themselves as part of an age grade in Lavialle – a first step in their realization of sources of identity beyond the household and kindred. Going to school, even for the younger children, marks the beginning of a symbolic understanding of Lavialle as a social unit, through their association with other children from Lavialle.

The primary school classroom
The content and timetable of lessons in French primary education are outlined in national policy documents. At the time of my fieldwork in Lavialle, the system was set up according to a timetable mandated in 1969 called "le tiers temps pedagogique." Its three major phases were: (1) French and arithmetic; (2) history, art, and social sciences, which, along

with other subjects, were referred to as "les activités d'éveil" (curiosity-awakening activities); and (3) physical education. In general, the first two subjects (French and arithmetic) were to be taught in the mornings, and the others in the afternoons. (See Halls 1976:82–4; Lewis 1985; and Vincent 1980.)[2]

Henri Juillard closely followed this curriculum for the most part. Mornings and early afternoons were devoted to arithmetic and French, and the rest of the day was spent on other lessons. The tone and format of the class changed from morning to afternoon, so that the first two subjects of arithmetic and French were taught in a more formal manner than were social studies and art. The class was divided among levels for arithmetic and French, but worked together for the afternoon activities.

Henri, called "Monsieur le maître" (Mr. Teacher) by the children, had organized the seating in his class into eight pairs of desks, with a girl and a boy in each pair. These were arranged into three rows, with the CM level children to the left of the room and the CE level children to the right. There were blackboards at the front of the class, and a small television overhead to the right. The teacher's desk was placed at the side, facing the students' desks. Some bookcases and other equipment were at the rear of the room. The classroom had an airy atmosphere, due to its high ceilings and the large windows which occupied most of the two longest walls. Through these windows, fields, passing tractors, and daily activities on nearby farms were in full view of the children and their teacher during the day.

The beginning of the school day was marked by a ritualized change of clothing. When the children arrived at school in the morning, they changed from their shoes or boots into slippers which were kept at school. In general, their clothing was casual and most girls wore slacks and overalls, as did the boys. Some of the children put small frocks over their clothing before entering the classroom. Their teacher often wore a white coat in class (similar to those worn by doctors or lab technicians).

Because Henri had four different grade levels to work with, he used a technique of switching back and forth among groups while teaching arithmetic and French. He would usually teach a lesson to one level, while the others read or worked out problems on their own. During a typical morning session, he began with the CM group working on French verb conjugations and the CE working on arithmetic. He helped the CE group work out some mathematical problems on the board while the CM group worked at their desks. Then, he got the CE group to do independent problems at their desks while he introduced a new verb form to the CM group. When students had finished their independent work, they took a school library book to the rear of the classroom, and sat on the floor to read. Henri's teaching style in handling the different age levels was reminiscent of the work of an orchestra conductor, and he showed a great facility for moving back and forth between the groups.

French and arithmetic lessons were taught with a serious and often severe tone. Henri offered little praise to children when they gave a right answer, and levelled harsh criticism for wrong answers. He would mock and ridicule students, who were expected to work hard in order to arrive at right answers. The emphasis in these lessons was on the individual learner, but the wider peer group was an essential source for ridicule from which the teacher attempted to draw. Although Henri taught the class as a group, each student was responsible for his or her answer independently, and there was no pairing of students to work on problems of arithmetic and French. His criticisms were usually aimed at individual students, rather than at the class as a whole. An arithmetic lesson with the CE group illustrates the teaching method used.

The arithmetic lesson

The teacher began to work out problems at the board with the CE group. They had their red notebooks open on their desks. As he worked out a problem of subtraction, the children copied it into their notebooks. After about 10 minutes of this activity, the teacher asked them to put away their notebooks in their desks and to bring out their slates. He distributed chalk.

The teacher then put a new problem on the board. He told the children that they were to work it out in their heads, write only the answer on their slates, and then hide it (either with their hands or by turning it over). Then, when he gave the signal they were to hold up their slates for him to see. He told them that they were to write clearly in the middle of the slate so that he could see well.

As he continued to write a problem on the board, the teacher told the children to "pay attention." Then, after giving them a few seconds to work it out, he shouted "OK, show them!" ("Montrez!") while banging an eraser on the blackboard as the signal. The children held up their slates, each anxious to see if he or she had gotten the right answer. The teacher looked at each slate in turn, saying either "yes" or "no" to each child, without other elaborating remarks. To one young boy, however, who consistently had problems with this activity, he was sarcastic. Once, when the child gave a wrong answer, he said only, "You call that an operative?" with no explanation or help.

About ten problems were worked out in this manner. At one point towards the end, the boy who was having trouble succeeded with a particularly difficult problem. The teacher only said "yes" in response to his correct answer, with no praise. When the children had finished with the problems, the teacher asked them to raise their hands to indicate the number of errors they had gotten. (They had been keeping score on their slates.) They were to raise their hands as he called out "all those with one error," "all those with two errors," etc. Again, no comments of praise or criticism accompanied this accounting. Afterwards, the teacher said only "OK," and asked them to put away their slates. They opened their notebooks and were started on some new problems, while he turned his attention to the CM group.

This lesson emphasized speed, quick thinking, and accuracy, in addition to its explicit intent of teaching arithmetic. Moreover, the children's ability to perform became known to both other children and the teacher, since the number of errors was made public. The emphasis was, thus, on individual performance in the context of a group audience. The teacher made no effort to coax the right answers from the students; it was each child's responsibility to come up with it on his or her own. This arithmetic lesson resembled a race, a sporting event, with its banging of the eraser on the blackboard and "ready, get set, go . . ." tone. It assumed a shared value of performing well in such a situation, and encouraged competition among peers.

The afternoon activities (Plate 7), in contrast to the morning lessons, were introduced in a more relaxed atmosphere, and often involved projects on which the children worked in groups. The children appeared to be more at ease, and, whereas they often whispered when talking to their teacher during the French and arithmetic lessons, they spoke in normal tones in the afternoons. A lesson from one afternoon shows the contrast between arithmetic/French and the *activités d'éveil*. This was a lesson on the train, in preparation for a trip to Normandy which the children were to take.

The train lesson

The teacher brought out a booklet about trains, copies of which were distributed among the children. These were publications of the SNCF (the national train system). He reviewed the booklet, showing that it told about the history of trains, different types of trains, and the types of things that one finds on a train. During this, the class was very eager and attentive. Several children left their desks and approached the teacher in order to better see the pages he was discussing and to make spontaneous comments. There was no discouragement of this behavior on his part. He showed photos of trains and discussed them.

The children were then told to take out their large loose leaf notebooks (the ones used for such activities). They were instructed to cut out certain photos specified by the teacher from the booklets. As they cut them out, the children chattered among themselves, checking on each other's progress and giving suggestions. Older children helped younger children.

Then the teacher told them how to arrange the photos in the notebooks. They were to paste them in. Titles, photos, and then captions would be placed in the notebooks. He began to write captions on the board for them to copy in their notebooks. At one point, he was asked to explain the phrase *le banlieu parisien* (Paris suburbs) when writing a caption about suburban trains – which he did.

Plate 7   *Children in the classroom.* Boys and girls sit while their teacher demonstrates a lesson in the afternoon. A poster on the wall encourages children to get fresh air. The children are seated in male/female pairs at wooden desks. This is a photo of the older children, in the primary classroom.

During the lesson, two older boys began to tease a younger boy about the way he was working, but a fourth boy reproached them and told them to leave him alone.

There was little criticism or tension during this lesson, as there had been during the arithmetic lesson. The atmosphere here was more relaxed, in that children were allowed to talk, to stand up, and to participate more spontaneously. This lesson did not involve right or wrong answers, as did the lesson in arithmetic. However, it did involve right and wrong ways to do things when carrying out instructions. The most important implicit lessons in this activity on trains were about remembering what had been explained, following directions, classifying knowledge, and neatness. The emphasis on group activities, in which the whole class participates, was, however, more in tune with Laviallois notions of peer solidarity than the individualistic bias of the arithmetic and French lessons.

It was during the afternoon that physical education took place (Plate 8). The students were taught calisthenics and had relay races. These activities

Plate 8   *Physical education in the playground.* The older children perform calisthenics outside toward the back of the playground. Two dairy farms lie just beyond the fence of the school, and are a constant reminder to the children of family life while they are at school. There was no play or sports equipment at the school, other than balls and old tires. One of the old outhouses can be seen at the far right of the photo. These were replaced by indoor plumbing for the children in 1981.

took place, for the most part, outside on the playground. Most of the subjects that the teacher chose for afternoon activities had to do with things unfamiliar to the children. The perspective adopted was usually that of an urban one. There were lessons on such subjects as: hygiene through the ages, cultural geography, and summer camps, as well as a series of lessons on the train. Once, when an educational television program on Mali was shown to the class, the teacher emphasized the differences between French urban society and this rural agricultural setting, rather than pointing out similarities between Lavialle and the village shown. The school newspaper, initiated in the spring of 1981 and sold to local inhabitants, did involve the children to some degree with their local milieu. But even in this case, the subjects covered were all suggested by the teacher, and the children worked closely under his supervision while they produced the newspaper.[3]

Classroom resistance

At the same time that Henri attempted to impose social control and values of competition in the classroom, with any group work closely supervised, the children devised methods of coping with and resisting his efforts. They adopted classroom strategies of cooperative behavior among peers that allowed them to resist the teacher's attempts to socialize them in ways that conflicted with family-based forms of socialization. These strategies constitute "everyday forms of resistance" because they were not openly confrontational; rather, they were subtle forms of "passive" resistance.[4]

The dominant strategy that the children developed toward their teacher was one of behaving in an overtly passive manner while actively pursuing social ties and aid from peers. The children did not openly resist schoolwork, and tried to provide proper answers in class and to complete homework assignments. In many ways, however, they did no more than what was expected of them.

The children behaved in class as a *group*, through cooperative behaviors that undermined the teacher's authority and influence. For example, the children often helped each other with problems when the teacher would leave the room, and older students guided younger ones. Whenever possible, the children made sure that their own work conformed to that of their peers. Rarely did the children go to the teacher for help when they did not understand something; most often, it was to other students that they turned. This is understandable, since the teacher might have mocked a student who had not followed instructions properly. From the child's perspective, the safest route was to rely on peers. Through this, the teacher's model of the individual learner competing with his peers for achievement was constantly undermined. Yet, Henri Juillard can also be seen as an agent in the process of reinforcing peer solidarity, since his behavior discouraged children from approaching him as individuals.

Two of the children's speech behaviors illustrate their passive resistance to the teacher. The first was their use of the third person pronoun (*on* or one) to refer to themselves, rather than the first person singular (*je* or I). This use of a more passive voice is common among inhabitants of Lavialle, who, as was discussed in chapter 3, use the *on* form to connote both "I" and "we." This speech form allows for a vagueness of meaning emphasizing the group rather than the individual. In the classroom, it subverted the emphasis on individual learning and achievement. The teacher often tried to correct the children in their use of this form. For example, he once asked a pupil who used the *on* form: "Why do you say *on*? Was it not you alone who did it? Come now, say *je*." In this case, Henri was trying to get the child to substitute the more individualistic "je" for the more inclusive and vague "on." Since the Laviallois highly value those who are "simple," modest, and who do not put on airs, for them the use of the first person, which accents the individual and his/her actions, is discouraged. The children were therefore caught between two linguistic codes, one at home and one at school. By using the more common "on," they resisted the school's code.

The children's habit of whispering, especially marked during the morning lessons, constituted another form of passive resistance. When they spoke in the presence of the teacher, either among themselves or directly to him, children whispered – seeming to adopt a posture of timidity and respect. They had learned to whisper from observing other children at the school. Although this behavior appeared to be passive, it had the effect of strengthening group ties among the children (all whispering) versus the teacher. Their whispering was discouraged by the teacher, who often asked his pupils to speak up and remarked to me that he found this behavior highly annoying. Whispering in class and using the *on* speech form were both cultural mechanisms pointing toward group, rather than individual, identity.

The lunchroom
The lunchroom was even more explicitly formal and ritualized than the classroom. At noontime, after being dismissed from class, the older children walked in single file upstairs to the lunchroom, speaking in whispers and waiting at the door until their teacher gave them permission to enter. The younger children then arrived in pairs of girls and boys, hand in hand, and also were required to wait at the door until given permission to enter the room.

The seating arrangement involved a separate table for the teachers, Lucette and me (when I was present); and three tables joined into a U-shape which opened towards the adults' table, where the children sat. As the children entered the room, each would take his or her cloth napkin from a container and be seated. At each place, Lucette would already have placed a slice of bread and a first course. The children began eating almost immediately upon entering, pouring themselves some grenadine mixed with water from the pitcher to drink. All of this was to be done in near silence.

The teachers did not address the children during the meal unless it was to discipline them. Lucette was responsible for the children during lunchtime, as part of her job as aide, and she would deal with any problems that arose among the children. As she served the meal and moved about their table, she would report back to Liliane about those children who were not eating enough (usually one of the younger children). Periodically, one of the teachers would rap upon the head table and tell the children to be more quiet ("Doucement!").

During our own conversation at the table, the teachers also expressed a concern for noise. On almost any matter that was being discussed among the four of us, one of the teachers would note that we should keep our voices down so that the children could not overhear our words. They were conscious that the children were the ears of their parents, and reported back to them. Henri Juillard usually ate quickly and left, to attend to either school-related work or some town council business. He interacted very minimally with the children during lunch and never rose to attend to their table. Liliane was more involved with the children but mainly only when there were problems that Lucette could not easily handle herself.

When a child wanted something at lunch, such as another slice of bread, he or she would rise from the table, raise up his or her right hand from the elbow only with the index finger up, and approach their schoolmistress, saying: "s'il vous plaît, Madame (or Maîtresse), si (or, est-ce que) je pourrai avoir un morceau de pain?" (May I please have another slice of bread, ma'am?) She would usually just nod in response; sometimes Henri would complain that the child had already eaten enough. This pattern was consistent for the children. I asked Liliane if she and Henri had taught the children to behave in this manner, and she replied that no, former teachers had, but that she and Henri had let it stand. The younger children had learned to do this from watching the older ones, she explained, and she had never had to instruct a child in this behavior.

A child who misbehaved at lunch was isolated from the others. This happened at least once a day. Naughty children were either sent out of the room into the hallway or made to stand and eat at the counter behind the teachers. Their "misbehavior" was never very disruptive in my perception, since I often did not even notice it and would be surprised to hear a child reprimanded and isolated. The slightest noise or action not immediately related to eating in an orderly manner was cause for disciplinary action. In general, it was boys who misbehaved in this context.

There were two lessons, closely related, being learned in the lunchroom, which might be considered part of the "hidden curriculum" of the school. The first was about the power hierarchy in the school; the second about middle class codes of etiquette. These are, of course, intertwined.

At lunchtime, power relations in the school were ritualized in a succinct form, and children learned about their relationship to outside forms of authority. Henri, who had the clearest authority role in the school, was not directly involved in serving food or attending to children. He almost ignored the children at lunch, and left early – a sign of his bureaucratic, impersonal style, and of his having more important things to do than sit in the lunchroom. Liliane, next in the chain of command, ordered Lucette about, and was responsible for maintaining the discipline. She did some nurturing when a child cried, but mainly left this to Lucette.

Lucette was clearly under the direction of the teachers, but was senior to the children in the local age-grade system. She was treated as a "servant" by the teachers in this context, and was frequently ordered about to carry out tasks by Liliane. Her manner was much more good-natured and humorous with the children than that of the teachers; still, she was expected by them to carry out her job in an orderly manner and to maintain the standards of discipline. The children realized that she was not on an equal footing with the teachers, and often tried to appeal to her if they had been punished by the teachers.

After lunch, when the teachers and most of the children had left, a few children were to stay behind and help Lucette clean up. The entire mood of the lunchroom changed to a less formal one at this time: the children stopped whispering, and joked around with Lucette and me. There was an atmosphere of "backstage" behavior (Goffman 1959).[5] The children viewed Lucette as a familiar and non-threatening figure, even though she worked at the school. They saw that she was just as much under the control of the teachers in their presence as they were (made evident by her change in behavior when the teachers were absent). The children were lowest in the official power hierarchy of the school. While adults chatted, the children were to remain quiet. They were set apart from adults, and distance was maintained through lack of interaction as well as space. Children were mixed together in the seating arrangement, with older and younger children, boys and girls, seated side by side. Their every action was under close surveillance, and they needed to get permission to get more food or do anything but eat. This was a context where social control was made explicit.

The authority of the teachers, and their role as powerful individuals in the school, were more clearly illustrated for the children in the lunchroom than in other, more diffuse contexts of school life. Here were together, in ritualized fashion, all of the actors of the school (except for Bernard, the driver). This did not create a sense of "solidarity" among all present, however (as it has been suggested that such school rituals do),[6] but rather, intensified and made clear the divisions between teachers and locals (Lucette and the children). The children were seeing how non-family members could impose constraints on their behavior that were not found at home. They saw someone who was an elder to them, Lucette, who had some local authority over them, also come under the control and close supervision of these teachers. This setting, rather than serving to reinforce school solidarity, intensified the solidarity of the children and Lucette vs. the teachers. The children were learning that there was a power hierarchy originating from outside of the family and community, embodied in the school, but that they could develop ways of resisting its hegemony through peer solidarity. The contrast between the formal rituals of the lunchroom and the "backstage" atmosphere with Lucette after the teachers left the room helped create a context for resistance in other settings of the school. When children joked with Lucette in the lunchroom after the teachers left, they were learning a model of the Laviallois who could participate in the school's structure while also questioning and challenging her place in it. When parents tried to eliminate the format in the lunchroom whereby children stayed behind and helped Lucette, during the dispute analyzed in the previous chapter, they unwittingly undermined some of the resistances to schooling and authority constituted in this setting.

The second lesson learned in the "hidden curriculum" of the lunchroom was more specifically related to the contrast between middle-class and "peasant" forms of self-control, manners, and politesse. Codes of etiquette are important markers of social status and position in France (see Bourdieu 1984). The children of Lavialle were learning in the lunchroom that the ways they ate at home were *not* socially acceptable to the teachers. All aspects of the meal in the lunchroom were highly formalized: napkins were used, permission had to be granted for a second helping, and food was served in an orderly manner involving several sequential courses. The values being imparted were "bourgeois," in many ways foreign to children from farm backgrounds. The rigidity and tension associated with eating in the school had no parallel with mealtimes at home – which were relaxed, informal, and simpler. The children were learning about completely different ways of behaving in social situations.

They were also learning that ways of behaving at home were devalued, and even unacceptable, in settings controlled by middle-class values, such as at school. In many ways, the lunchroom was symbolically run like the ideal upper-middle-class "bourgeois" household (especially one based on a nineteenth-century model). The patriarchal father in this model, as portrayed by Henri, was stern and distant with his children. The mother (Liliane), aided by a servant, would oversee the household, upholding the father's authority. Children would be expected to be silent and obedient, and to demonstrate self-control.

The reasons for this nineteenth-century "bourgeois" style in a lunchroom of a late twentieth-century rural school in France have much to do with the nineteenth-century origins of the "form" of primary schooling, which have been perpetuated in the lunchroom despite reforms in the classroom. Since the lunchroom is not a state-supervised activity, its traditions are not subject to "official" control. Lavialle's school has only had a lunchroom since the 1960s, but the form adopted there was taken from lunchrooms in other schools, which are also strongly rigid and hierarchical. The teachers in Lavialle continued this form both because it was "traditional" in the wider French school culture, and because it was a convenient way to control the behaviors of the children. It was part of the cultural knowledge (Anderson-Levitt 1987) of French teachers about how to manage the lunchroom. Even though it might not conform to the more progressive educational models of French educational experts, this lunchroom behavior is perpetuated in Lavialle because it is part of a culture of schooling informally passed on by teachers and pupils.

Lunch at school contrasts in important ways with meals at home. This was evident in social relations as well as in the content of the meals. While regional identity is conveyed through family meals, national identity was more relevant in the school. The food was not Auvergnat, no cheeses were served, and it came mostly from a frozen food service that delivered to the school. Children ate a variety of foods that are standard fare for French schools, and while not unknown to the Laviallois, were not commonly served at home. The menu was decided by the teachers, rather than by families or by Lucette, the cook. The bread was always the long, white baguette-style bread associated with urban life in France. At home, farm families often ate rounded loaves of darker bread.

Although lunch is the most formal meal served at home, the behaviors of children are much less constrained than they are at school, and the behaviors of their parents were much less strict than those of the teachers. Family meals were generally relaxed, and seen as a break from labor. Fathers, although expressing their authority over the family by sitting at the head of the table, were not distant, as was Henri. They served the bread, symbolizing their role in nurturance and in subsistence activities, and often spoke to children and teased them during the meal. There was no strict division between the old and the young at the table, and children sat side by side with adults at home. The emphasis on manners and the use of napkins at school contrasted with the absence of these in most homes.

The social form of the lunchroom is part of school culture, and reflects the necessity of feeding a large group of children as efficiently and quickly as possible. The teachers wanted the children to be quiet so that they would eat, not talk, and also wanted to school them in proper manners. The distinction between meals at school and at home is most likely a universal in state systems of education, where schooling is standardized and formalized. In those situations such as Lavialle, where class distinctions come into play, however, these differences are brought more sharply into relief.

Recess
In contrast to the explicit social control exercised in the lunchroom, recess was the time of most "freedom" and intensified peer interaction. If the weather was good, the children went out into the schoolyard behind the school to play; if not, they stayed in the building, but were not closely supervised during this time and could develop their own play activities in the halls. Both classes took recess at the same time, so that all of the children were together, as in the lunchroom. One or more of the teachers was always present, but they would spend this time reading or chatting among themselves. Attention would be given to the children only if a behavioral problem arose (as was the case in the lunchroom), but this was rare during recess (in contrast to the lunchroom). The teachers considered this to be a break for themselves as much as for the children.

I never saw a teacher suggest an activity during recess, nor did I observe a child at a loss for something to do. Recess had been more closely supervised by adults in previous years. About six years before I did my fieldwork, a local woman who helped at the school used to teach the children dances and songs (many of them traditional ones that she had learned as a child). Some of the children remembered this, but they did not perform such activities spontaneously.

The children's play was, for the most part, divided along sex and age lines, with some cooperation among groups. Sometimes older children would organize younger children in a game, since they did not do this on their own. Age-grading was, thus, an important factor in the games, which, in turn, reinforced different statuses among the children. In one game, for example, two five-year-old boys were playing with two four-year-old boys. The younger boys were ghosts, the older ones explained to me. If they caught the older boys, they, too, would become ghosts. When the older boys shouted "cabane!", they would be in a safe place. During their explanation of the game to me, the older boys repeatedly referred to the younger boys as "the little kids" (even though they were only one year younger). A favorite game in winter involved the building of snow houses from blocks of snow, or from snow rolled into balls. Usually, the older boys in the school supervised, and the other children (both boys and girls) helped. All groups played together in this communal project, and the authority of the older boys to direct was never questioned or threatened by older girls or younger boys.

One of the most important aspects of the child culture in the school was the game of marbles.[7] This was a time for passing on local school tradition, since this game had been played in the school for generations. The children were very knowledgeable about changes in the game and in the type of marble used since the time of their grandparents' years in the school. This game provided the children with an important point of continuity with the past: teachers had changed, the content and form of lessons had changed, but the game of marbles had remained a constant form passed on from child to child and from parent to child.

The game was played by both girls and boys, but in separate teams, and only by the older children. The younger ones eagerly watched the matches, and boys and girls would watch each others' games. The game of marbles emphasizes manual dexterity, a good spatial sense, and is mostly a physical and not verbal activity. The children seemed to appreciate the skill involved, and to enjoy improving their skills. Just as important as the game itself, however, were the marbles themselves. They were collected and traded, and were prized possessions. All of the children knew where to buy the best marbles. Some of the children would show off marbles from their collection that had belonged to an older relative. Since it was played exclusively by children in Lavialle, this game provided the children with an important, tangible link between their childhood and that of their elders.

During recess, the children thus had an opportunity to perpetuate and re-invent a local "culture of childhood" in Lavialle. Despite elements of recess that favored group ties among the children, however, it was an integral part of the schooling process, and not entirely in opposition to it. Recess had a structure that differed from out-of-school play, and which conveyed different meanings to children. Play at home was not discontinuous with other activities for children; at home, work and play were not clearly separate activities. Each blends into the other on a farm. For example, children might play a chasing game while their parents were working in the fields, and the parents might even join in for a moment. At school, there was a clear distinction between the rigid discipline and adult supervision of the classroom and lunchroom, and that of the play-time of recess. It was the contrast with the other two contexts that gave meaning to the relative freedom that the children had in recess. Children were being encouraged through these contrasts to compartmentalize their lives and activities into "work" and "play," in keeping with the values and needs of an industrial society – but not, necessarily, the life that they all would enter.

Not only were the children learning lessons about the division between work and play, however. They were also learning about and reproducing their own local culture through recess activities, as they shared knowledge about childhood and its history in Lavialle. Recess represents the interweaving of home and school life for children in Lavialle, which differs from the polarities between home and school that are reinforced in the lunchroom and classrooms. Because of its physical location outside, at the borders of the school and the farms, the activity of recess constitutes a marginal, in-between region connecting families to the state. The playground represents the sphere of contact between the two realms of a child's life, and the culture of local childhood that is perpetuated there helps to undermine the other messages of the school which devalue local culture, but does so under the watchful eye of the state.

Learning to be Laviallois, learning to be French
The behaviors of Lavialle children at school result in low educational achievement, and contribute to a levelling of school performance among them. Few students excel in school, and many do poorly. As I showed in chapter 7, the overall educational levels of children in Lavialle are lower than those of other children in the region. This outcome arises from a combination of factors, however, and is not simply the result either of the repressive school *or* of family environments that do not support the school. The children of Lavialle know that their parents want them to learn their lessons at school and, in particular, to gain good basic skills of reading and arithmetic. However, the climate in which the learning occurs conflicts with notions of a well-behaved (*sage*) Laviallois child: one who does not openly compete or disrupt social situations, and one who remains loyal to familial concerns.

An understanding of the link between educational strategies and poor school performance in Lavialle lies in a rethinking of the prominent dichotomy in the literature on schooling between "school" and "home." Local culture permeates the school in various ways, and the school has been part of Lavialle for over one hundred years. The school and home environments of the children of Lavialle have always existed in relation (and reaction) to each other. Children are, in a sense, caught between the hegemony of the family and the hegemony of the state, and their strategies reflect the need to cope with these conflicting demands.

The families of Lavialle have developed successful strategies of forming strong attachments to regional identity and to the kindred among children, in order to perpetuate the family farm as a viable social and economic unit and reinforce ties to rural life. The children's behaviors at school are part of an overall attempt to keep the state "at bay" in Lavialle. They constitute practice in forms of social manipulation – expressed through the concept of *debrouiller* – used in Lavialle to protect local interests and identity in the face of outside threat. The children engage in a balancing act through which they try to appease both the teachers and their parents. This is similar to the tactics and strategies adopted for generations by adults in Lavialle to straddle national and regional forms of culture and meaning.

Through their schooling experiences and coping strategies, the children in Lavialle practice *debrouillage* ("making out" and "making do"). Total cooperation with the teachers might result in better school performance for the children in primary school. From the children's point of view, however, they would lose both parental and peer support if they excelled in school. Given the teachers' impersonal, often sarcastic modes of interaction with the children when they had schooling difficulties or resisted schooling forms, and given the obstacles facing farm children in higher levels of schooling, it seems reasonable that the children identified more strongly with their families and peers than with the teachers. This is particularly the case for males, for whom the social distance between their fathers and Henri was greater than that between Lucette or Liliane and their mothers. Boys misbehaved more often than girls at school, and resisted the school and teachers more than did girls. One little girl played school at home after school, and told me that she wanted to become a teacher. Her older brother would take over her family's farm, and she was encouraged in her studies by her parents. Even those girls who were likely to become farmers were more acquiescent in Henri's classroom than were boys.

Children in Lavialle learn to cope with two opposing behavioral codes during the school years: that of home and that of school. They rarely display overt challenges to the teachers (this would have been unacceptable to both their parents and their teachers). However, they adopt several forms of "hidden" or "everyday" resistance to the school and teachers. Both girls and boys engage in tale-telling and criticism of the teachers with their parents after school (which is why the teachers were so careful to be discreet during their own conversations). They whisper and use the *on* form of speech in class to subvert the teacher's individualizing strategies. They solicit peer aid and solidarity whenever possible during class, lunch, and recess. And, the children perpetuate a "culture of childhood" at the school that reinforces local integrity and tradition in the face of the centralized and standardizing school system.

Everyday life in Lavialle's school reflects the negotiation and manipulation of power relations not just between adults and children, but between national and local levels. Schooling in Lavialle is, furthermore, a process involving not just an "official" agenda and a "hidden curriculum," but a complex interweaving of local and national agendas. The children received a variety of messages at school. In the classroom, the emphasis was on the intentional teaching of various literacy skills and moral values. In the lunchroom, the emphasis was on middle-class codes of etiquette, historically based bourgeois family forms, and self-control. During recess, the emphasis was on the division between work and play, peer interaction, and on the culture of childhood in Lavialle. As the children moved throughout the space and time of the school day, they had to negotiate their identities with each other and with the teachers in these different contexts.

There were many processes at work in Lavialle's school, but for the most part, schooling experiences reinforced the boundaries between home and school. This was emphasized by teachers as well as by students. In adopting the oppositional stance of their elders toward teachers, the children contribute to this process. Schooling contributes to the shaping of local and regional identities in opposition to national and state-based systems of meaning and control in Lavialle. It also, however, teaches children how to juggle these identities.

10

Conclusions: persistence, resistance, and coexistence

The three terms of persistence, resistance, and coexistence each serve as a shorthand for ways of looking at regional or ethnic identity in plural societies. Each also infers as its opposite some type of cultural extinction or erasure. These terms present different perspectives on cultural identity, however, with different implications for an understanding of identity in Lavialle. They complement each other when used together.

The notion of cultural persistence has been around for a while in anthropological discourse, and suggests that certain minority cultures or indigenous peoples are resilient in the face of pressures from dominant cultures to conform or disappear. This concept is related to an older notion of cultural survival in anthropology, and it can sometimes be used to suggest an essentialist view of cultures as intact and surviving, rather than changing in response to dominant cultures. Persistence is, however, a worthwhile concept, because it prompts questions about why certain cultures remain viable and others do not, and encourages us to question the whole process and nature of cultural survival.

The notion of resistance has become fairly popular as a way to talk about relationships between subordinate cultural groups and dominant cultures, and, in the context of identity, stresses the refusal of social groups to change in certain ways. It also may infer the active assertion of alternative identities among subordinate peoples. Resistance suggests that cultural identity must be actively maintained in the face of pressures from dominant culture to conform, and that survival can be a struggle. Resistance is a useful concept for highlighting the political nature of the struggles involved in cultural persistence and cultural identity. Cultures can persist because of resistance, because culture and power are closely linked. A perspective informed by the notion of resistance differs from one positing that persistence is due to inertia or "backwardness." The notion of resistance can also point attention to emergent cultural forms or identities that result precisely from contact with hegemonic cultures. The danger with using resistance exclusively as a way of talking about cultural identity is, however, that one may neglect to notice ways in which the maintenance of one cultural identity does not always entail the complete rejection of, or resistance to, another.

A third concept, coexistence, implies that cultural identity in nation-states can be multiple. Social actors can make use of both a regional or ethnic identity and a national identity. In the US, this may seem to be a fairly commonplace perspective. However, the tendency in France has often been to assume that the nation would eventually erase all cultural difference. Persistent regional identity is, consequently, viewed either as a symptom of some type of survival of archaic folk culture (which will eventually disappear) or as the result of militant movements of resistance to national French culture. My study of Lavialle shows, in contrast, that there can be (to use a linguistic model) cultural diglossia in France. I am not alone in observing this – other anthropologists have also observed these issues in France (Mark 1987 and Rogers 1991).

One hundred years after the nationalist program of universal primary education was first instituted in France, I carried out fieldwork in a remote mountain community in France. I have described this research in this book. What I found in Lavialle was a profound sense of regional Auvergnat identity which was nuanced by identities connected to kinship, age, gender, and class. I found that the families in Lavialle, despite pressures from the school system, had found a way to socialize their children to be both Auvergnat and French. They had not, as Weber (1976) concluded, made a transition from "peasants into Frenchmen." They had forged an identity that allowed the coexistence of both rural Auvergnat identity and French national identity.

I have concluded from this that the important question to ask about French society is not whether or not, or to what degree, it is culturally diverse, but, rather, how it is that people learn to manage diverse identities, to be both Auvergnat and French. Lavialle has persisted as a viable farming community in a changing French economy, when many other villages were abandoned, because it has been able to resist aspects of French dominant culture that threatened its existence. Persistence, resistance, and coexistence are all part of this story.

The ways in which the small family farms of Lavialle have responded to the French educational system over the past 100 years have been the major theme of this book. Families and children in Lavialle use strategies of both resistance and accommodation to shape the role and meaning of schooling. They do so within the constraints of a highly stratified system of education that has, historically, offered few opportunities to peasant children. Given their limited power within the school itself, Lavialle families have developed means to influence education from the outside. They have adopted socialization strategies that stress local cultural meanings, and have presented challenges to teachers in those realms of schooling in which there is some local control. Although French primary schools are national institutions, Lavialle's school is a social space within and around which people have found ways to be both Laviallois and French.

This book has described the ways in which the Laviallois have persisted as a vital rural community with a strong sense of local identity at the same time that they have participated in national institutions, like the school. Families in Lavialle, defined in terms of both the household and wider kindred, have adopted socialization strategies that are both reactive – aimed at controlling the influence of the school and teachers on their children, and active – aimed at strengthening the attachment of children to families and rural life. These strategies are based upon the close link between family and farm in Lavialle. During years of rural decline, urbanization, and industrialization in France, in which the percentage of farmers in the total work force decreased to 8%, Lavialle has weathered changes, and families there have been able to attract children to farming careers in order to perpetuate households and farms. They have also been able to keep those who leave active in local affairs, returning to participate in and support community life.

The desire to preserve family ties and family property in Lavialle is based on the importance of farming as a social and economic system. The small dairy farms of Lavialle require a constant renewal of generations willing to take over farms as well as a ready supply of kin to help with seasonal labor and less regular activities, such as barn-raising. Kin are also important participants in ritual activities and religious festivals – including funerals, marriages, and holidays. Even though most children in Lavialle will not become farmers, the Laviallois have adopted socialization strategies which ensure that many will do so and that those who do not will maintain their ties to the *commune* and their kin (*les nôtres*).

The role of schooling in this context of family economies has varied in different historical periods. Schools in Lavialle have acquired local meanings and have been used in local political struggles, despite the fact that they were national institutions. Families have used different strategies to influence the education of boys and girls, heirs and non-heirs. The role of education in Lavialle has been constrained by the economic and cultural strategies of families.

The history of education in Lavialle that I have traced here does not show a linear process of modernization and progress through schooling. There are recurring themes of conflict between families and teachers. Although opposition to teachers and schools is a constant theme in Lavialle's history, it was more intense during some historical periods than in others, and in some sections of the *commune* it was more marked than in others. This opposition has not been based entirely on economic factors, such as the need for child labor, but also arises from resistance to the school as a "social form" – which communicates bourgeois models of behavior, gender roles, and values.

I have traced continuities in Lavialle's school from its configuration in the 1870s as a one-room school taught by a poor and unhappy schoolmaster, M. Brun, and attended by the children of "indifferent" peasant parents, to its manifestation as a two-room school taught by a young suburban couple fearful of parental reprisals in the early 1980s. In some ways the similarities between the two schools, given their distance in time, are striking. Lavialle is still a community of family farmers and the teachers still live at the school, depend upon the *commune* for adequate facilities, and hope for the goodwill of cooperative parents.

These similarities should not overshadow important changes, however, in both the education system and Lavialle during the intervening years. In many ways, the meanings of schooling at the time of Monsieur Brun's school bear little resemblance to those surrounding the school of Henri and Liliane Juillard. The school is no longer a relatively new and "alien" institution, but one through which most people have passed during their youth. It is now a symbol of communal identity as much as it is a symbol of outside forms of power. The family farms of Lavialle have gone through several periods of rural decline and have been transformed into less labor-intensive units. Children are no longer needed to work on farms, and their role in the family is increasingly tied to sentimental and emotional values (see also Segalen 1983; Prost 1981; Minge-Kalman 1978). In addition, social stratification within the *commune* has lessened at the same time that the population as a whole has become increasingly inserted into the wider class structure.

During the twentieth century, schooling in Lavialle has become less of a local institution in the formal, administrative sense, but its importance to individual lives and to the overall social life of the *commune* has grown.

Schooling =
Local
Meaning

Schooling has become increasingly entrenched in local meanings at various levels – that of individual experience (since each person passes through it for some period of time), the family (for whom the formal education of children is now intertwined with overall economic strategies), and the *commune* as a whole (now that the school is one of the few symbols available to characterize Lavialle as a "community").

Boundaries between home and school have widened since the time of Brun's school, when the classroom was in an old farmhouse and the schoolmaster carried on his own subsistence farming to supplement his income. These boundaries are accentuated within and outside of school, both through the dissemination of urban, bourgeois values among the teachers and through counter-narratives to schooling imparted to children through family-based forms of socialization.

Why do these boundaries persist? Why don't family meals reinforce the same codes of etiquette inculcated at school, and why haven't parents encouraged their children to be more competitive at school? Why is it that families continue to resist these social forms and to socialize their children at home with other values? Why haven't the efforts of generations of teachers in Lavialle transformed the Laviallois into more willing clients?

Teachers'
answers

As I have argued elsewhere (Reed-Danahay and Anderson-Levitt 1991), the teachers in Lavialle would reply that this is because parents are "backward" and traditional. Teachers in Lavialle have been criticizing parents for over a century for their failure to meet middle-class norms, and have long complained that the parents of brighter pupils have discouraged them from educational achievement. Henri and Liliane Juillard were frustrated by the lack of parental interest in their attempts to encourage summer camp attendance, to bring some entertainment into Lavialle with a movie series, and to use innovative teaching methods – all of which, the teachers felt, would improve the chances for educational success among Lavialle children. They felt undermined by parental criticisms, and what they viewed as lax methods of child-rearing.

Discontinuity
between
Home &
School
Culture

Discontinuity between the culture of the school and the culture of the home is an important theme in educational research and thinking. Critics of schools wish that schools were more like the home environments of children from minority populations, while teachers, and those associated with the parent education movement, seem to wish that life at home could become more like school. I have given ample evidence in this book to support the conclusion that there are extreme discontinuities between home and school in Lavialle. It is not enough, however, to suggest that the low educational achievement of children in Lavialle is due to such differences. The more important issue is that of how and why such discontinuities have been perpetuated, as well as contradicted, in Lavialle.

Neither the school, despite its official "transcript" (Scott 1989), nor the families of Lavialle, have truly worked to transform the Laviallois into middle-class citizens. Teachers have used critiques of rural families to legitimize the bourgeois cultural models which inform both the hidden and overt curriculum of the school, and, thereby, to reinforce and justify the subordinate status of the Laviallois (Reed-Danahay and Anderson-Levitt 1991). They have rationalized the low educational achievement of Laviallois children in terms of the attitudes of families, rather than attributing it to wider structural inequalities in French society. The gap between home and school is not created solely through the resistance of families in Lavialle. It is also the product of the middle-class form of the school, which changes with national trends. Just when the Laviallois had come to accept certain types of authority roles in teachers and certain forms of teaching methods, the newer, more "progressive" methods of Freinet and less authoritarian teaching behaviors entered the scene. Families in Lavialle do not resist the school because of "backward" cultural values, but because they have articulated a culture of opposition to the school as a social form promoting the values, language use, and codes of etiquette of the dominant culture.

The aims of the school in Lavialle are not in absolute conflict with those of families; it is the "form" of the school that has created resistance, as well as the behaviors of individual teachers. Parents approach the school with a fairly specific agenda in mind: it should impart a basic level of instruction to children that will enable them to be knowledgeable enough to run profitable farms, and to pursue viable skilled occupations in the region if they do not become farmers. Farmers need to be aware of agricultural innovations and bureaucratic guidelines; they also need to keep records of their business. Literacy skills are now recognized as vital to this, and parents are supportive of the idea of education when it relates to the imparting of such practical knowledge and skills. The education of girls in skills of bookkeeping is, for instance, highly desired. Despite their support for education, however, parents in Lavialle do not, quite realistically, see it as an avenue for great social mobility. Nor do they want it to encourage their children to leave their native region or denounce familial background.

The opposition of Laviallois families to schooling is connected to overall economic and cultural strategies. Parents do not trust the school for many of the same reasons that they do not trust other outside influences

ences. Not only teachers, but social workers, tax collectors, bankers, and all state bureaucrats are resisted by the Laviallois not simply because they introduce change, but because they threaten to undermine the strength of relations of reciprocity and exchange between members of the local group.

Lavialle parents' increased interest in and, in a sense, dependency upon, schooling has intensified their frustrations at their lack of control over both their children's futures and the schooling process. As strategies of state control over children and schooling have intensified, so have strategies for tempering this control. Just as power has been increasingly transformed in the modern French state into "symbolic violence" (Bourdieu and Passeron 1990) so, too, has resistance to it become more subtle. Bourdieu defines symbolic violence as a form of violence that "allows force to be fully exercised while disguising its true nature as force and gaining recognition, approval and acceptance by dint of the fact that it can present itself under the appearances of universality – that of reason or morality" (Bourdieu 1990:84–5). Resistance in Lavialle is articulated with the concept of *debrouiller* (Reed-Danahay 1993a), which also disguises itself, just as, Bourdieu suggests, does power.

Debrouiller is used in Lavialle to express the ability to be resourceful, clever, or cunning in difficult situations. Rather than evoking the particular action of resistance, *debrouiller* expresses the skill involved in harboring (and subtly displaying) mistrust and animosity toward elites like teachers, while maintaining sufficient relations with them to ensure that their connections and power are not directed against children. Along with other concepts, like "everyday" resistance and practice (Scott 1985 and Certeau 1988), or "social poetics" (Herzfeld 1985), *debrouiller* expresses the artful ability to create and to manipulate cultural meanings and situations. It involves a subtle mixture of both accommodation and resistance, and does not make a clear-cut distinction between the two. The notion of *debrouiller* implies that power has more to do with the ability to "make out" or "make do", than with one's social status.

What occurs in Lavialle's school is not simply a mirror of social relations outside of the school, nor a function of broad structural conditions. Rather, it is a site for the production of those relations and conditions. School in Lavialle is a place where children learn how to manipulate and deal with agents of the state, and to maintain local cultural identity through participation in a national-based institution. When children in Lavialle's school use passive forms of resistance, these cannot easily be attributed to the same sort of "penetration" of the dominant ideological system described by Willis for the lads (Willis 1981a; see also Scott's dis-

School in Lavialle is...

cussion of "penetration" 1985:318–22). They are young children just learning social norms and ideologies. They are, nevertheless, social agents, rather than being passive vessels of inculcation by teachers. It is, unfortunately, rare for children to be discussed in political analyses, except in such passive terms, as recipients of socialization.

The children of Lavialle (as social agents) have developed means of "coping" with the contradictions between school-based models of the person and of social relations' and home-based models. These constitute mostly "passive," everyday forms of resistance to the teachers and school, which are culturally constructed at the local level. They are informed by the cultural models found outside of school, among their families. Adults and children in Lavialle influence education both through a defensive posture of resistance to certain aspects of the school as a "social form" and through active strategies reinforcing local identity and social life. Families reinforce ties among kin through important life-cycle transitions, and teach the importance of regional identity and local social life through everyday routines.

The study of education in Lavialle that I have offered in this book is intended to speak not only to issues of identity in France or even in Europe, but also to wider issues of social agency and cultural diversity. I have not meant to romanticize the resistance of the Laviallois, and have drawn as much upon their own models of manipulative behavior (as expressed in the concept of *debrouiller*) as I have drawn from those of other analysts. Resistance is closely connected to power, and represents a way to influence and a form of control. All of social life reflects the tension between resistance and compliance, with power residing not in one or the other, but in the negotiation between the two.

I have made no claims in this book that Lavialle is a "typical" rural community in France. Nor have I made dire predictions concerning Lavialle's imminent demise. The inhabitants of Lavialle are, like so many people in different parts of the world, trying to "make it." They are trying to survive in a marginal position while both participating in and being subject to cultural and economic processes of an increasingly global scale. They adapt to changes, rather than resist them altogether. It is in light of the adaptive, coping strategies of the Laviallois that schooling must be considered. The wider implications of this study derive not, therefore, from the particular combination of power and resistance in Lavialle, but from a recognition that families actively use and shape institutions like schools in different ways in different social contexts.

Notes

1: Introduction: journey to Lavialle

1. Lavialle is a pseudonym, as are all other local names used here. When dealing with the level of the department or region, I return to "real" names.
2. The other students and I were, to use Merton's terms, recently resurrected by Hannerz (1992:252–5), "cosmopolitans" in contrast to the "locals" of Lavialle.
3. See Kelly (1984) on the education of elites and French colonial education in West Africa.
4. A *commune*, as I will explain more fully later, is the smallest administrative unit in France. Although a *commune* may constitute one city or town, in the case of Lavialle it encompasses a central village and surrounding hamlets. It roughly corresponds to the type of rural settlement known in the United States as a "township." I have retained the use of the French term here, however, in order to highlight the differences between rural life in France and the US, and, in particular, the centralization of the French government and educational system.
5. On the importance of landscape markers such as mountains for the construction of social identity, see Crumley and Marquandt (1987).
6. A "rural" *commune* is officially defined in France as one with a population of less than 2,000 that is not located in an urbanized zone.
7. As Pierre Bourdieu suggested to me, French farmers have an easier time talking about sex than about education (personal communication, 1981).
8. My name was an amusing source of puns for the Laviallois. My nickname, "Debbie," it was pointed out, sounded like *débile* in French (which means mentally defective). On the other hand, "Déborah," it was jokingly suggested, sounded like *des beaux rats* (or, handsome rats). A popular French song about a woman named "Déborah" had been widely played on radio stations soon before my arrival in Lavialle, and, therefore, my formal name was more familiar and readily adopted than my nickname.
9. I have explored these issues elsewhere, in a comparison of Pierre Bourdieu's writings on French education and on Algerian peasant society, in which I argue that Bourdieu presents an "occidentalized" view of French culture by pairing it with rural Algeria (see Reed-Danahay 1995).

214

2: Theoretical orientations: Schooling, families, and power

1. This is not unlike Willis' argument that "cultures live their own damnation and . . . a good section of working class kids condemn themselves to a future in manual work" (1981a:174).

2. Although Willis is usually referred to as a "resistance" theorist, his overall theoretical framework ultimately rests upon a theory of social reproduction. He is concerned with the ways in which resistance and cultural practice lead to social reproduction, and, therefore, is not as far from Bourdieu as he claims (Willis 1981b).

3. See Abu-Lughod (1990) for a critique of "the romance of resistance" in contemporary ethnography, which also borrows from Foucault. My own reading of Foucault, however, sees him as granting more weight to processes of resistance than does Abu-Lughod.

3: Cultural identity and social practice

1. See also Strathern 1981: xxix on villages as "imagined."

2. The priority of the household over the *commune* as a source of identity in France contrasts with the importance of the "village" as a key symbol in rural England. The prevalence of large-scale capitalist farms in England, with a more marked class structure of landowners and laborers, may have encouraged closer identification with the village unit than was the case in France, especially in areas of small-scale family farming (Strathern 1981 and 1982).

3. See Cowan (1990) on dance and gender in Greece.

4. The phrase "rural neighborhoods" (*quartiers ruraux*) was first suggested to me by historical geographer André Fel (personal communication).

5. Marc Prival, a French ethnographer of the Auvergne region, suggested to me during my fieldwork that a good test of my assimilation in Lavialle would be if my claim to a share of the timber in the village of Lavialle would be accepted – something I never, however, carried out.

6. Jolas and Zonabend (1977) similarly describe differences among hamlet sections – "the tillers of the field" and "the woodspeople" – in a symbolic analysis of tendencies toward differentiation and unity in a Burgundian *commune*.

7. House names in Lavialle, while more private, are not the only labels of place in France imbued with intense meaning. In his discussion of street names in old neighborhoods of Paris, Certeau refers to them as "remaining relics of meaning" (1988:105). I am not sure that it would be accurate, however, to call Lavialle colloquial house names "relics of meaning," since they have important meanings *in the present*.

8. See also Goffman (1961) and Certeau (1984). I have elaborated upon the theme of *debrouiller* as a form of resistance elsewhere (Reed-Danahay 1993a).

9. Values of "cunning" in European society have been identified in other ethnographies and, as Belmonte (1979) points out, relate to the picaresque tradition. Belmonte describes the importance of cunning (*la furbizia*) among the under-class in Naples as "a stance which is maintained toward society as a whole, not only toward members of other classes but equally toward one's neighbors, kinsmen, and friends" (1979:143–44). Similarly, Herzfeld details the use of notions of cunning (*poniria*) among Cretan sheep-thieves, and

writes that it "signifies the conventionally disrespectful attitude that Greeks bring to their dealings with those in power" (1985:2).

10. I do not mean to imply here that other French people do not use the term *debrouiller*; rather that the Laviallois associate it with particular local behaviors and stances towards the outside. They also associate the dance they call *la bourrée* with local and regional culture, even though it is found in other parts of France as well. This does not, however, negate its meaning to the Laviallois.

11. Resourcefulness is also an important value among rural inhabitants of Kentucky, who refer to it as "the Kentucky Way" (Halperin 1990). Like *debrouiller*, this notion refers to the idea of "making do" in difficult situations and overcoming hardships, and is closely associated with regional identity and "insider" status. Comparisons between rural Kentucky and rural Auvergne are particularly apt since the populations in both mountain regions were historically poor and isolated, and promote strong kin ties.

4: *Les nôtres*: families and farms

1. This discussion of census material uses the term "household" for the French census term *le ménage* (defined by the census as those persons who occupy the same lodgings as a principal residence). These people are not necessarily all related. The "family" is defined by the census as groups of no fewer than two individuals, comprising a couple (or individual parent) and their unmarried children of less than 25 years of age. The census therefore defines *ménage* as a household consisting of one or more nuclear families so defined, or of unrelated individuals, or a mixture. These official terms do not have the same meanings as concepts of household and family in Lavialle.

5: From child to adult

1. I avoid the use of the terms "formal" vs. "informal" socialization to express the differences between practices at school and out of school, although this is a common usage in the literature on home–school relationships. There are "formal" and "informal" aspects to socialization in school *and* at home, and the equation of "formal" with school tends to support a monolithic view of the French educational system. (Recent work in the field of literacy similarly challenges such a dichotomy when dealing with literate vs. non-literate cultures – see Akinnaso 1991). It might be better to think in terms of "everyday" practices vs. "ritualized" practices (Certeau 1988). For the purposes of this study, I use the terms "locally-based" or "family-based" vs. "school-based" socialization.

2. See also Zonabend (1980: 100–44) for a historical description of childhood in Burgundy from a life cycle perspective.

3. Neville (1984), drawing upon the work of Solon Kimball and her own research on American families, has usefully pointed to the importance of family-based rituals for cultural transmission and learning in contexts of social change.

4. Both Zonabend (1979) and Wylie (1975) note more community-wide involvement with baptism in the rural communities they studied than I observed in

Lavialle. The regions in which their studies were conducted (Burgundy and Provence), however, were much less isolated from urban centers and received better health care sooner than Lavialle. It may be that baptism may not receive a great deal of attention in Lavialle because in the not-so-distant past there was a high infant mortality rate there. An alternative explanation, however, is that the family's claim (rather than that of the church or community) over the child is stronger in Lavialle than in these other communities, due to the prevalence of small-scale family farming.

Family over Church [handwritten annotation]

5. The coffee drunk by the Laviallois is not the strong "expresso" coffee served in Parisian cafes and in southern France. It resembles American coffee in strength, and is drunk in tall ceramic cups. The making of coffee, always freshly ground, is an important female ritual of hospitality. At breakfast, the Laviallois drink *café au lait* from a bowl, but not at other times of the day.

6. I attended one such *fête des enfants* in a small town in the Limagne region near Clermont-Ferrand. This involved a large carnival and parade orchestrated by the school as the celebration of childhood. It appeared to express and reinforce strong identification between the community, families, and the school. Although this town had many farmers, it was more open to urban influences, and the educational strategies of families there were much different from those in Lavialle. The farms were larger, and dependent upon cereal cultivation. Many of the farm children pursued higher education, and few sons and fewer daughters (even when the only heir) were willing to join their parents on the farm.

7. Badone (1989: 217–18) notes similar concerns about this ceremony and the end of religious participation in rural Brittany.

8. I recognize that the original Church liturgy of these rituals expressed more the children's symbolic marriage to the Church, than that of the sacrament of marriage. However, the striking resemblance in older photos of clothing worn for marriages and first communions, as well as parallels between the two rituals, point to the social meaning of *la première communion* as a dress rehearsal for marriage.

9. *Brioche*, a delicate and decorative egg-based bread, is eaten on special occasions in Lavialle.

10. Curious onlookers from Clermont-Ferrand and its environs who attended the festival trivialized it as a piece of picturesque folklore. A common attitude toward village life among urbanites was expressed to me by one young man from the city (unrelated to anyone in Lavialle) who asked, when he learned that I was an American living in Lavialle, "How can you *stand* to live here year-round?"

11. A distance eloquently articulated by Hélias (1978) in his memoir of childhood and education in Brittany.

6: Schooling the Laviallois: historical perspectives

1. Jules Ferry served as Minister of Foreign Affairs in France from 1880 to 1885. His role in French imperialism is less publicized and was less popular than his role in education at home. (See Furet 1985; Power 1944; and Ageron 1985.) The history of the relationship between Ferry's roles in education and coloni-

alism is yet to be written, and I cannot, unfortunately, do justice to this topic here.

2. This period of French schooling has received a great deal of attention by historians, given its importance in nationalist ideology. The centennial celebration of the Ferry laws in 1981 renewed interest in the Third Republic's educational achievements. See Le Groupe de Travail 1981; Furet 1985; Gildea 1983; M. Ozouf 1963; J. Ozouf 1967; Stock-Morton 1988; Weber 1976; and Zeldin 1980.

3. Accounts of the urge to improve education after this demoralizing defeat bear a striking resemblance to post-Sputnik American educational rhetoric, as well as to more recent concerns in the United States about the superiority of Japanese education.

4. On the so-called "clandestine" schools, see also Gildea (1983:210–11); Heywood (1988:66); Furet and Ozouf (1982:101–17).

5. See also Heywood (1988:65–6), for a related discussion of village teachers (*prétendus-instituteurs*) in the early 19th century, and Singer (1983:109).

6. There is, however, mention of schools in the nearby town of Grosbourg in the early 18th century (CRDP 1977).

7. The *garde-champêtre* (literally, guardian of the fields; similar to a sheriff) is employed by each *commune* to keep order in any disputes over land or animals that might occur. Lavialle still has one today.

8. Schoolmasters commonly took on this task to earn supplemental income, especially in the early years when their salaries were so low. The local teacher was also, however, often one of the few literate inhabitants in rural villages, and so fulfilled many roles that required literacy skills. (See Day 1983; Singer 1977; and Reboul-Scherrer 1989.)

9. A narrowing of the population attending schools accompanied the rise of mass education. Both younger children and adults who had previously attended educational institutions were excluded in many cases from public schooling. (See Ariès 1962; and Kaestle and Vinovskis 1978.)

10. For a comprehensive overview of primary education in France since the 1950s from the perspectives of both French and American scholars, see Anderson-Levitt *et al.* 1991. Also helpful are Halls 1976; Lewis 1985; Prost 1968 and 1981; and Vincent 1980.

11. The *tiers-temps* timetable for lessons introduced a three-part division between the subjects of French, math, and what were called *activités d'éveil* (including, art, science, and social sciences). It was replaced with a back-to-basics curriculum in the late 1980s. On recent reforms in French primary education, see Anderson-Levitt *et al.* 1991.

12. This is in contrast to the situation in other regions of France, such as Normandy, where teachers have been recruited from the south of France for decades. These teachers feel themselves to be culturally different and their accents are markedly southern, which furthers school-family distance. (This information is based on my discussions with teachers in a Norman primary school; see also Henriot-Van Zanten 1990.)

7: Families and schools

1. Weiler (1988) argues that the lack of substantive reform in the French educational system during the past thirty years, especially problems associated with implementation, are related to the weakening legitimacy of the French state.
2. This is a common feature of the French educational system. In *lycées*, for example, teachers of different status sit at separate tables in the cafeteria and will not speak to younger, less "senior" or less well qualified teachers.
3. The choice of wine as a drink for children may appear odd to some readers, but according to my Laviallois informants, it was common in previous years. Wine was believed to "fortify" children as well as adults. This practice has only declined in recent years, accompanied by a change of attitude. There were stories of families within recent memory who had served wine to children – with the added warning, however, that this is bad for children and encourages mental deficiency.
4. On the phenomenon of a high proportion of male bachelors in rural France during this period, see Bourdieu (1962).
5. McDonald notes a similar reticence to admit the use of regional languages, in this case Breton, among public teachers in Brittany (1989:235–6).
6. In a similar case of apparent sabotage, McDonald notes that two "mysterious" fires earlier in the century plagued a convent in an anti-clerical section of a Breton rural *commune* (1989:227).
7. Although I was not able to interview former teachers from this school, and must depend upon the recollections of local families and former students, my experience with the other two schools suggests that there is not a sharp contrast between teacher and family perceptions of their relationships.

8: The politics of schooling

1. Anderson-Levitt's (1989) research on urban French teachers' criticisms of families provides an interesting contrast to the situation in rural Lavialle. In the urban context, teachers focused more on what they saw as "family problems" – such as divorce, alcoholism, and immorality – rather than the mistrust, indifference, and backwardness attributed to families in Lavialle over the years. Our two cases are compared in Reed-Danahay and Anderson-Levitt (1991).
2. I have chosen to refer to the teachers in this chapter as Henri and Liliane, rather than Monsieur and Madame, since I was on a first-name basis with them. More formal terms of address were, however, used by most parents and all of the children, who used "Monsieur and Madame Juillard" or *le maître* and *la maîtresse*. Some parents addressed the teachers by first name in face-to-face situations (and many others only when speaking about them), but the vast majority of people used the more polite form of Monsieur and Madame Juillard.
3. A general description of French teacher unions, although now a bit dated, is given in Clark (1967). According to Hall (1976), only about 8% of teachers are politically active in France. See Delwasse (1980) and Duclaud-Williams (1983) for some useful descriptions of opposition to the Haby Reforms.

4. Here is an example of the contrast between what Scott (1990) calls the "hidden" transcripts of subordinate peoples and the "official" transcripts of public discourse.
5. Gender segregation also occurs in church, where women sit in the front and men stand or sit at the rear during Mass. The parents' seating pattern differs from that of their children in the classroom, who are placed by the teacher in male–female pairs.
6. The contrast between women's private and public gender roles was well illustrated in drinking behavior. At the Christmas party for families at Lavialle's school, at which refreshments were organized by a local cafe owner and the female teacher, women were served sweet white wine and men were served red wine. Liliane Juillard told me that this was all that women in Lavialle would drink, and she saw this as indicative of their old-fashioned mentality. During my visits with families, however, I observed many occasions at which women drank red wine (sometimes diluted with some water). I also observed discussions between husbands and wives over farming decisions in which the women took an active role.
7. In his study of local government in France and Italy, Tarrow (1977) reports the common practice in rural French *communes* of electing mayors who are in some senses outsiders. This has advantages for the community in that the mayor has more outside contacts than most members, but, also, can serve as a "figurehead" for actual political maneuvering at the local level. This pattern was replicated in Lavialle through the election of two non-farmer, non-natives, to the parent committee. It was also evident in the election of a new mayor in Lavialle in 1982 who was a non-native who had married into a Lavialle farm family. Town council members are, however, almost all from local kindreds.
8. This is a common feature of rural local politics, in France (Rogers 1991:111–14) and elsewhere (see especially Herzfeld 1985: 92–122 and Scott 1985: 133–4).
9. Incidentally, the next mayor of Lavialle, elected in 1982, was a Socialist farmer, showing the political expediency of the Laviallois. They realized the advantages of having a mayor who was a member of the party in power at the national level.

9: Everyday life at school

1. The school calendar varies from department to department in France, so that starting dates in the fall are not consistent throughout the nation. This was implemented to stagger the dates of the famous French migration to the south in the summer.
2. Reforms in 1985, after my fieldwork, abolished the *activités d'éveil* and replaced these with a back-to-basics curriculum that has since been implemented. (See Anderson-Levitt *et al.* 1991 for more recent changes.)
3. Henri's unwillingness to bring subjects of local significance or relevance into the classroom was marked. French anthropologist Françoise Zonabend had suggested to me that I ask the class to create local calendars and other local documents, as she had done in Burgundy. This was totally resisted by Henri,

who felt that such an activity was irrelevant to the curriculum. Any narratives or drawings related to family life that I asked the children do for my research had to be carried out as homework.

In addition, Henri never felt it appropriate to bring up the subject of the French elections in class, even though the year of my fieldwork was a Presidential election year. He told me that he viewed such current events as inappropriate to the curriculum, but also hinted that he feared parental reprisals if he raised any controversial topic. The lack of attention to the local setting of the school in the curriculum in Lavialle's school may, therefore, be related as much to teacher fears of parental reprisals for interfering with local matters as to concern for keeping close to the prescribed curriculum.

4. See Reed-Danahay (1987a) for an earlier discussion of classroom strategies of resistance in Lavialle.
5. My participation in such "backstage" contexts was crucial to research. It helped in the development of rapport with the children, and eventually their parents. Had I confined my observations to the classroom, and not interacted with children less formally in other contexts, I would have been perceived as a similar authority figure to the teachers. I also would have missed a wide range of behaviors among the children that were not exhibited in the classroom and other "formal" contexts of school.
6. Research on schooling contexts considered to be "communal," particularly in small towns and rural settings, has focused on ritualized bases of solidarity (see Peshkin 1978 and Hostetler and Huntington 1971). Rituals in schooling have recently received increased attention in the literature (see Handelman and Shamgar-Handelman 1990 and McLaren 1986).
7. Augustins (1988) also provides an analysis of the game of marbles in French elementary schools. See also Reed-Danahay (1986).

Bibliography

Abélès, Marc. 1991. *Quiet Days in Burgundy: A Study of Local Politics*. Trans. A. McDermott. Cambridge: Cambridge University Press; Paris: Editions de la Maison des Sciences de l'Homme.

Abercrombie, Nicholas, Stephen Hill, and Bryan S. Turner. 1980. *The Dominant Ideology Thesis*. London: George Allen and Unwin.

Abu-Lughod, Lila. 1990. The Romance of Resistance: Tracing Transformations of Power Through Bedouin Women. *American Ethnologist* 17 (1): 41–55.

Ageron, Charles-Robert. 1985. Jules Ferry et la colonisation. In F. Furet (ed.) 1985: 191–206.

Akinnaso, F. Niyi. 1991. Schooling, Language, and Knowledge in Literate and Nonliterate Societies. *Comparative Studies in Society and History* 34(1): 68–109.

Allatt, Patricia. 1993. Becoming Privileged: The Role of Family Process. In Ing Bates and George Riseborough (eds.) *Youth and Inequality*, pp. 139–59. Buckingham and Philadelphia: Open University Press.

Althusser, Louis. 1971. Ideology and Ideological State Apparatuses: Notes Toward an Investigation. In *Lenin and Philosophy*, pp. 127–86. Trans. B. Brewster. New York: Monthly Review Press.

Anderson, Benedict. 1991 [1983]. *Imagined Communities: Reflections on the Origin and Spread of Nationalism*. Revised edition. London: Verso.

Anderson, R.D. 1975. *Education in France, 1848–1870*. Oxford: Clarendon Press.

Anderson-Levitt, Kathryn M. 1987. Cultural Knowledge for Teaching First Grade: An Example from France. In George D. Spindler and Louise Spindler (eds.) *Interpretive Ethnography of Education at Home and Abroad*, pp. 171–94. Hillsdale, NJ: Lawrence Erlbaum.

1989. Degrees of Distance between Teachers and Parents in Urban France. *Anthropology and Education Quarterly* 20 (2): 97–117.

1994. Common Visions: Knowledge for Teaching First Grade in France and the United States. (book manuscript)

Anderson-Levitt, Kathryn *et al.* 1991. Elementary Schools in France. *Elementary School Journal* 92 (1): 79–95.

Anglade, Jean. 1971. Paulin Chauvet, Maître d'Ecole en Lozère (1878). In *La Vie quotidienne dans le Massif Central au XIXème siècle*, pp. 213–27. Paris: Librairie Hachette.

Apple, Michael. 1979. *Ideology and Curriculum*. London: Routledge and Kegan Paul.

1986. *Teachers and Texts: A Political Economy of Class and Gender Relations in Education*. New York: Routledge and Kegan Paul.

Ariès, Philippe. 1962. *Centuries of Childhood: A Social History of Childhood*. New York: Vintage Books.

Augustins, Georges. 1988. Jeux de billes: lieu de la raison, lieu de la passion. *Ethnologie française* 18(1):5–14.

Badone, Ellen. 1989. *The Appointed Hour: Death, Worldview, and Social Change in Brittany*. Berkeley: University of California Press.

Baker, Donald and Patrick J. Harrigan (eds.). 1980. *The Making of Frenchmen: Current Directions in the History of Education in France, 1679–1979*. Waterloo, Ontario: Historical Reflections Press.

Bastide, Huguette. 1969. *Institutrice de village*. Paris: Denoël Gonthier.

Baudelot, Christian and Roger Establet. 1971. *L'Ecole capitaliste en France*. Paris: François Maspero.

Behar, Ruth. 1986. *Santa Maria del Monte: The Presence of the Past in a Spanish Village*. Princeton: Princeton University Press.

Bell, Colin and Howard Newby. 1974 [1971]. *Community Studies: An Introduction to the Sociology of the Local Community*. New York: Praeger.

Belmonte, Thomas. 1979. *The Broken Fountain*. New York: Columbia University Press.

Belperron, R. 1978. *On a sauvé l'école du village*. Paris: Editions Syros.

Berger, Suzanne. 1972. *Peasants Against Politics: Rural Organization in Brittany 1911–1967*. Cambridge: Harvard University Press.

Bernot, Lucien and René Blanchard. 1953. *Nouville: Un village français*. Paris: Institut d'Ethnologie.

Bertho, Catherine. 1980. L'Invention de la Bretagne: genèse sociale d'un stéréotype. *Actes de la Recherche en Sciences Sociales* 35:45–62.

Boissevain, Jeremy. 1975. Introduction: Towards a Social Anthropology of Europe. In J. Boissevain and J. Friedl (eds.) *Beyond the Community: Social Process in Europe*, pp. 9–18. The Hague: European-Mediterranean Study Group, University of Amsterdam.

Boli, John and Francisco O. Ramirez. 1986. World Culture and the Institutional Development of Mass Education. In John G. Richardson (ed.) *Handbook of Theory and Research for the Sociology of Education*, pp. 67–90. New York: Greenwood Press.

Boli, John, Francisco O. Ramirez and John W. Meyer. 1985. Explaining the Origins and Expansion of Mass Education. *Comparative Education Review* 29(2):145–70.

Bourdieu, Pierre. 1962. Celibat et condition paysanne. *Etudes Rurales* 5–6: 32–135.

1972. Les stratégies matrimoniales dans les système de reproduction. *Annales: Economies, Societés, Civilisations* 4–5(Juillet-Oct): 1105–25.

1977a. Une class objet. *Actes de la Recherches en Sciences Sociales* 17/18:2–5.

1977b. *Outline of a Theory of Practice*. Trans. R. Nice. Cambridge: Cambridge University Press.

1979. Les trois états du capital cultural. *Actes de la Recherches en Sciences Sociales* 12 (5): 61–113.

1984. *Distinction. A Social Critique of the Judgement of Taste.* Trans. R. Nice, Cambridge, MA: Harvard University Press.

1990. From Rules to Strategies. In *In Other Words*, pp. 59–75. Trans. Matthew Adamson. Stanford: Stanford University Press.

Bourdieu, Pierre, Luc Boltanski, and Monique de Saint-Martins. 1973. Les stratégies de reconversion: les classes sociales et le système d'enseignement. *Information sur les Sciences Sociales* 12 (5): 61–113.

Bourdieu, Pierre and Jean-Claude Passeron. 1964. *Les héritiers, les étudiants et la culture.* Paris: Editions de Minuit.

1990 [1977]. *Reproduction in Education, Society and Culture.* Trans. R. Nice. London: Sage Publications.

Bowles, Samuel and Herbert Gintis. 1976. *Schooling in Capitalist America.* New York: Basic Books.

Carles, Emilie. 1977. *Une soupe aux herbes sauvages.* Paris: France Loisirs.

Carrier, James. 1992. Occidentalism: The World Turned Upside-Down. *American Ethnologist* 19:195–212.

Certeau, Michel de. 1988 [1984]. *The Practice of Everyday Life.* Trans. S. Randall. Berkeley: University of California Press.

Charles, Frederic. 1991. France. In Maggie Wilson (ed.) *Girls and Young Women in Education: A European Perspective,* pp. 67–90. Oxford: Pergamon Press.

Cheverny, M. 1981. Les effectifs des classes primaires. *Le Monde de l'Education* (Mars):55–6.

Clark, James M. 1967. *Teachers and Politics in France. A Pressure Group Study of the Federation de L'Education Nationale.* Syracuse, New York: Syracuse University Press.

Clark, Linda L. 1984. *Schooling the Daughters of Marianne: Textbooks and the Socialization of Girls in Modern French Primary Schools.* Albany: SUNY Press.

Cleary, M.C. 1989. *Peasant, Politicians and Producers: The Organization of Agriculture in France since 1918.* Cambridge: Cambridge University Press.

Clout, Hugh D. 1989[1985]. *Western Europe: Geographical Perspectives.* 2nd edition. New York: Wiley.

Cohen, Anthony P. (ed.). 1982. *Belonging: Identity and Social Organisation in British Rural Cultures.* Manchester: Manchester University Press.

1987. *Whalsay: Symbol, Segment and Boundary in a Shetland Island Community.* Manchester: Manchester University Press.

Cohen, Yehudi. 1970. Schools and Civilizational States. In J.F. Fischer (ed.) *The Social Sciences and the Comparative Study of Educational Systems,* pp. 55–147. Scranton: International Textbook Co.

Colburn, Forrest D. (ed.). 1989. *Everyday Forms of Peasant Resistance.* Armonk, New York and London: M.E. Sharpe, Inc.

Coombs, Fred S. 1978. The Politics of Educational Change in France. *Comparative Education Review* 22 (3): 464–503.

Cowan, Jane. 1990. *Dance and the Body Politic in Northern Greece.* Princeton: Princeton University Press.

C.R.D.P. 1977. *L'Enseignement sous l'ancien régime en Auvergne: Bourbonnais, et Velay*. Clermont-Ferrand: Centre Régional du Documentation Pédagogique.

Crumley, Carole L. and William H. Marquardt (eds.). 1987. *Regional Dynamics: Burgundian Landscapes in Historical Perspective*. San Diego: Academic Press.

Cuisinier, Jean and Martine Segalen. 1986. *Ethnologie de la France*. Paris: Presses Universitaires de France.

D'Amato, John. 1988. "Acting": Hawaiian Children's Resistance to Teachers. *Elementary School Journal* 88 (5): 529–44.

Daucé, P., G. Jegouzo, and Y. Lambert. 1972. Education et mobilité professionelle des enfants d'agriculteurs: premières analyses. *Economie Rurale* 31–46.

Day, C.R. 1983. The Rustic Man: The Rural Schoolmaster in Nineteenth Century France. *Comparative Studies in Society and History* 25: 26–49.

Delbos, Génévieve. 1982. Leaving Agriculture, Remaining a Peasant. *Man* 17:747–65.

Delwasse, L. 1980. Le sabotage des conseils d'école. *Le Monde de l'Education*. (Oct.): 50–4.

Detienne, Marcel and Jean-Pierre Vernant. 1978. *Cunning Intelligence in Greek Culture and Society*. Trans. J. Lloyd. Atlantic Highlands, NJ: Humanities Press.

Donzelot, Jacques. 1979. *The Policing of Families*. Trans. R. Hurley. New York: Pantheon Books.

Duclaud-Williams, R. 1983. Centralization and Incremental Change in France: The Case of the Haby Educational Reform. *British Journal of Political Science* 13: 71–91.

Esman, M.J. (ed.) 1977. *Ethnic Conflict in the Western World*. Ithaca: Cornell University Press.

L'Exode Rural vu par L'I.N.S.E.E. 1979. Clermont-Ferrand: INSEE and CRDP.

Fabian, Johannes. 1983. *Time and the Other: How Anthropology Makes its Object*. New York: Columbia University Press.

Fédération des Délégués Départementaux de l'Education Nationale. 1977. *L'Ecole en milieu rural*. Paris: Imprimèrie Gelbard.

Fel, André. 1962. *Les Hautes Terres du Massif Central: tradition paysanne et économie agricole*. Clermont-Ferrand: Publications de la Faculté des Lettres et Sciences Humaines de Clermont-Ferrand.

1977. Petite Culture 1750–1850. In Hugh Clout (ed.) *Themes in the Historical Geography of France*. New York: Academic Press.

Foley, Douglas E. 1990. *Learning Capitalist Culture*. Philadelphia: University of Pennsylvania Press.

Foster, C.R., ed. 1980. *Nations Without a State*. New York: Praeger.

Foster, Stephen W. 1988. *The Past is Another Country: Representation, Historical Consciousness, and Resistance in the Blue Ridge*. Berkeley: University of California Press.

Foucault, Michel. 1978. *The History of Sexuality*. Volume I: *An Introduction*. Trans. R. Hurley. New York: Pantheon Books.

1982. Afterword: The Subject and Power. In Herbert Dreyfus and Paul Rabinow, *Beyond Structuralism and Hermeneutics*, pp. 208–226. Chicago: University of Chicago Press.

Furet, François (ed.). 1985. *Jules Ferry: Fondateur de la République*. Paris: Editions de l'Ecole des Hautes Etudes en Sciences Sociales.

Furet, François and Jacques Ozouf. 1982. *Reading and Writing: Literacy from Calvin to Jules Ferry*. Trans. La Maison des Sciences de l'Homme and Cambridge University Press. Cambridge: Cambridge University Press; Paris: Editions de la Maison des Sciences de l'Homme.

Gambetta, Diego. 1987. *Were They Pushed or Did They Jump? Individual Decision Mechanisms in Education*. Cambridge: Cambridge University Press.

Geertz, Clifford. 1973. *The Interpretation of Cultures*. New York: Basic Books.

Giddens, Anthony. 1984. *The Constitution of Society*. Berkeley: University of California Press.

Gildea, Robert. 1983. *Education in Provincial France 1800–1914*. Oxford: Clarendon Press.

Giroux, Henri. 1983. *Theory and Resistance in Education*. South Hadley, MA: Bergin and Garvey Publishers, Inc.

Goffman, Erving. 1959. *The Presentation of Self in Everyday Life*. New York: Doubleday and Co.

  1961. *Asylums: Essays on the Social Situation of Mental Patients*. New York: Anchor Books.

Goubert, Pierre. 1986. *The French Peasantry in the Seventeenth Century*. Trans. I. Patterson. Cambridge: Cambridge University Press.

Graff, Harvey. 1979. *The Literacy Myth: Literacy and Social Structure in the Nineteenth Century City*. New York: Academic Press.

Green, Andy. 1990. *Education and State Formation. The Rise of Education Systems in England, France and the USA*. New York: St. Martin's Press.

Grew, Raymond and Patrick Harrigan. 1991. *School, State and Society: The Growth of Elementary Schooling in 19th Century France – A Quantitative Analysis*. Ann Arbor: University of Michigan Press.

Grignon, Claude. 1968. Les Jeunes Ruraux à l'Ecole. *Economie Rurale* 75: 81–90.

  1975. L'Enseignement agricole et la domination symbolique de la paysannerie. *Actes de la Recherche en Sciences Sociales* 1(janv.): 75–97.

Grillo, Ralph. 1985. *Ideologies and Institutions in Urban France: The Representation of Immigrants*. Cambridge: Cambridge University Press.

Le Groupe de Travail de la Maison d'Ecole à Montceau-les-Mines 1981. *Cent ans d'école*. Scyssell: Camp Mellon.

Halls, W.D. 1976. *Education, Culture, and Politics in Modern France*. Oxford: Pergamon Press.

Halperin, Rhoda. 1990. *The Livelihood of Kin: Making Ends Meet 'The Kentucky Way'*. Austin: University of Texas Press.

Handelman, Don and Lea Shamgar-Handelman. 1990. Holiday Celebrations in Israeli Kindergartens. In Don Handelman, *Models and Mirrors: Towards an Anthropology of Public Events*, pp. 162–89. Cambridge and New York: Cambridge University Press.

Hannerz, Ulf. 1992. *Cultural Complexity: Studies in the Social Organization of Meaning*. New York: Columbia University Press.

Heath, Shirley Brice. 1983. *Ways with Words: Language, Life and Work in Communities and Classrooms*. Cambridge: Cambridge University Press.

Hélias, Pierre-Jakez. 1978. *The Horse of Pride: Life in a Breton Village*. Trans. J. Guicharnaud. New Haven: Yale University Press.

Henriot-Van Zanten, Agnes. 1990. *L'école et l'espace local: Les enjeux des Zones d'Education Prioritaires*. Lyon: Presses Universitaires de Lyon.

Herzfeld, Michael. 1985. *The Poetics of Manhood: Contest and Identity in a Cretan Mountain Village*. Princeton: Princeton University Press.

1987. *Anthropology Through the Looking-Glass: Critical Ethnography in the Margins of Europe*. Cambridge: Cambridge University Press.

Heywood, Colin. 1988. *Childhood in Nineteenth-Century France*. Cambridge: Cambridge University Press.

Hobsbawm, Eric. 1992 [1983]. Mass-Producing Traditions: Europe 1870–1914. In Eric Hobsbawm and Terence Ranger (eds.) *The Invention of Tradition*, pp. 263–307. Cambridge: Cambridge University Press.

Holland, Dorothy and Margaret A. Eisenhart. 1990. *Educated in Romance: Women, Achievement, and College Culture*. Chicago: University of Chicago Press.

Hostetler, John A. and Gertrude E. Huntington. 1971. *Children in Amish Society: Socialization and Community Education*. New York: Holt, Rinehart, and Winston.

I.N.S.E.E. 1980. L'Appareil Scolaire en Auvergne, *Le Point*. Clermont-Ferrand: I.N.S.E.E.

Jegouzo, Guenhaël and Jean-Louis Brangeon. 1976. *Les paysans et l'école*. Paris: Editions Cujas.

Joanne, P. 1899. *Dictionnaire géographique et administratif de la France*. Paris: Librairie Hachette et Cᵗᵉ.

Jolas, Tina and Françoise Zonabend. 1977. Tillers of the Field and Woodspeople. In Robert Forster and Orest Ranum (eds.) *Rural Society in France: Selections from the Annales*, pp. 126–51. Trans. E. Forster and P. M. Ranum. Baltimore: Johns Hopkins University Press.

Kaestle, Carl F. and Vinovskis, M. 1978. From Apron Strings to ABCs: Parents, Children, and Schooling in 19th Century Massachusetts. In John Demos and S.S. Boocock (eds.) *Turning Points: Historical and Sociological Essays on the Family*, pp. 539–80. Chicago: University of Chicago Press.

Kelly, Gail. 1984. Colonialism, Indigenous Society, and School Practices: French West Africa and Indochina, 1918–1938. In Philip G. Altback and Gail P. Kelly (eds.) *Education and The Colonial Experience*, 2nd edition, pp. 9–32. New Brunswick: Transaction Books.

Kelly, Gail and Carolyn M. Elliott (eds.) 1982. *Women's Education in the Third World: Comparative Perspectives*. Albany: State University of New York Press.

King, Nancy. 1982. Children's Play as a Form of Resistance in the Classroom. *Journal of Education* 164 (4): 320–9.

Kondo, Dorinne. 1990. *Crafting Selves: Power, Gender, and Discourses of Identity in a Japanese Workplace*. Chicago: University of Chicago Press.

La Blache, Virginie. 1990. La class, c'est la vie. *Le Monde de l'Education* 175(Octobre): 44–5.

Lareau, Annette. 1989. *Home Advantage: Social Class and Parental Intervention in Elementary Education*. New York: Falmer Press.

LeBlanc, J. 1975. *Les motivations et les problèmes des éleveurs du Massif Central.* Riom: CT-GREF Groupement de Clermont-Ferrand.

Lehning, James R. 1980. *The Peasants of Marles: Economic Development and Family Organization in Nineteenth-Century France.* Chapel Hill: The University of North Carolina Press.

Leichter, Hope J. 1979. Families and Communities as Educators: Some Concepts of Relationship. In Hope J. Leichter, *Families and Communities as Educators*, pp. 3–94. New York: Teachers College Press.

Lewis, H.D. 1985. *The French Education System.* New York: St. Martin's Press.

LeWita, Beatrix. 1988. *Ni vue ni connue: approche ethnographique de la culture bourgeoisie.* Paris: Editions de la Maison des Sciences de l'Homme.

Lightfoot, Sara Lawrence. 1978. *Worlds Apart: Relationships Between Families and Schools.* New York: Basic Books.

Lynch, Katherine A. 1988. *Family, Class, and Ideology in Early Industrial France: Social Policy and the Working-Class Family, 1825–1848.* Madison: University of Wisconsin Press.

Manry, André-Georges. 1974. *Histoire de l'Auvergne.* Toulouse: Edouard Privat.

1987. *Histoire des Communes de Puy-de-Dôme.* Le Coleau: Editions Horvath.

Mark, Vera. 1987. In Search of the Occitan Village: Regionalist Ideologies and the Ethnography of Southern France. *Anthropological Quarterly* 60(2):64–70.

Martin, Emily. 1987. *The Woman in the Body: A Cultural Analysis of Reproduction.* Boston: Beacon Press.

Mayeur, Françoise. 1981. *De la Revolution à l'école républicaine.* Tome III: *Histoire Générale de l'enseignement et de l'education en France.* Paris: G.-V. Labat.

Maynes, Mary Jo. 1985a *Schooling for the People.* New York: Holmes and Meier.

1985b. *Schooling in Western Europe: A Social History.* Albany: SUNY Press.

McDonald, Maryon. 1989. *We Are Not French! Language, Culture, and Identity in Brittany.* London and New York: Routledge.

McLaren, Peter L. 1985. The Ritual Dimensions of Resistance: Clowning and Symbolic Inversion. *Journal of Education* 167 (2): 84–97.

1986. *Schooling as Ritual Performance: Towards a Political Economy of Educational Symbols and Gestures.* London: Routledge and Kegan Paul.

Mendras, Henri. 1970. *The Vanishing Peasant: Innovation and Change in French Agriculture.* Trans. J. Lerner. Cambridge: MIT Press.

Mendras, Henri (with Alistair Cole). 1991. *Social Change in Modern France: Towards a Cultural Anthropology of the 5th Republic.* Cambridge: Cambridge University Press.

Meyer, John. 1977. The Effects of Education as an Institution. *American Journal of Sociology* 83(1):55–77.

Minge-Kalman, Wanda. 1978. The Industrial Revolution and the European Family: The Institutionalization of 'Childhood' as a Market for Family Labor. *Comparative Studies in Society and History* 29(3):454–67.

Ministère de l'Education. 1981. *L'Ecole publique à cent ans.* Paris: L'Imprimérie Lancry.

Mitterauer, M. and R. Seider. 1982. *The European Family.* Trans. K. Osterveen and M. Horzinger. Chicago: University of Chicago Press.

Morin, Edgar. 1970. *The Red and the White: Report from a French Village*. Trans. A. M. Sheridan-Smith. New York: Pantheon Books.

Motley, Mark. 1990. *Becoming a French Aristocrat: The Education of the Court Nobility 1580–1715*. Princeton: Princeton University Press.

Moulin, Annie. 1991. *Peasantry and Society in France Since 1789*. Trans. M.C. and M.F. Cleary. Cambridge: Cambridge University Press.

Nadel-Klein, Jane. 1991. Reweaving the Fringe: Localism, Tradition, and Representation in British Ethnography. *American Ethnologist* 18(3):500–17.

Neville, Gwen Kennedy. 1984. Learning Culture Through Ritual: The Family Reunion. *Anthropology and Education Quarterly* 15(2): 151–66.

Ogbu, John. 1982. Cultural Discontinuities and Schooling. *Anthropology and Education Quarterly* 13 (4): 290–307.

Ortner, Sherry. 1984. Theory in Anthropology Since the Sixties. *Comparative Studies in Society and History* 26:126–66.

Ozouf, Jacques. 1967. *Nous les maîtres d'école. Autobiographies d'instituteurs de la belle époque*. Paris: Julliard.

Ozouf, Mona. 1963. *L'Ecole, l'église, et la république, 1871–1914*. Paris: Armond Colin.

1984. *L'école de la France: Essais sur la Revolution, l'utopie et l'enseignement*. Paris: Editions Gallimard.

1985. Unité nationale et unité de la pensée de Jules Ferry. In F. Furet (ed.): 59–72.

Parman, Susan. 1990. *Scottish Crofters: A Historical Ethnography of a Celtic Village*. Fort Worth: Holt, Rinehart, and Winston.

Peshkin, Alan. 1978. *Growing Up American: Schooling and the Survival of Community*. Chicago: University of Chicago Press.

Petonnet, Colette. 1973. *Those People: The Subculture of a Housing Project*. Trans. Rita Smidt. Westport, CT and London: Greenwood Press, Inc.

Poitrineau, Abel. 1979. *Le Diocèse de Clermont*. Paris: Editions Beauchesne.

Pourrat, Annette. 1976. *Traditions d'Auvergne*. Verviers, Belgium: Marabout.

Power, Thomas F., Jr. 1944. *Jules Ferry and the Rennaissance of the French Empire*. New York: King's Crown Press.

Price, Roger. 1987. *A Social History of Nineteenth-Century France*. New York: Holmes and Meier.

Prost, Antoine. 1968. *Histoire de l'enseignement en France, 1800–1967*. Paris: Librairie Armond Colin.

1981. *Histoire générale de l'enseignement et de l'education en France*. Volume IV: *L'école et la famille dans une societé en mutation (1930–1980)*. Paris: Nouville Librairie de France.

Rapp, Rayna. 1986. Ritual of Reversion: On Fieldwork and Festivity in Haute Provence. *Critique of Anthropology* 6(2): 35–48.

Rapport sur La Situation de l'Enseignement Primaire dans le Puy-de-Dôme pour l'Année 1944–45. N.D. Unpublished Report. Clermont-Ferrand: L'Inspection Académique.

Reboul-Scherrer, Fabienne. 1989. *La Vie quotidienne des premiers instituteurs 1833–1882*. Paris: Hachette.

Reed-Danahay, Deborah. 1986. Educational Strategies and Social Change in Rural France. Unpublished Ph.D. Dissertation. Brandeis University.

1987a. Farm Children at School: Educational Strategies in Rural France. *Anthropological Quarterly* 60 (2): 83–9.

1987b. Gender Differences in Regional Identity in Rural France. Paper presented at the New England Women's Studies Association Conference, Hartford, CT.

1991. La production de l'identité régionale: L'Auvergnat dans le Puy-de-Dôme rural. *Ethnologie Française* 21 (1): 42–7.

1993a. Talking about Resistance: Ethnography and Theory in Rural France *Anthropological Quarterly* 66(4): 221–9.

1995. The Kabyle and the French: Occidentalism in Bourdieu's Theory of Practice. In James Carrier (ed.) *Occidentalism: Images of the West.* Oxford: Oxford University Press.

Reed-Danahay, Deborah and Kathryn M. Anderson-Levitt. 1991. Backward Countryside, Troubled City: Teachers' Images of Families in Rural and Urban France. *American Ethnologist* 18 (3): 546–64.

Reiter, Rayna Rapp. 1972. Modernization in the South of France: The Village and Beyond. *Anthropological Quarterly* 45:35–53.

Rogers, Susan Carol. 1987. Good To Think: The "Peasant" in Contemporary France. *Anthropological Quarterly* 60(2):56–63.

1991. *Shaping Modern Times in Rural France.* Princeton: Princeton University Press.

Rosenberg, Harriet G. 1988. *A Negotiated World: Three Centuries of Change in a French Alpine Community.* Toronto: Univ. of Toronto Press.

Sahlins, Peter. 1989. *Boundaries: The Making of France and Spain in the Pyrenees.* Berkeley: University of California Press.

Schnerb, Marion. 1937. *L'Enseignement primaire dans le Puy-de-Dôme avant et après la loi Guizot.* Clermont-Ferrand: Imprimérie Générale Jean de Bussac.

Schonfeld, William R. 1971. *Youth and Authority in France: A Study of Secondary Schools.* Beverly Hills, CA: Sage Publications.

Scott, James C. 1985. *Weapons of the Weak: Everyday Forms of Peasant Resistance.* New Haven: Yale University Press.

1989. Everyday Forms of Resistance In Forrest D. Colburn (ed.): 3–33.

1990. *Domination and the Arts of Resistance: Hidden Transcripts.* New Haven: Yale University Press.

Segalen, Martine. 1983. *Love and Power in the Peasant Family.* Trans. S. Matthews. Chicago: University of Chicago Press.

1986. *Historical Anthropology of the Family.* Trans. J.C. Whitehouse and S. Matthews. Cambridge: Cambridge University Press.

1991. *Fifteen Generations of Bretons: Kinship and Society in Lower Brittany, 1720–1980.* Trans. J.A. Underwood. Cambridge and New York: Cambridge University Press.

Sider, Gerald M. 1986. *Culture and Class in Anthropology and History.* Cambridge: Cambridge University Press.

Sieber, R. Timothy. 1979. Classmates as Workmates: Informal Peer Activity in the Elementary School. *Anthropology and Education Quarterly* 10(4):207–35.

Singer, Barnett. 1977. The Village Schoolmaster as Outsider. In Jacques Beauroy *et al.* (eds.) *The Wolf and the Lamb: Popular Culture in France,* pp. 189–208. Saratoga, CA: Anma Libri.

1983. *Village Notables in Nineteenth-Century France: Priests, Mayors, and Schoolmasters*. Albany: State University of New York Press.

Singleton, John. 1974. Schools and Rural Development: An Anthropological Approach. In P. Foster and J.R. Sheffeld (eds.) *Education and Rural Development*. The World Year Book of Education, pp. 117–36. London: Evans Bros. Ltd.

Sirota, Regine. 1988. *L'Ecole primaire au quotidien*. Paris: Presses Universitaires de France.

Smith, Gavin. 1989. *Livelihood and Resistance: Peasants and the Politics of Land in Peru*. Berkeley: University of California Press.

Spiegel, Sanda Jo. 1978. Education and Community in a French Village. Unpublished Ph.D. Dissertation. University of California, Berkeley.

Stack, Carol B. 1974. *All Our Kin: Strategies for Survival in a Black Community*. New York: Harper and Row, Publishers.

Stock-Morton, Phyllis. 1988. *Moral Education for a Secular Society: The Development of Morale Laïque in Nineteenth-Century France*. Albany: SUNY.

Strathern, Marilyn. 1981. *Kinship at the Core: An Anthropology of Elmdon, A Village in North-West Essex in the Nineteen-Sixties*. Cambridge: Cambridge University Press.

1982. The Village as an Idea: Constructs of Village-ness in Elmdon, Essex. In Anthony P. Cohen (ed.) *Belonging*, pp. 247–77. Manchester: Manchester University Press.

Strumingher, Laura S. 1983. *What Were Little Girls and Boys Made Of? Primary Education in Rural France 1830–1880*. Albany: State University of New York.

1985. Square Pegs into Round Holes: Rural Parents, Children and Primary Schools; France 1830–1880. In Marc Bertrand (ed.) *Popular Traditions and Learned Culture in France*, pp. 133–148. Saratoga, CA: Anma Libri.

Le Système Educatif en France. 1978. Paris: C.N.D.P. Tardieu, Ambrose. 1877. *Grand dictionnaire historique du Département du Puy-de-Dôme*. Moulins: Désrosiers.

Tarrow, Stanley G. 1977. *Between Center and Periphery: Grassroots Politicians in Italy and France*. New Haven: Yale University Press.

Terrail, Jean-Pierre. 1992. Destins scolaires des sexe: Une perspective historique et quelques arguments. *Population* 47(3):645–76.

Thabault, Roger. 1971 [1945]. *Education and Change in a Village Community: Mazières-en-Gâtine 1848–1914*. Trans. P. Tregear. New York: Schocken Books.

Tilly, Louise A. 1980. Individual Lives and Family Strategies in the French Proletariat. In *Family and Sexuality in French History*. Robert D. Wheaton and Tamara Haraven (eds.), pp. 201–33. Philadelphia: University of Pennsylvania Press.

Tilly, Louise A. and Joan W. Scott. 1978. *Women, Work, and Family*. New York: Holt, Rinehart and Winston.

Turner, Victor. 1969. *The Ritual Process: Structure and Anti-Structure*. Chicago: Aldine Publishing Company.

Van Gennep, Arnold. 1909. *The Rites of Passage*. Trans. M. B. Vizedom and G. L. Caffee. London: Routledge and Kegan Paul.

Villin, Marc and Pierre Lesage. 1987. *La galerie des maîtres d'école et des instituteurs, 1820–1945*. Paris: Plon.

Vincent, Guy. 1980. *L'Ecole primaire française. Etude sociologique*. Lyon: Presses Universitaires de Lyon.

Vincent, Joan. 1990. *Anthropology and Politics: Visions, Traditions, and Trends*. Tucson: The University of Arizona Press.

Wallace, Anthony F.C. 1961. Schools in Revolutionary and Conservative Societies. In F. L. Gruber (ed.) *Anthropology and Education*, pp. 25–54. Philadelphia: University of Pennsylvania Press.

Weber, Eugen. 1976. *Peasants Into Frenchmen: The Modernization of Rural France, 1870–1914*. Stanford: Stanford University Press.

Weiler, Hans. 1988. The Politics of Reform and Nonreform in French Education. *Comparative Education Review* 32 (3): 251–65.

Wheaton, Robert. 1975. Family and Kinship in Western Europe: The Problem of the Joint Family Household. *Journal of Interdisciplinary History* 4–5 (Spring): 601–28.

Willis, Paul. 1981a [1977]. *Learning to Labor: How Working Class Kids Get Working Class Jobs*. New York: Columbia University Press.

1981b. Cultural Production is Different from Cultural Reproduction is Different from Social Reproduction is Different from Reproduction. *Interchange* 12(2 & 3): 48–67.

Wilson, Thomas M. and M. Estellie Smith (eds.) 1993. *Cultural Change and the New Europe: Perspective on the European Community*. Boulder, CO: Westview Press.

Wylie, Laurence. 1963. Social Change at the Grass Roots. In Stanley Hoffman *et al.* (eds.) *In Search of France*, pp. 159–234. New York: Harper and Row, Publishers.

1975 [1957]. *Village in the Vaucluse*. 3rd Edition. Cambridge: Harvard University Press.

Young, Michael and Peter Willmott. 1962 [1957]. *Family and Kinship in East London*. Baltimore, MD: Penguin Books.

Zeldin, Theodore. 1980. *France 1848–1945. Intellect and Pride*. Oxford: Oxford University Press.

Zonabend, Françoise. 1979. Childhood in a French Village. *International Social Science Journal* 33 (3): 492–512.

1980. *La memoire longue: temps et histoire au village*. Paris: Presses Universitaires de France.

Index

Cambridge Studies in Social and Cultural Anthropology

Editors: ERNEST GELLNER, JACK GOODY, STEPHEN GUDEMAN,
MICHAEL HERZFELD, JONATHAN PARRY

N (To explore)

* An American researcher's lens
  - She acknowledges her bias early on.

* Book reviews of this text

Printed in the United States
R1559000003B/R15590PG34185LVSX00003B/1}

9 780521 616171